Beyond the Dysfunctional Family

Jews, Christians and Muslims in Dialogue With Each Other and With Britain

Edited by
Tony Bayfield, Alan Race,
Ataullah Siddiqui

*Incorporating the dialogical fruits of
the Manor House Abrahamic Dialogue Group (1993–2010)*

Copyright © 2012
Tony Bayfield, Alan Race, Ataullah Siddiqui
All rights reserved

Published by
The Manor House Abrahamic Dialogue Group
London

ISBN-10: 1468167472
ISBN-13: 978-1468167474

CONTENTS

INTRODUCTION
Tony Bayfield, Alan Race, Ataullah Siddiqui

PART ONE
Three Traditions in British Context

1.	How Did the Jewish Community Come to be Where it is Today? *Michael Hilton*	13
2.	How Did the Christian Community Come to be Where it is Today? *Elizabeth J Harris*	31
3.	How Did the Muslim Community Come to be Where it is Today? *Dilwar Hussain*	55

PART TWO
Encounters in Dialogue

4.	Jewish-Christian Dialogue	
(a)	A Jewish Reflection on Relations with Christians and Christianity *Rachel Benjamin*	85
(b)	A Christian Reflection on Relations with Jews and Judaism *Jane Clements*	93
(c)	A Muslim Eavesdropper on Jewish-Christian Dialogue *Humera Khan*	101
5.	Christian-Muslim Dialogue	
(a)	A Christian Reflection on Relations with Muslims and Islam *Shanthikumar Hettiarachchi*	107
(b)	A Muslim Reflection on Relations with Christians and Christianity *Sughra Ahmed*	115
(c)	A Jewish Eavesdropper on Christian-Muslim Dialogue *Miriam Berger*	123
6.	Muslim-Jewish Dialogue	
(a)	A Muslim Reflection on Relations with Jews and Judaism *Abdul Jalil Sajid*	129
(b)	A Jewish Reflection on Relations with Muslims and Islam *Norman Solomon*	137
(c)	A Christian Eavesdropper on Muslim-Jewish Dialogue *Marcus Braybrooke*	147

PART THREE
Sharpening Dialogue through Critical Thinking

7.   Me, My Jewishness, Modernity and Other Faiths   155
Tony Bayfield

8.   Religious Absolutism, Violence and the Public Square   183
Alan Race

9.   Faith and Engagement: a Reflective Journey   201
Ataullah Siddiqui

10. In the Footsteps of Dinah: a Feminist   217
Perspective on Jewish/Christian/Muslim Dialogue
Elizabeth Tikvah Sarah

PART FOUR
Analysing Our Encounters

11. Differences and Common Ground   241
Tony Bayfield, Alan Race, Ataullah Siddiqui

PART FIVE
Looking to the Future

12. The Platform Statement (2005) – a Staging Post   269
A Group Agreement (1)

13. Recommending a Way Forward   275
A Group Agreement (2)

Biographies of Contributors   291

Index   299

*This book is dedicated to John Bowden,
a founder-member of the Manor House
Dialogue Group, whose commitment to
dialogue was inspirational.*

INTRODUCTION

Tony Bayfield, Alan Race, Ataullah Siddiqui

When Jews, Christians and Muslims sit down to talk to one another what should each say to the others? The three traditions are often grouped together as 'Abrahamic religions', which is shorthand for drawing attention to some sense of relatedness – historically, theologically and existentially – between them. However, although all three traditions look to Abraham as a foundational figure in religious symbolic memory, each configures and projects that symbolism differently, and it is this which has fuelled an intense rivalry, witnessed throughout history, between them. Herein lays the difficulty for the conversation. Jews, Christians and Muslims are siblings – albeit distant ones – yet they have displayed all the features of a dysfunctional family. What they have to say to one another therefore will be conditioned by all of the associated traits of fractious family values – antagonism, jealousy, suspicion and even murderous violence. We say this, notwithstanding the recognition that there have been some limited periods in history when relationships have been less tortured.

This book, however, is predicated on the belief that relationships between the Abrahamic traditions do not have to remain trapped in dysfunctionality. Jews, Christians and Muslims have influenced one another in differing degrees through time, for good as well as ill, and in ways which have yet to be fully documented. This suggests that each cannot give a full account of its own soul without reference to the others. Furthermore, theologically speaking, the notion of an

Beyond the Dysfunctional Family

'Abrahamic' family conjures up a shared ethos which might be roughly coined as 'prophetic ethical monotheism'. Such an ethos emphasises, among other features: the basic goodness of the material world (none of us believes in Manichean dualism) – such that rocks, plants, animals, human beings, and the mysterious universe itself all exist for the purposes of God's praise; history as the adventurous journey for freely establishing justice, peace and the moral life in community and between peoples; and religious devotional practice which celebrates our responses to the summons of a divine invitation to spiritual awareness and human fulfilment. There is much that is shared among us, as well as much that is mutually strange. A great deal of the dialogue between us is about exploring both shared and confusing terrain.

A second assumption of this book is the unhesitating belief that the future of our world is to be a shared future which applauds diversity as such: cliché as it is, we live in a global village. If this is one of those unargued-for assumptions about contemporary reality which underpins rational argument, it strikes us as being nevertheless entirely reasonable and difficult to dismiss. The many sides of what is intended by the term 'globalisation' confirm it as valid. In this light, Abrahamic interfaith dialogue can be viewed as a sub-set of the many dialogues, across many divides, which will be necessary for building our shared global future.

The participants in this Abrahamic dialogue have accepted that theological permission for engagement with the sibling others has long been granted and claimed. We do not think of one another as evil, immoral, religiously benighted or intellectually deluded. By 'permission' we mean that our traditions hold out an expectation that the mysterious reality we name variously as Adonai, Heavenly Father, Allah, has more to communicate than has been glimpsed so far through one lens alone. The universalist sense of the sacred, which the distinctive heart of each of the three traditions opens up, leads us to think so. We might simply ask, 'What has the Divine Mystery been up to beyond our walls?' Expressed more mundanely, as a matter

Introduction

of fact interfaith dialogue is beginning to shape the next historical phase of an unfolding religious apprehension of life, in which people of different traditions both affirm their distinctiveness and their interdependence.

We learn from one another. Better still: we propose that we learn more of 'God' through our openness to one another than in our isolations. To this extent, this book looks to the fruits *of* dialogue beyond the mere 'permission' *for* dialogue.

This book of dialogue is the result of at least fifteen years of patient listening in trust, engagement with one another through human empathy, and the willingness to confront and be confronted. We have experimented in walking in the shoes of one another. As the taken-for-granted truths of our religions can be among the most intransigent of our convictions, traditionally to be defended at all costs, undertaking such dialogical openness is not an easy journey to make. Therefore we do not talk of dialogue glibly; its art, we have discovered, has to be learned and re-learned with every precious encounter. In the process it comes to be cherished as a gift, rooted in hard-won friendship, experienced often as frustrating and fragile, yet ultimately life-changing. At times it seems like the only antidote to the jealousies of sibling rivalry.

Over this period we have become acutely aware that interfaith relationships are not forged in a cultural vacuum; there is always context. Our traditions have shaped and been shaped by the civilisations of which they have been a part and this is no less true of the present. Consequently, we have identified the following factors in our present-day context as having been significant for the dialogue between us.

1. The historical experiences of loss and the subsequent anxiety over survival

Jews understandably feel this the most. But Muslims too are aware of a different kind of decline and many admit to a loss of intellectual vitality from its medieval heyday and especially since the collapse of the Ottoman empire through Western

Beyond the Dysfunctional Family

colonialism. Mainstream Christians too are beginning to experience a different kind of loss: under pressures of modernity/post-modernity the explicit influence of their beliefs and practices in British society are seemingly less relevant to many.

2. British uncertainties about shared values, identity, social cohesion and multiculturalism

Membership of the European Union and increased migrations have brought people from many different cultural, ethnic and religious backgrounds to these shores. In turn, religion as a primary marker of identity has risen up to become important for many. The impact of this growing sense of religious plurality has unsettled Britain as a secular modern liberal democracy. Changes in some city demographics have meant that civic and government authorities have had to become more pro-active in respect of taking seriously the religious identities of its citizens.

3. Polarisation between 'Religious' and 'Secular'

As Britain experiences the effects of religious plurality, at the same time there is an increase in public declarations of atheism and agnosticism. This inevitably gives the impression that there is a strong polarisation between religious believers and non-believers, yet this is unlikely to be the case. The real facts of citizens' allegiances are generally harder to establish, in spite of the impression created through much media reporting and debates. As it is, many religious believers exercise a form of 'provisional secularism' in daily life, and many secularists admit to interest in spiritual questions.

4. Polarisation between 'Conservative' and 'Liberal' religious voices

Both of these tendencies are the result of reactions to critical thinking stemming from the modernity of the European Enlightenment and deepened by postmodernity. At one extreme there is so-called Fundamentalism and at the other what might be called Religious Non-Realism, though the labels can easily be

Introduction

disputed. Interfaith dialogue began with liberal-minded voices but is now gradually being taken up by more conservative voices. Precisely how 'tradition' is balanced against the assumption of religious authenticity in the other, expected in dialogue, remains a key question for all dialogue practitioners.

5. *Religiously-motivated violence*

This is the factor of context which has dominated discussion of religion and interfaith dialogue for the first decade of the twenty-first century. It represents the shadow side of competitive thinking in religious commitment and it cannot be wished away. Any dialogue between religions which does not tackle this problematic area will not be worth the paper on which it is written. Because of the terrorist attacks in the USA in 2001 and in Britain in 2005, and in many parts of the world, Muslims have had to bear the brunt of the criticism. But the perpetration of violence is no respecter of tradition; there are no 'pure' religions in this respect.

If the dialogue reflected in this book is concerned with relations between the three Abrahamic traditions it is also keen to engage with debate about the critical role which religions might play in society. It explores not only the dysfunctionality within the family but seeks to open up how a new relationship between the three might contribute to British society as a whole. This involves us in delving into some history, facing new challenges regarding evolving identity and theological convictions in the light of critical thinking, setting out some parameters for cooperation between us, and requesting changes from our political classes if they are to respond creatively to persistent religious convictions in society generally. This is a tall order and in order to understand how this all coheres in one book let us now outline how the book should be read.

First, what the book does not do. It does not collect together a set of interesting reflections which can be read in any order and which may or may not have some intrinsic relationship between them. That is a tried and tested format which has merits, but it is

5

Beyond the Dysfunctional Family

not ours. For this book is both the story of people committed to a process and the result of the process itself thus far. Therefore it is both an interactive narrative of human voices and a contribution to Abrahamic interfaith understanding. As I hinted earlier, it is best described as a first fruits of dialogue.

It is important to grasp that there is a momentum within the developing narrative of the book. Each of the sectional Parts build on what preceded it. Individual contributions were subject to the scrutiny of the dialogical process at every stage. Attentive listening was followed by the offering of corrective responses, which in turn resulted in revision and resubmission to the group's collective responsibility. That is to say, the logical progress of the book's narrative was 'owned' by the whole group, and it was this which enhanced our sense of 'Abrahamic' relatedness, historical honesty, present-day challenges and dialogical credentials throughout. It will be easier to see the effectiveness of the building-block approach of this process if we briefly spell out the substance of each section, as follows:

• **Part One** has three contributors tell their stories of what it 'feels like' to be Jewish, Christian and Muslim in Britain today in the light of what they each inherit from recent history: what makes them rejoice and what turns them fearful, what projections for the future might look like. They tell them as personal accounts yet with an eye to their communities. This is necessary scene-setting for dialogue, as well as profoundly revealing about how history has shaped who we are.

• **Part Two** follows by delving interactively into some dialogical encounters as such. Individuals from two different communities offer their glad acceptances of and remaining puzzles about each other, while a third party from the remaining community listens in as an eavesdropper and responds accordingly. What is the relevance of your conversation for me?, the eavesdropper might be asking. Bilateral conversations often reveal aspects of dialogue which generic conversations easily gloss over, and so the aim here is to bring out issues and questions which are important in our newly emerging shared journey of mutual

Introduction

learning and identity-in-relationship. These conversations can only of course be a snapshot of what Jew, Christian and Muslim might say to one another. But enough is said to raise a curtain on some significant matters.

• **Part Three** takes up the challenge of critical thinking, again from the three confessional faith standpoints, but includes also a view from a feminist perspective. This is the section which seeks to deepen the questions between us by injecting challenging notes of theological and philosophical critique. So issues such as the following are brought to the fore: revelation and truth in religion; the role of scripture; the possibility of meaningful communication between us; how violence has intervened between us; exclusivity regarding gender relationships and whose experience counts when listening to the past and imagining the future; absolutism in religious identity, as an historic given and a present threat; how we might present ourselves to society in ways which command credibility; the impact of modernity/ postmodernity on all of us. This section begins to recognise that dialogue entails that perhaps we do not live out of tradition alone, important as tradition may be.

• **Part Four** takes the dialogue a stage further as a deliberate exercise in self-critical reflection: it analyses the previous three sections, highlights emerging themes, reveals points of agreement/disagreement, draws the reader's attention to the historical and theological reasons for dysfunctionality and its potential healing, and sets the scene for how Jews, Christians and Muslims might cooperate positively for the good of society, as they see it. It weaves together both process and content as a piece of whole dialogical cloth in a remarkable manner which is rarely present in other texts of dialogue.

• **Part Five** recalls an earlier stage in the evolving life of the group and presents what we called then our 'Platform Statement' (2005).[1] This was the result of intensive discussions in the years immediately following the 9/11 terrorist attacks in the USA in 2001. Not everyone in the group which has

Beyond the Dysfunctional Family

produced this book was party to those discussions but all are happy to endorse the Platform as a dialogical marker on the way to subsequent conversations and preoccupations. We include it here particularly because of its courage in tackling the relationship between so-called religiously-motivated violence and religious identity. Finally, this section looks to the necessary changes that will be required both in how our three traditions separately and together approach their roles in society and in how the organs of political governance approach the religions in modern democracies, if the future is to be more secure than what is often envisaged.

All in all, this book represents an attempt to unsettle some boundaries, as all dialogue does. Its scope reflects the experiences of those who have contributed to it, but we trust that its significance is not limited to those individual accounts themselves. We believe that interfaith dialogue is no longer a luxury only for those so inclined. Moreover, it is not just for the sake of social cohesion or improved international relations that dialogue is necessary. Dysfunctionality requires the therapeutic healing of history's scars at many levels, including the theological. Therefore interfaith dialogue invites us to move beyond tolerance in order to embrace a form of interactive acceptance of one another, even as paradoxically we might not comprehend fully or agree with all that the others stand for.

Authentic interfaith dialogue overcomes both the loneliness of isolated monologue and the confusion of deadening relativism in matters of religious truth. It accepts that what remains is the conversation between us. If this book of Abrahamic dialogue helps to stimulate that dialogical process in others along new adventurous avenues then it will have fulfilled a major part of its purpose.

A note on language

Precise definitions of terms in religious discourse are seldom easy to formulate. In the context of cross-faith discussion the scope for misunderstanding is inevitably increased. On the

Introduction

whole, we have not tried to enforce a strict policy on the use of language and trust that clear meanings are evoked within the context of the various contributions themselves. As it is, there are no agreed conventions even on the use of terms such as 'faith(s)' and 'religion(s)' and their cognates 'interfaith' and 'interreligious'; and the same could be said for other terms such as 'secular' and 'secularism'. This book is written from the perspectives of those who are practising believers and therefore, when terms such as 'faiths' or 'religions' are used, it is generally intended that these apply generically to living communities of spiritual commitment, each with their inward and outward dimensions, their cognitive, affective, social and historical aspects. Finally, the terms 'interfaith' and 'interreligious' do not indicate a new religion formed as an amalgam of ingredients from our three different religions; rather, it should be understood after the manner of 'international', which is the cooperation and interaction between nations.

NOTES

1. *Welcome and Unwelcome Truths Between Jews, Christians and Muslims: A Platform Statement from a Dialogue Group of Jews, Christians and Muslims* was previously published in a journal associated with each of the Abrahamic traditions and with interfaith dialogue: *MANNA* No 86, Winter, 2005 (Jewish); *Modern Believing*, No 47, July 2006, pp. 6-10 (Christian); *Encounters, Journal of Inter-Cultural Perspectives*, Vol 10, Nos 1&2, 2004, pp. 119-122 (Muslim); *Interreligious Insight*, Vol 3, No 2, April 2005, pp. 78-81 (journal of the World Congress of Faiths, London, UK, and Common Ground, Lake Forest, USA).

PART ONE

Three Traditions in British Context

1

How Did the Jewish Community Come to Be Where it is Today?

Michael Hilton

The memory remains vivid in my mind to this day. In the early summer of 1955, a shy four year old boy was led by his mother into the dark panelled headmaster's study at Quainton Hall School, Harrow. Father Montague Eyden, the Headmaster, was an unmarried Anglican priest in the Anglo-Catholic tradition. He had done much to develop the school's links with the Church of England Shrine of *Our Lady of Walsingham* in Norfolk. The school had been founded by his mother in 1897, and "Mont" (as he was known) devoted his whole life to it. He expected all the boys to attend daily services in the school chapel, dedicated to St Francis, where boys knelt for prayers. On the wall behind the altar hung a large crucifix, backed by a large coloured cloth of which the colour varied according to the time of the liturgical year. And here was I, a young Jewish boy, coming for interview. There were few Jewish primary schools in those days, and very many schools had a Church connection. Mont was a kindly man and certainly not averse to accepting a few Jews into his school. But he expected them to conform and attend Chapel with the other boys. In the post-war Jewish community of those days there were rumours of a "Jewish quota", a strict limit on the numbers of Jewish boys who would be likely to be accepted at this and other schools. My mother had told me of the quota, and how that meant I had to do especially well at answering the questions. I counted from one to twenty correctly, and answered a few other questions. But then I stopped, and gazed with great curiosity at the portraits on the wall. Mont interpreted this

Beyond the Dysfunctional Family

curiosity as an intelligent inquisitiveness, and accepted me into his school.

And so, throughout my formative years, although secure in my identity as a Liberal Jew, I attended far more Christian prayers than Jewish ones. Like many children, we were often irreverent. Just before the entrance to the Chapel was a holy water stoup. As we went in, each boy dipped his finger into the water. The more pious used it to make the sign of the cross on their foreheads, while the rest of us, including the Jewish boys, just dipped in our fingers and then flicked the water at each other. Mont probably did not know of this irreverence, but he certainly saw us as different. He himself taught Scripture lessons to the twelve-year olds who formed his Sixth Form (It would now be called Year 8). He would often read from the Gospel of John of Jesus' encounters with "the Jews", and as he came to this phrase, he would look across at his Jewish pupils, as if identifying us with those Jews of old. But there was no hostility in his gaze, just a hope that one day we might see the error of our ways and come to understand the true faith.

STUDY AND SYMPATHY

In Britain in the 1950s, there was a wave of sympathy for Jews which came directly out of knowledge of the Holocaust and an awareness of Jewish suffering. I and my generation benefited from growing up at that time. There were the traditional theological arguments, but I never felt myself hated. In those days my spiritual home was the Liberal Jewish Synagogue, a vast cavern of a building opposite Lord's in St John's Wood. Prayer was very formal, and meant little to me. Much of traditional Judaism had been discarded there, along with Zionism, kosher food, bar mitzvah and the festival of Purim. All of these I grew up without experiencing, but because I knew little about any of them, I didn't miss them. My Judaism was important to me, because it was about rigorous honesty, a secure and loving family, and being different from the Christian boys at school. I failed to

How Did the Jewish Community Come to Be Where it is Today?

learn Hebrew mainly through my own lack of interest, but also because of educational difficulties caused by poor teaching and poorly implemented policies. In the early 1960s some Liberal synagogues suddenly changed from the traditional Ashkenazi to the Israeli way of pronouncing Hebrew, which left my own class, and I suspect our teachers, really confused. Instead of a bar mitzvah, I had, along with the rest of my class, a Jewish confirmation ceremony at the age of 15, inconveniently timed to take place a couple of weeks before my GCE O Level exams. It is not surprising that my school exams took priority.

The first visit I remember making to an Orthodox United Synagogue was in Kenton in June 1967. This was during the Six Day War, when my father took me to a rally in support of Israel. People really thought Israel was about to be destroyed. There was a mass panic among Jews round the world. We were urged to rally round and to sacrifice as much as we could to the cause. Being a teenage non-Zionist pacifist, the rally meant absolutely nothing to me. It was only many years later that I came to realise how unusual and how untypical of Anglo-Jewry were my attitudes at that time.

Study was my route back. At Oxford, the air was full of it. A few friends got together and called a meeting of what we called 'The Non-Jewish Jew Society', a place where students unsure about their Jewish identity could meet and talk. Forty students turned up to the first meeting held in my college room, but we soon settled down to a group of six or eight. The name of our group came from an essay by the Marxist writer Isaac Deutscher. But we never studied Deutscher or Marx. We invited the young Reform rabbis Jeffrey Newman and Michael Goulston as guest speakers, and they encouraged us to explore the classic Jewish text 'Sayings of the Fathers'. Here was a world of aphorism and proverb, of witty and thoughtful sayings. It soon became apparent that study of such texts was limited without knowledge of Hebrew.

A year or two later, as I enjoyed the leisurely life of a graduate student in those days, the opportunity arose. Without even

15

Beyond the Dysfunctional Family

leaving Oxford, it was easy to immerse myself in Hebrew texts and traditional Judaism. My first visits to Israel gave me a deep love of a country where, in spite of my non-traditional Jewish upbringing, I felt immediately at home. After I moved to London and became a housing officer, my Jewish studies continued, with the help of friends who were studying to be rabbis at Leo Baeck College. They invited me to join them at Bendorf in Germany at the annual Jewish-Christian-Muslim conferences held there for students. The conferences in 1980 and 1981 were the first occasions I had met Muslims, and I was keen to go again. But when I asked to go in 1982, Rabbi Jonathan Magonet explained that places were limited, and that priority was given to Leo Baeck College students. Did he, I wonder, anticipate what would happen? In 1983 I was back at Bendorf, this time as a student rabbi. It was my dialogue with other faiths which took me into the rabbinate, not the other way around.

My studies at Leo Baeck College not only enabled me to enjoy a career as a congregational rabbi, but also led to my own scholarly contributions to dialogue. In 1986, Father Gordian Marshall, a Dominican I had met at Bendorf, invited me to lead a study week with him at the Ammerdown Centre in Somerset. For our first week, we placed Gospel and Rabbinic texts side by side, and discovered both similarities and contrasts. Those who studied with us, both Jews and Christians, found themselves looking at the development of their own faith in a new light. Our studies were written up as a book, *The Gospels and Rabbinic Judaism: A Study Guide* (SCM, London 1988). I have been leading occasional dialogue weeks there ever since. In 1991, Muslims joined the Ammerdown week for the first time. Every two or three years, when these weeks take place, I have learned more about the very real historical connections between our three faiths. Since the advent of Christianity, both Judaism and Christianity have been shaped by dialogue. Since the advent of Islam, all three faiths have been shaped by interaction with the others. Many imagine that all such encounters have been hostile ones, but over the centuries, friendly encounters have shaped

How Did the Jewish Community Come to Be Where it is Today?

our respective cultures and practices more than hostility. Even Jews living as a small minority in medieval Europe had many friendly encounters with Christians, leading to the cultural exchanges I detailed in my book, *The Christian Effect on Jewish Life* (SCM Press, London, 1994).

The Abrahamic dialogue group which has produced this book has been an important part of my life for a little under twenty years. We have met three or four times a year, and many have arrived or left the group. But I do not think that anyone has left untouched by the encounter. Particularly after 9/11, our efforts to grapple with religious hatred showed us clearly that we have much more in common than what divides us. But dialogue is always complex, and we have often become painfully aware of the profound differences that exist *within* each of our three faiths. This too we have shared.

We live today in a difficult and uncertain world. As part of my research for this account, I asked a dozen suburban Jews to take a few minutes out from a committee meeting to share what they thought were the issues of concern for Anglo-Jewry today. The answers came thick and fast. 'We are a diminishing community, full of apathy and assimilation.' 'People think there are millions of Jews in Britain.' 'When I say I'm Jewish, people look at me in a condescending way.' 'We are blamed for what happens in Israel.' 'They think all Jews are rich.' In the face of such comments, Jews have different reactions. One is to argue and debate. One is to hide, for most Jews are not readily identifiable, and it is often not necessary to admit to being Jewish. A third reaction is to respond by asserting positive affirmations of Jewish identity. These three responses are not mutually exclusive: many may respond differently depending on their self-confidence and their view of the situation.

VARIETIES OF INSECURITY

There is a feeling among Jews in Britain that we have never outgrown a centuries old sense of being victims of hatred.

Beyond the Dysfunctional Family

Today, that feeling is commonly fed by media reports on the Arab-Israeli conflict. On a hot day in the summer of 2006, I went into a supermarket to buy a sandwich, and picked up a copy of *The Independent*. When I got to the till, the cashier unfolded it and there splashed across the whole of the front page, was a picture of a dead Lebanese baby. The cashier visibly shivered. "It makes you go cold, looking at that," she said. And she stopped and crossed herself before carrying on. I remember feeling physically sick. Never before, not even during those scripture lessons at school, had I felt such a strong sense of discomfort at being a Jew in Britain. It was caused by the revulsion I saw all around me at Israeli action in Lebanon.

I discussed the newspaper reports with an official from the Community Security Trust. 'How could the media be so irresponsible?' I asked. 'Don't they realise that pictures like that, day after day, week after week, increase hatred of the Jewish community?' The answer I got was a sobering one. 'The media do indeed realise their responsibilities,' he replied. 'I have seen much worse pictures that they don't print at all.'

The Israeli incursion into Lebanon came to an end. Remarkably, the United Nations organised a cease-fire and it held. Recriminations continued in Israel but not in Britain. We British Jews went back to being a warm and cosy community – until similar news reports came from Gaza in early 2009. That too passed, but no doubt there will be more such disturbing episodes. There is a wide gap between how the media regards us when Middle East events are in the news and when they are not. On the positive side, our customs and way of life are far better known in the outside world than when I was a child. Books and the media give accurate information, Judaism is taught in schools across Britain and the community organises public cultural and educational events. The Jewish community is well-known and largely respected. But there is also a depth of hatred that wasn't there before. The effect of the political tensions are such that synagogues and schools have their security rotas, and religious services and Sunday school classes take place in buildings with

How Did the Jewish Community Come to Be Where it is Today?

trained security personnel on duty. No Jewish day school is without its security guards, and on school outings boys from orthodox schools will be likely to wear a secular baseball cap rather than a *kippa* identifying them as Jewish. Thus confidence is tempered with fear. At any time, the next news report might bring back that sense of being victimised.

An additional sense of insecurity is brought about by an awareness that the community is shrinking. In the 1950s there were thought to be 450,000 Jews in Britain. In 2001, the first time a question about religion appeared on census forms, the number was discovered to be 267,000 (Census 2001). In the 1950s there were Jewish communities scattered across the country, but now many of the smaller communities have completely disappeared, and the Jews of Britain live mainly in the larger cities, in particular London (65%), Manchester and Leeds. Within London, the largest communities are in the north-west of the metropolitan area, especially the London Borough of Barnet, home to almost 1 in 5 British Jews, and yet with huge Jewish religious diversity within this small area. The most visible *Haredi* (ultra-Orthodox) community with men mainly dressed in traditional black clothes is small, comprising only 8.5% of the British Jewish community and located mainly in Barnet and Stamford Hill in London and in Salford in Greater Manchester. But some academics dispute these particular census figures. According to a report from the University of Manchester, the ultra-Orthodox in 2008 account for 18% of the Jewish population of London, and almost three-quarters of the live births nationally, with an average of 7 children per family.[1] The one section of the community which is really growing is the one least engaged with British society's public life, and this fact alone increases the discomfort of the rest of the community. In an increasingly secular society, it feels to many Jews that our community is becoming more polarised, and those who occupy the middle ground are becoming fewer in number and less influential.

Analysis of the 2001 census data shows that one quarter of all married Jews reported that their spouse was either of a

Beyond the Dysfunctional Family

different faith or of 'no religion'. Intermarriage is nothing new: it has been estimated that one in twelve British people have a Jewish ancestor. But intermarriage is undoubtedly increasing, and the community is gradually becoming more diverse. There are conflicting and contradictory trends, as has been pointed out in a published analysis of the data:

> The Census data present a paradox. While on the one hand they allow us to look at the entire Jewish population as a single group, they reveal that no single group actually exists; rather it is a collection of multiple subgroups defined in myriad ways... Whether one looks at location, age, nationality or any other marker, there is no single 'Jewish community' but a complex array of overlapping tiers... These data ultimately challenge certain facts and myths that many have cherished: that of the Jewish nuclear family, the homogenous Jewish household, the Jewish housewife, the married Jewish couple or the universally successful and prosperous Jewish citizen.[2]

This huge variety represents a great change from the early twentieth century model of assimilation and acculturation. That trend still exists, but exists alongside a considerable section of the community which sees itself as a confident part of a multicultural society in Britain. There are far fewer Jewish children now who attend Church of England schools like mine. My own children, like most today, have attended Jewish primary schools, where they have gained a knowledge of Hebrew and of Jewish literature and traditions which my generation never had. But unfortunately, it is all too easy for such easy confidence to spill over into a fear of the other. A *Jewish Chronicle* article lamented the shortage of Jewish primary school places, and the author stated that several of her friends would "consider emigration" if their children did not get a place.[3] It is impossible to imagine such a comment appearing even ten years ago. The paradox is clear. Parents scrambling to get their children into Jewish schools are led on not just by their commitment to Judaism or by the high quality of the schools, but also by an increased fear

How Did the Jewish Community Come to Be Where it is Today?

of an outside world hostile to Jews, and fear of their children being isolated Jews in a non-Jewish school.

NEW CHALLENGES

This sense of an outside world that is often hostile has been a common experience of Jews in Europe for centuries. In the past, the threats from outside have been tempered and counterbalanced by the warmth of Jewish home and communal life, with its rich culture, literature, rituals and spirituality. But today, that home life is under threat, from assimilation, divorce, and simply forgetfulness of the religious aspects of the tradition. In today's Jewish home, inherited family custom may be a stronger component of Jewish life than religious ritual practice. The spiritual meaning of Jewish festivals takes second place to the recipes. The Jewish children I teach in my synagogue have a better knowledge of Hebrew and of Jewish festivals than I had as a child, but their sense of their own Jewish identity is often weaker. Many grow up admiring Judaism as part of their family's history, but feel no need to preserve it for their family's future. In the twenty-first century, the relationship of a Jew with the community may not be straightforward. For many, being part of the community may be regarded as a spare time activity, analogous to a hobby.

A Jew is likely to identify more closely with the community at some times than at others, or with some aspects of religious life more than others. In the modern world we frequently compartmentalise different aspects of our lives, and this can lead to a dissociation between religion and the outside world. Even the way we care for each other has become professionalised and institution-based. There are many excellent Jewish care homes for the elderly, but they are not staffed by Jews. The community donates money and others do the work. That strong sense of community, preserved for so long and still there for so many other minority groups, seems to be going. A sense of personal commitment has been lost from this important aspect of traditional religious duty.

Beyond the Dysfunctional Family

Even belief in God has become partitioned off from the day-to-life that religious belief is meant to enrich. God is not a normal topic of conversation within the Jewish community. Many define the British Jewish community today as an ethnic minority rather than a religious group.[4] Belief in God may be separate from an individual's knowledge of Jewish laws and traditions, both of which may influence attitudes and behaviour. Prayers tend to follow set texts and the tradition of personal and spontaneous prayer is ignored by many. Thus at times of crisis the Jew in Britain today comes face to face with questions of doubt and questions of faith which are unfamiliar. When confronted by suffering, many may not know where to look for guidance.

The past lives on inside us. My own childhood memories are part of me. Many of those older than me remember terrible times. In Britain today there are still many elderly Jews who were refugees or survivors of the Nazi era. Although they are not alone amongst ethnic minority groups who have witnessed or experienced or survived genocide, their experiences relate directly to their Jewish backgrounds. Typically, they have spent their working lives achieving as much as they can. Activity helped to suppress distressing thoughts of their past. However, in older people, as activity lessens, there is more time to think and reflect and this can cause distress. For some survivors, authority figures such as people in uniform may be a symbol of suspicion and persecution rather than help and support. Sixty years on, adjusting to illness in old age when loss of control over one's actions and life may become daily challenges, causes difficulties for survivors. Their children too, the so called "second generation," may also have a strong sense of being victims. This helps to explain the sense of being unsafe felt by many in the Jewish community, and the deep sense of insecurity felt when Israel is under attack or involved in military conflict. As Tony Bayfield has put it: 'Most Jews believe that the destruction of Israel would finally bring about the end of Jews and Judaism. That fear is one of the dominating forces in Jewish life.'[5]

Not everything is negative. There is a Jewish cultural Renaissance in Britain. There are more Jewish music, theatre

How Did the Jewish Community Come to Be Where it is Today?

and films than ever before. In December each year, the Limmud conference attracts two thousand Jews, nearly 1% of Anglo-Jewry, for a taste of Jewish learning and culture. Celebration of the joyful aspects of Jewish life, which has sustained Jews for centuries, is still the norm in Jewish homes, synagogues and community centres. The community continues to shrink, but if it eventually disappears it will not be for lack of effort or opportunity. If there were in the future no Jews in Britain, what difference would it make to British society? Would individual Jews who have contributed to this country be remembered as Jews?

THE INFLUENCE OF OTHER FAITHS

Because Jewish identity can be ethnic, cultural or national instead of religious, and because Judaism is not a missionary religion, the Jewish relationship with other faiths is diverse. As with other faith groups, there are fundamentalists who believe they are in possession of the only truth. But most Jews are pluralist, accepting the traditional teaching that for both Jews and non-Jews it is righteous deeds that lead to salvation. 'The pious among the nations will merit a share in the World to Come.'[6] Dialogue has shaped Judaism in the past, and that process is likely to continue. Unlike Judaism and Christianity, Judaism has not looked to one historical figure alone for its source of inspiration. Alone among traditional faiths, Judaism dates its years from the imagined date of the creation of the world. All world history is part of our heritage, and every era provides inspiration for the next. Problems arise only when the past is allowed to veto the present, when the tradition becomes resistant to change.

Successive British governments have viewed Jews as a model of good integration. This is undoubtedly because we have been doing it for centuries, living as minorities in Christian Europe and the Muslim world. Our generation is clearly not the first to grapple with such issues. In medieval Europe, when Jews were a small minority in Christian societies, it was necessary to reach

Beyond the Dysfunctional Family

such accommodation with them as they could. Daily buying and selling was vital to survival. But how could such daily trade with Christians be reconciled with a tradition that was often wary of other faiths? The Torah itself was intolerant of idolatry, calling for the destruction not only of the idols themselves but also of the people who worship them. In the classical rabbinic period of the early centuries of the Christian era, the laws of *Avodah Zarah* ('strange worship') governed the tense relationships between Jews and pagans. Although intolerant by modern standards, the rabbis who formulated the detailed rules began to recognise the practical importance of establishing peaceful relationships between communities of different faiths living side by side. But even so, they prohibited trade between Jews and pagans on pagan festival days, lest the Jew be thought to be offering some kind of support. In twelfth-century France, this gave those studying such rules a problem. In their time, Jews traded openly with Christians all the time, and virtually every day had been designated a Christian saint's day. Despite this, the French scholars known as *tosafists* managed to reconcile their community practice with the ancient rules:[7]

> It is puzzling, what kind of permission people find in our world to negotiate business on the actual days of the Christian feasts. Nearly every day in their calendar is a saint's day and every week they have their Christian day, so trade should always be prohibited!

However, after detailed discussion, a surprising conclusion is reached:

> The reason for the permission seems to us that we accept that the Christians among us do not actually worship idols, and because of this there is a leniency. .. and in any case, Rabbenu Tam[8] explains "it is forbidden to do business with them" specifically with reference to the actual items used for idolatry. We are not here dealing at all with ordinary buying and selling, which is certainly permitted.

How Did the Jewish Community Come to Be Where it is Today?

I quote this detailed example because we are not used to thinking of the twelfth century as a liberal age. Yet dialogue, debate and even religious innovation were flourishing at that time. Today, we need to rediscover debates like this from the past as examples of good practice, at a time when we face the new challenges of living alongside many other faiths in close proximity. With the small size of the Jewish community and its patchy locations, most non-Jews in Britain will never actually meet a Jewish person, and misunderstandings about the community, and the use of stereotyped beliefs and images is not uncommon. In areas with a high immigrant population from countries in Europe Africa and Asia with very small Jewish communities, this situation is further compounded.

It sometimes feels as if such good practices from the past are little understood by Jews today. The respect and understanding shown by those of other faiths when they visit a synagogue or meet Jews does not encourage us to rethink. We are happy to demonstrate the ceremonies, ritual objects and antiquity of our faith, but allow dialogue to reinforce our preconceptions about our history instead of challenging them. Few Jews, for example, take an interest in those features of Christian life which are part of the history of Judaism. Much interfaith dialogue helps to preserve the untrue myth that the Judaism of ancient times has continued virtually unchanged. Those early European Jewish scholars who discussed whether it was permitted to trade with Christians lived on the threshold of a rich period of innovation when many familiar Jewish practices were borrowed from the Church. We frequently use the Yiddish term *shul* for a synagogue, probably borrowed by Jews from their Christian neighbours who saw the young boys going there for classes. The commemoration of the anniversary of the death of a relative with the lighting of a memorial candle is a legacy of the Crusades.[9] The custom of lighting two Shabbat candles was borrowed from the Church in the middle ages. There was an ancient custom of lighting a lamp in the home for Shabbat, but the norm had been a single oil lamp.[10] As the *Encyclopedia Judaica* points out,

25

Beyond the Dysfunctional Family

the widespread employment of candles in the rites of the Catholic Church encouraged their use among medieval Jewry.[11]

In many ways, in contrast to that creative period of Jewish borrowings from Christianity, our dialogue today is sterile and impoverished. We discuss theology and history, but do not wish to see any real impact of dialogue on our culture and customs. So frightened are we by the impact of a secular society, that we react by clinging the more tightly to our traditions, to the extent that our rituals become fixed and unmoving. The medieval Jew managed to borrow memorial and Sabbath candles, but a Jew today who purchases a 'Chanukkah bush' for his living room is regarded with suspicion. A better understanding of the relationship between our three faiths through history leads to the inevitable conclusion that our histories are impossibly intertwined. To advance dialogue we therefore need to find creative ways of expressing our commitment to live side by side. We have to move outside the small dialogue world, and present practical solutions to the ever increasing number of families and households which contain within them those who have allegiance to different faith groups. We have hardly begun the work of freeing ourselves from the prejudice and suspicion which prevents such solutions.

DIALOGUE WITH THE SECULAR

Like all faiths, we are also in dialogue with the secular world. Having a secularised society is no guarantee of tolerance, and to those of us engaged in contact between faith communities it sometimes seems that we are more tolerant and respectful of each other than many non-believers are of any of us. However, as Jews we recognise that we ourselves are far more than just a faith community. Those who identify as Jews today do so in many different ways, many of them cultural or secular. Our dialogue with the secular world begins within our own communities. In Israel, there are many tensions between secular and religious Jews. In Britain, that divide seems less

How Did the Jewish Community Come to Be Where it is Today?

painful, probably because we do not have religious and secular Jewish politicians jockeying for position in the UK Parliament. Secularism in the UK certainly has a voice. The National Secular Society objects to public funding for faith schools and hospital chaplains. Such debates do not have an echo within the Jewish community. Most of those Jews who are not in favour of faith schools are worried about exclusiveness and the creation of social and ethnic tensions, not about the teaching of religion as such. Hence the importance of involving as many Jews as possible in dialogue, representing all shades of opinion and all sections of the community. Informally, very many are already involved. In schools, in the health service, in business and elsewhere Jews and non-Jews work side by side and exchange views. In smaller Jewish communities, parents may find themselves as a Jewish representative asked to give a talk or presentation about an aspect of Jewish life to a child's class. In larger Jewish communities, there are official representatives involved in helping to form education, health and other public policies, and in presenting the views of the community to local councils, MPs and government.

On Christmas Eve 2005, half a century after my school interview, I found myself back in the Headmaster's study at Quainton Hall School. The pictures had changed, but the dark wooden panelling was just as I remembered it. The Headmaster, Desmond Banister, was training in his spare time to be a Church of England minister. Like 'Mont', he was part of the Anglo-Catholic tradition, but unlike his predecessor, Desmond had to write about another faith as part of his training. I work as a rabbi locally and he had found out that I was an Old Boy of the school, and asked me to help. We spent a happy morning together discussing Judaism and Jewish-Christian relations. Jews are no longer the only non-Christian faith represented at the school – there are many Sikh, Hindu and Muslim students, and Harrow has become the most religiously diverse borough in Britain. There is a real willingness among Christian ministers to reach out to other faiths as equals, in a way I could not have imagined as a child. In the summer of 2009, Desmond left the school to take up full time ministry in a local Church. We are still in touch.

Despite our multi-faith society, and despite a much greater awareness on the part of clergy of many traditions, most children in the UK still learn about other faiths from books or other media, without real contact and visits. Similarly, most Jewish day schools have in the past taught little or nothing about faiths other than Judaism. If we really want tolerance and dialogue to grow we actually have to create something new and shared. As a society we are learning to understand that having diverse faiths means more than respecting difference, and that we are all enriched by the real knowledge that comes from knowing each other. We have to search behind our differences for the unity that can bind us. We have to trust each other more and we have to be aware as individuals of the spiritual longing that exists in all of us. We have to be more aware of our shared experiences as human beings, experiences of alienation, of migration, of loneliness, of love, of searching. Jews are used to being a small minority in societies which have other concerns. Today, we are all minorities in some aspects of our lives.

NOTES

1. Yaakov Wise (2008) 'Historic decline in Jewish population reversed', 20 May, http://www.manchester.ac.uk/aboutus/news/display/?id=3612, accessed April 2009.

2. David Graham, Marlena Schmool, and Stanley Waterman (2007) *Jews in Britain: A Snapshot from the 2001 Census.* London: Jewish Policy Research.

3. Miriam Shaviv (2008) 'Take Education More Seriously', *Jewish Chronicle*, 27 June, p. 31.

4. S Cohen and Keith Kahn-Harris (2004) *Beyond Belonging: the Jewish identities of moderately engaged British Jews.* London: Jewish Policy Research. p. 70.

5. Tony Bayfield (2007) 'The Jewish Experience in Britain' in Ed. Alex Bigham *Having Faith in Foreign Policy.* London: Foreign Policy Centre. p. 41.

How Did the Jewish Community Come to Be Where it is Today?

6. Maimonides, *Mishneh Torah*, Hilchot Melachim 8:11, based on *Babylonian Talmud*, Sanhedrin 105a.

7. *Tosafot* on *Babylonian Talmud*, Avodah Zarah 2a. Older printed editions were forced to change the references to Christians. These were restored by the modern editor Adin Steinsaltz in his edition.

8. Rabbenu Tam, pp. 1100-1171, Aube, North East France.

9. Abraham Millgram (1971) *Jewish Worship*. Philadelphia: Jewish Publication Society. p. 448.

10. Michael Hilton (1994) *The Christian Effect on Jewish Life*. London: SCM Press. pp. 179-182.

11. Meir Ydit (1972) 'Candles' in *Encyclopedia Judaica*, Jerusalem: Keter, 5:117.

2

How Did the Christian Community Come to Be Where it is Today?

Elizabeth J Harris

In 1939, as the Second World War began, my father registered as a conscientious objector, convinced, as a member of the Student Christian Movement (SCM), that the teaching of Jesus was not compatible with military action. He was influenced by his own father, who had returned disillusioned from the First World War, convinced that a war-free world could be built through the Labour Party and the Co-operative Movement. When the horror of the holocaust emerged, he 'recanted' from his pacifism. He decided that pacifism, at its best, was a personal vocation and that the fight against the Nazis had been necessary. Throughout his life, I believe, he retained a sense of guilt that he had not fought against Hitler – a 'heavy burden' he called it, in his diaries.

In this personal reflection on how the British Christian community has come to be where it is today and what it looks like to me, a 'liberal' Christian committed to building respect between faiths, I begin in the 1940s with the debate over pacifism. My father was not alone. Many young Christians in the SCM became conscientious objectors. Some remained so after the war. Others realised that war was sometimes necessary in the face of greater evil, in this case, the demonic policies of Nazi Germany against Jews and those perceived as deviant from an Aryan 'norm' – policies made possible because of centuries of Christian anti-semitism, seen, for instance, in Martin Luther's infamous tract, *On the Jews and their Lies*, which was included in a 1936 edition of Luther's work published under the Nazis.[1] The idealistic young men who, in 1939, insisted that military force

31

Beyond the Dysfunctional Family

was incompatible with Christianity perhaps did not realise what this legacy had spawned in Nazi-dominated Europe.

Some Christians, however, were better informed. In the 1920s, the London Society for Jews and Christians was formed. In 1934, the General Assembly of the Church of Scotland recognised the 'age-long sufferings of the Jewish people' and, aware of current anti-semitism, declared that their ill-treatment was 'abhorrent'.[2] This prepared the ground for the work of Christians such as William Simpson (Methodist), Kathleen Freeman (Anglican) and James Parkes (Anglican), which led to the founding of the Council of Christians and Jews in 1942.[3]

Only a minority of Christians, however, knew about the Council. More influential were the writings of Dietrich Bonhoeffer (1906-1945), a German Lutheran pastor, who was hanged by the Nazis for conspiring against Hitler, barely a month before the war ended. His *Letters and Papers from Prison*, published in English in 1953, posed, according to Keith Clements, 'a unique challenge to Christianity to take a prophetic stance towards any misuse of political power'.[4] It inspired a generation of Christians to reflect on the relationship between Christianity and radical political opposition. Christian involvement in anti-nuclear demonstrations in the 1950s at Aldermaston, headquarters of Britain's nuclear weapons initiative, including the march from London to Aldermaston in 1958, was inspired by such writings.

THE 1950s

As the 1940s ceded to the 1950s, a minority of Christians were also aware of a growing diversity of belief in Britain, apart from the Jewish presence, and a growing academic interest in 'comparative religion'. Firstly, there was an underlying fascination with the 'East' going back, at least, to Victorian Britain, when Edwin Arnold's evocative poem on the Buddha, *The Light of* Asia (1879), went into numerous editions, novels by H. Rider Haggard, Marie Corelli and Rudyard Kipling played with religious concepts such as reincarnation and *karma*, and

How Did the Christian Community Come to Be Where it is Today?

movements such as the Theosophical Society were formed.[5] By the 1950s, this had lead to a sizeable number of western converts to Buddhism.[6] Secondly, Christians in urban areas such as Liverpool, London, Woking and Cardiff were aware of a Muslim presence. Liverpool and Cardiff had vibrant Muslim communities well before the 1950s. In fact, British convert to Islam, Abdullah Quilliam, had founded the Liverpool Muslim Institute and British Muslim Association in 1887, two years before the opening of the Woking mosque in 1889.[7]

The interest in 'comparative religion' had largely arisen from the colonial encounter with religions in Asia and Africa. In 1938 Edwin James published an introduction to the subject, followed by A C Bouquet in 1941.[8] How to react to this theologically was becoming significant, in a context in which the exclusivism of the Dutch theologian, Hendrik Kraemer,[9] was still influential and teaching at many theological colleges was heavily influenced by the thought of Karl Barth.[10] Were the 'other' religions of the world misguided, 'human' attempts at reaching the transcendent or traditions with much to teach Christians about the divine?

This was the context into which I was born, in 1950, a child of the Methodist manse. Food was still rationed. There was depression and poverty. New clothes were rare. The Christian churches in the 1950s, however, were confident and evangelistic. From 1950-53, as a young minister in Sacriston, a mining village in County Durham, my father lead a Methodist group in song and proclamation at 10.00 pm on Sundays, outside the cinema, near to a pub. Similar acts of witness were happening elsewhere, often involving Christians who had taken the 'pledge', a declaration that they would never touch alcohol. Churches were full at this time. Sacriston had two large Methodist Churches with membership in hundreds. However, there were many non-churchgoers, who were keener on the pub than worship. Even in the 1950s, Christians were aware of a growing secularism with roots in Britain's class history and challenges to Christian belief from science.

Also in the 1950s a cultural diversity different from traditional distinctions between Scottish, Welsh, Irish and English became

Beyond the Dysfunctional Family

part of the experience of some urban Christians. As a young child, in the mid 1950s, I was unaware that my father, now in Middlesbrough, opened up the club facilities of one his churches to new migrants from the Caribbean. He later wrote, 'The venture thrived for quite a while, but none of these (the newcomers from the Caribbean) dared to attend a Sunday service'.[11] This pattern was to become familiar. Black Christian communities emerged that felt too alienated from the 'white' church to join it for worship.

For the majority of Christians, awareness of religious and cultural diversity came later. In the late 1950s, when we were living in Stanmore, in North West London, I remember being embarrassed at junior school because my father was a Methodist minister. Most of my classmates had no religious faith. Secularism had deepened. My best friend came from what might be called a post-Christian home. Significantly, I cannot remember if there were Jews or Muslims at this school. I am sure there must have been – but I don't remember them, although I knew what a synagogue was, and possibly a mosque. And religious education classes only taught Christianity. However, for those who were open to engaging with religious diversity, new resources were beginning to appear, developing the earlier works of comparative religion scholars and missionaries.[12] For instance, in 1956, Kenneth Cragg's *The Call of the Minaret* brought Islam into the homes of many Christians, awaking some to the possibility of real dialogue.[13] This was followed in 1957 by *An Introduction to Asian Religions*, by Methodist scholar, Geoffrey Parrinder.[14]

If I had attended the Stanmore school in the 1960s, my story might have been different. For it was then that the religious landscape for British Christians truly began to change as Hindus, Jains, Muslims and Sikhs from South Asia came to Britain to meet shortfalls in the workforce alongside further migration from the Caribbean. It was also a time of new theological thinking and debate. Bonhoeffer continued to inspire liberal Christians but there were new writers too. John Robinson's (1919-1983) *Honest to God* first appeared in 1963 and sold a million copies. It hurt

How Did the Christian Community Come to Be Where it is Today?

some Christians because it questioned traditional images of God but energized others, particularly those seeking new ways of thinking about the divine in an increasingly secular age.[15] Just a couple of years later, Harvey Cox's *The Secular City* appeared, which not only grappled with secularism but also growing religious diversity.[16] Again, it disturbed some and inspired others.

At a political level in the 1960s, there was growing indignation among Christians at the global inequalities between rich and poor. The British Empire may have become a Commonwealth but there was no common wealth. A plethora of initiatives emerged. The one that touched me, as a university student in Lancaster, was Third World First, a student organisation founded in 1969.[17] Its initial focus was raising money for the poor but it soon began educating people about the causes of poverty through its magazine, *The Internationalist* (from 1973, *The New Internationalist*), which gained support from Christian organisations such as Christian Aid, the Methodist Church and the Quaker-inspired Cadbury and Rowntree Trusts. *The New Internationalist* connected with politically conscious Christians and secularists with articles about oil power, the sugar trade, Bolivian miners, world health, and multinationals and baby food. Its readers were also likely to have read two other influential writers, Franz Fanon and Paulo Freire. Fanon (1925-1961), as he was dying from leukaemia, published *Les Damnés de la Terre*, translated into English as *The Wretched of the Earth* in 1963. It was a revolutionary anti-colonial book, written in the context of the Algerian independence struggle. The Brazilian Freire (1921-1997), in his 1970 book, *Pedagogy of the Oppressed*, championed an education that was an empowering act of freedom, a means of transforming the world.

For students like me who leaned towards socialism and avidly read *The New Internationalist*, the times were both exciting and disturbing, as the 1960s became the 1970s. There was the legacy of the Vietnam War, on one hand, and the socialism of Fidel Castro's Cuba, on the other. There were liberation struggles in some African countries and promising developments in

Beyond the Dysfunctional Family

newly independent countries – Tanzania, for example, under the socialist Julius Nyerere. There was also hope in the Chile of Salvador Allende – to be crushed in 1973, with the killing of Allende and the installation of General Pinochet.

Not all Christians, though, were of my ilk. The majority were more influenced by the internationally known evangelists of the time, such as Billy (William Franklin) Graham (1918 -), American Southern Baptist, who visited Britain in 1954, 1966, 1984-5 and 1989, preaching the need for each person to claim salvation through faith in Jesus Christ alone.

At an international level, change was coming in all sections of the church. In the Roman Catholic Church, the Second Vatican Council from 1962-65 stimulated a period of remarkable change, most markedly in the areas of liturgy, theology and relationships with other faiths. The key document for the latter was *Nostra Aetate* (*In Our Time*). Released in 1965, it took a broadly inclusivist view, stating:

> The Catholic Church rejects nothing that is true and holy in these religions. She regards with sincere reverence those ways of conduct and of life, those precepts and teachings which, though differing in many aspects from the ones she holds and sets forth, nonetheless often reflect a ray of that Truth which enlightens all men.

The document also decried 'displays of anti-Semitism'.

For some other churches, change was led by the World Council of Churches (WCC), a body founded in 1948.[18] Significant was the Council's World Assembly held in Uppsala in 1966. With 704 delegates from 235 member churches and the theme, 'Behold I Make All Things New', it declared that, 'churches need a new openness to the world in its aspirations, its achievements, its restlessness and its despair'.[19] It had a harder political edge than previous Assemblies and new Council programmes resulted, including the Programme to Combat Racism, which focussed particularly on apartheid in South Africa, and, in 1970, the Sub-unit on Dialogue with People of Living Faiths and Ideologies,

36

How Did the Christian Community Come to Be Where it is Today?

headed by the Indian theologian, Stanley Samartha (1920-2001).

In 1969, a study work camp for young adults was held in Uppsala as a follow-up to the 1966 Council. This included the study of prophets such as Amos and Hosea, and the political struggle for liberation in Guinea Bissau. I was one of two British participants and its effect on me was seismic. I had been at the point of rejecting all religion. Uppsala 1969 changed that. For if religion could be about justice for the poor, political involvement and prophets who said, 'But let justice roll down like waters, and righteousness like an ever-flowing stream' (Amos 3: 24), I was interested. It was the content, though, that was important to me at that point, not the fact that it came from a Jewish source.

THE 1970s

To conclude that, by the 1970s, a gap was emerging in British Christianity between liberal Christians, energized by the new emphases in the WCC, and evangelical Christians, concerned with personal salvation and evangelism, would be too simplistic. Evangelicals were also turning to social justice issues. Key to this was Ronald Sider's 1977 book, *Rich Christians in an Age of Hunger*, which surveyed the Bible, extracting portions that spoke of a Christian's duty to help the poor.[20] It is still a best seller.

Parallel to this, a revolution was taking place in the teaching of religion in Higher Education – a movement away from the comparative study of religion towards the study of religion through the eyes of believers. Among the pioneers was Edwin Oliver James, who took the Chair of History and Philosophy of Religion in Leeds, in 1936,[21] as well as Geoffrey Parrinder, Andrew Walls and Frank Whaling.[22] And the Canadian scholar, Wilfred Cantwell Smith (1916-2000) was an undoubted influence.[23] The change was most noticeable at Lancaster – one of the new campus universities, opened in the 1960s to cater for a rising number of school leavers. Here, Ninian Smart created a Department for Religious Studies. The word 'Theology' was

Beyond the Dysfunctional Family

omitted. Rejecting 'the comparative study of religion', which, so often, meant the study of religion through Christian lenses, Smart pioneered a phenomenological approach, which sought to respect the authority of the believer. His 1969 book, *The Religious Experience of Mankind*[24] was a turning point for many. It certainly inspired me, when I read it in the late 1970s.

For Christians, the 1970s was a pivotal decade for other reasons too. Firstly, there was ordination of women to the ministry. In the nineteenth century, women became deaconesses in several Christian denominations but were not, generally, ordained as ministers or priests. In 1925, however, the Baptist Union of Great Britain and Ireland took the decision formally to accredit women ministers. Other denominations took a long time to follow – 1968 for the Church of Scotland and 1974 for the Methodist Church in Britain.[25] Women in these churches were energised by this change but not over-optimistic. They knew that formal recognition of women's ministry did not mean equality between women and men in the leadership of the church. The struggle for that still continues. Yet, by the 1970s, the first steps had been made in some Christian churches. I can remember my father taking pride in the fact that he was among the first Methodist Superintendents (a minister having oversight of a group of churches) to request a woman minister.

Secondly, Christians were realising that the Afro-Caribbean presence in Britain was not unproblematic. In 1976, the British Council of Churches (BCC) published, *The New Black Presence in Britain: A Christian Scrutiny*.[26] It identified seven elements in the 'disorder' within 'the black communities': large numbers of potentially creative young people stigmatised by spending years in ESN (Special Needs) schools; larger numbers emerging as semi-literate school-leavers; young people without roots and without hope; conflict between these young people and the police and other control agencies; parents incurring humiliation and blame for not caring for their children or for dealing with them too harshly; the co-opting of potential leaders into 'organisations that are intended to control discontent and to do

38

How Did the Christian Community Come to Be Where it is Today?

ambulance welfare work'; the white working class clamouring for repatriation and denial of citizenship to black people, and black people working harmoniously alongside white people on the factory floor but being excluded from working men's clubs.[27] The churches were encouraged not only to 'alleviate the hardships of black people' but to express fellowship with 'newly established churches', to establish a centre for Black Art and to intervene in the education of black people.[28]

The BCC was also addressing religious diversity. In 1974, Lamin Sanneh was commissioned to write a survey of Islam in the UK, which resulted in a Presence of Islam in Britain Advisory Group, chaired by the Rt Revd David Brown, Bishop of Guildford.[29] Then, in April 1977, the BCC Assembly instructed its Executive Committee, in co-operation with the Conference of British Missionary Societies (CBMS), to establish a way of helping the Churches and their agencies to promote a creative Christian response to the religiously plural character of the world community. As a result, the Committee for Relations with People of Other Faiths (CRPOF) was founded. Its first meeting, in May 1978, had the Rt. Revd David Brown in the Chair and Revd Kenneth Cracknell, Methodist minister, as Executive Secretary.[30]

The first members of CRPOF were mainly people who had come close to 'other' faiths during overseas missionary service and who had returned eager to encourage their home churches to establish courteous inter faith relationships. Kenneth Cracknell travelled the length of Britain, networked with national and international inter faith bodies, and wrote booklets that tackled biblical material head-on, particularly 'difficult' verses such as John 14.6 ('I am the way, and the truth, and the life. No one comes to the Father except through me').[31] He also encouraged encounter:

> ...all the reading in the world cannot replace that sense of joyful, personal discovery that takes place when two or more people of different religious commitments really begin to listen to each other. God has now opened the way for that experience to so many of us in Britain today.[32]

Beyond the Dysfunctional Family

The United Reformed and Methodist Churches were among the first individual Christian denominations to engage with Britain's new religious reality. For example, the Methodist Church's Division for Social Responsibility, at the end of the 1970s, published, *Shall we greet only our own family?* Recognising the theological diversity among Methodists, it sought to change attitudes, by offering biblical material to support an ethic for inter faith relations based on love. It set out five tasks: understanding the Gospel; sorting out our motives; accepting responsibility; improving our knowledge of other faiths; understanding our neighbours.

Marcus Braybrooke, an Anglican priest who was committed to the Council of Christians and Jews and the World Congress of Faiths (founded in 1936), was also beginning to publish in the 1970s.[33] His output was to become prolific, championing inter faith dialogue as a pilgrimage towards truth as well as the concept of a global ethic.[34]

At grassroots level, however, many Christians were either apathetic or resistant. Those actively involved in inter faith initiatives were in the minority and could feel very isolated. For instance, Ivy Gutridge, a lay Methodist woman, who was eventually granted an MBE for her services to inter faith understanding, became 'note-taker' of the Wolverhampton Inter Faith Group in 1974 and remained until 1998. She often spoke about how misunderstood she felt at the beginning. She was not alone. Those involved in the new inter faith groups were ignored or criticised by the majority of Christians.

For me personally, though, the 1970s was an exciting time. Encounter between faiths was not yet, for me, a priority. It was a new attitude towards mission that excited me. Gone was the view that the West would save the rest. Intercultural learning, partnership between the 'North' and 'South', and western Christians receiving from newer overseas churches was now being stressed. Entering this movement, wanting to learn from 'the other half of the world', I taught English in Jamaica for two years. For the first time, I experienced being in an ethnic minority. For the first time, I immersed myself in the 'other'. It

40

How Did the Christian Community Come to Be Where it is Today?

was a tough but amazingly rich experience. And I did learn much more than I gave. I was not alone – other young adults were having similar experiences. It was part of the spirit of the 1970s and the Christians involved brought back to Britain an enthusiasm for multiculturalism and a wish to enliven British Christianity.

My first post in Britain, when I returned, was in a comprehensive school in Brent, a London borough with one of Britain's highest percentages of black and Asian children. Enthusiastically, I taught books written by non-white authors, such as Linton Kwesi Johnson and V S Naipaul. My Jamaica experience paid dividends and the excitement I felt was characteristic of the decade. An optimism was present – that Britain could set an example in dealing positively with cultural diversity, in spite of warnings from bodies such as the British Council of Churches.

THE 1980s

If the 1970s was a decade of enthusiasm among the minority of Christian pioneers of intercultural and inter faith understanding, then the 1980s was one of consolidation and development. It was in a changing political atmosphere. In 1979, the Conservative Party gained power under Margaret Thatcher, issuing in a decade that would highlight the individual rather than the community. In April 1981, the first Brixton riot – a violent confrontation between black youths and police – took place, followed in 1985 by further riots in Peckham, Toxteth (Liverpool) and, again, Brixton. The limited optimism of the 1970s faded, to be replaced by anxiety about fragmenting communities and Britain's lessened moral credibility, an anxiety that was not helped by the belligerent rhetoric that accompanied the Falklands War in 1982.

CRPOF, at the beginning of the decade, was examining how the WCC 1979 document on inter faith relations could be made more accessible. Four principles for inter faith dialogue were consequently offered to the churches: Dialogue begins when people meet each other; Dialogue depends on mutual

41

Beyond the Dysfunctional Family

understanding and mutual trust; Dialogue makes it possible to share in service to the community; Dialogue becomes the medium of authentic witness.[35] The last contained an ambiguity that the Committee were well aware of. For the Committee, 'authentic witness' was not proselytisation. It was about relating to others in a way that was true to the gospel injunction to love one's neighbour. The ambiguity, however, made the guidelines more acceptable to the majority of Christians, for whom witness meant evangelism. In the years that followed, a number of Christian denominations formally accepted the principles. But the ambiguity it created remains with us to this day.

The 1980s was also a decade when the pioneers of the 1970s felt compelled to write more than in-house booklets. 1983 saw *Christians and Religious Pluralism* by Anglican priest, Alan Race.[36] It introduced a three-fold typology to describe the attitudes Christians took to religious plurality: exclusivism, inclusivism and pluralism, Race himself taking a pluralist position. This was followed in 1985 by *The Bible and People of Other Faiths* by Sri Lankan Methodist minister, Wesley Ariarajah, then Director of the Dialogue Sub-Unit of the WCC.[37] In 1986, Kenneth Cracknell drew together his experience at the BCC in *Towards a New Relationship: Christians and People of Other Faiths*.[38] And in the Roman Catholic Church, Gavin D'Costa published, *Theology and Religious Pluralism: The Challenge of Other Religions*, taking an inclusivist position.[39] These books were different one from another but all challenged exclusivist readings of the New Testament and Christian tradition and sought to draw people into positive relationships with people of other faiths.

At the same time, several Christian denominations appointed national inter faith officers. The Church of England appointed Mrs Mary Tanner (thus extending her primary role which was in intra religious dialogue about Christian unity), who was followed by the Revd Christopher Lamb, and the Methodist Church appointed the Revd Martin Forward. (Both Christopher and Martin offered a specialism in Islam). Within the Roman Catholic Church in England and Wales, Bishop Charles

How Did the Christian Community Come to Be Where it is Today?

Henderson was the pioneer, establishing the Bishops' Conference Committee for Other Faiths in 1984. Over the next years, the Church of England, with its commitment to pastoral care to the nation as a whole, produced a series of informative pamphlets concerned with themes such as theology for dialogue, use of church buildings for prayer with other faiths, and mixed faith marriages. A parallel series of leaflets on inter faith dialogue, and the faiths within England and Wales, was also produced by the Roman Catholic Church. This period saw a wave of creative responses from the institutional churches, waking up to new realities.

As this was happening, I was developing my own commitment to inter faith relations. Having left teaching, I was a staff member of the ecumenical agency, Christians Abroad, encouraging others to cross cultural barriers. And it was through my enthusiasm for this that I saw the further challenge – crossing religious barriers. I joined the fledgling Harrow Inter Faith Group and the World Conference on Religion and Peace. Eventually, through a serendipitous series of events, I left Christians Abroad to study Buddhism in Sri Lanka, on a scholarship from the World Council of Churches.

When I travelled to Sri Lanka I did not know that an American Roman Catholic professor of theology, John S Dunne, had used the expressions 'passing over' and 'coming back' to describe one form of interreligious encounter.[40] All I knew was that I wanted to immerse myself in Buddhism so that I could see the world through Buddhist eyes. Only such an immersion, I decided, would do justice to Buddhism and to global religious plurality. Initially I thought that I would stay one year. I stayed eight, gaining a doctorate in Buddhist Studies from a Sri Lankan University.

In Sri Lanka, I learnt at the feet not only of Buddhists but also of Christian pioneers of inter faith relations such as Dr Aloysius Pieris s.j. and Dr Michael Rodrigo o.m.i. I drew deeply from the wells of Buddhist spirituality and did indeed move towards seeing the world through Buddhist eyes. I 'came back' to Christianity but not to the same place. I wholeheartedly joined those Christians for whom an exclusivist theology based

43

Beyond the Dysfunctional Family

on Christian superiority is unacceptable and also the smaller band of those who have been so enriched by another religion that they continue to draw from its wisdom.

My journey into Buddhism was just one example of the multiple religious journeys that some Christians were taking in the twentieth century, challenging easy definitions of Christian identity. Now, in the twenty first century, further complexity is emerging, for instance within the self-definition of children of inter faith marriages and in those who openly claim a hyphenated religious identity: Buddhist-Christian, Christian-Hindu, and so on.

Returning to the 1980s, a key moment for inter faith relations in Britain was the establishing of The Inter Faith Network for the UK in 1987. The prime movers were Kenneth Cracknell and Brian Pearce, a retired civil servant, already involved with CRPOF. The imagination of Christians gave it birth, but Christians were not its gatekeepers. It was owned and managed by its members: faith communities, inter faith groups and bodies, and educational institutions. Its impact on the churches was initially not great. In 1993, however, the Network agreed a Code of Conduct, which several Christian denominations formally adopted. It stressed respect, courtesy, honesty and self restraint in inter faith relations. When, in 1996, I became Secretary for Inter Faith Relations for the Methodist Church, it delighted me that I could point Methodists towards the Code and say, 'this is what your own Church has agreed ...'

In other arenas, gaining an equal playing field for members of different faiths was not so easy. The prison service was one. The Church of England was the gatekeeper with those at the top resisting change. Some faiths were willing to work with this; others were not. Particularly vocal was the Angulimala Trust, the Buddhist organisation that mediated the provision of Buddhist prison chaplains. Led by a convert from the Church of England, it demanded a greater share in the central management of prison chaplaincy. Change eventually came. The difficulties that the prison service faced, however, was indicative of a general fear amongst Christians that the identity of Britain as a Christian country would be lost.

The Satanic Verses affair in 1988 and 1989 fuelled this fear. Comfortable Christians in the south of England were shocked and confused at the Muslim reaction to Rushdie's book.[41] To see a public book burning on the streets of an English town (Bradford) struck many as alien, non-British, unfathomable. Could religion evoke such destructive passion? Was this what Islam was? And wasn't such passion a sign that Muslims could not integrate? In Bradford, Christians such as the Revd David Bowen, of the United Reformed Church, worked tirelessly to mediate between communities. The publication that resulted was a masterpiece of empathetic yet robust intervention.[42]

THE 1990s

As the 1980s turned into the 1990s, however, there was still a significant movement among Christians towards greater openness to religious plurality. And this movement continued. If a snapshot was taken of, say, 1998, it would show: a lively Churches Commission for Inter Faith Relations (successor to CRPOF) linked to Churches Together in Britain and Ireland (successor to the BCC); a vigorous Christian involvement in the Inter Faith Network for the UK; local inter faith groups and local groups of the Council for Christians and Jews; a Christian Inter Faith Practitioners Association (successor to the Association for Ministerial Training in a Multi-Faith Society founded in the 1980s); and church discussion groups willing to use theological resources on inter faith relations. Christians were also involved in a new initiative, the Three Faiths Forum, founded in 1997 by Sir Sigmund Sternberg (Jewish), Dr Zaki Badawi (Muslim) and the Revd Marcus Braybrooke.

In the 1980s there were some signs that the theological training world wanted to take inter faith theology more seriously. For example, Alan Race at the Southwark Ordination Course and Andrew Wingate at the West Midlands Theological Training

Beyond the Dysfunctional Family

Course created space for theological reflection about religious plurality in their courses. By the 1990s some Theological Colleges were also beginning to include inter faith relations in their curricula, although it was too often relegated to the periphery – an Easter school here, a weekend there. I was sometimes invited to contribute to one. Yet, Christians involved in inter faith relations were still painfully aware that many in their churches still found moving beyond an exclusivist theology difficult. Why? Was the legacy of the missionary tradition of the British Empire too strong? Was the Alpha Course – a course designed to introduce new, lapsed or unenthusiastic Christians to an exclusivist Christian message – becoming just too successful? Was popular literature about the persecution of Christians overseas making Christians disbelieve what inter faith enthusiasts said? Or was hymnody and liturgy that still implied that only Christians held the key to salvation to blame? All of these factors, I believe, contributed, plus a growing awareness that the number of Christians in Britain would decline dramatically in the next century.

Many in the churches may also have recognised the fear and suspicion of Islam that a 1997, Runnymede Trust report, *Islamophobia: A Challenge for us all,* revealed. Significantly, three years before, there had been a similar report on anti-Semitism.[43] Some would have agreed with those who were calling multiculturalism into question. Jenny Taylor, a committed Christian, for instance, was arguing that the multicultural policies of local and national government were leading to the toleration of child marriage and forced marriage, educational absenteeism and the existence of geographical territories where different ethical and social norms prevailed.[44] Some may even have been influenced by The National Front, which, in the 1990s, was beginning to appeal to fears concerning Islam to illustrate why their racist policies were sound.

As the 1990s moved towards the millennium and the twenty first century, therefore, a retrenchment in inter faith relations on the Christian side was noticeable. Inter faith groups from

How Did the Christian Community Come to Be Where it is Today?

the 1970s onwards had been predicated on the enrichment that could come from encounter, conversation and in-depth meeting. This emphasis did not die. Christians, including me, continued to stress the need for inter faith learning. Others worked to resist the influence of the National Front in Lancashire and Yorkshire. Yet, other elements connected with retrenchment were entering, fuelled by several factors, including a change of government policy towards faith communities, fear amongst some Christians that Christian identity was under threat and pressure from some Christian communities overseas. All these factors remain important in the present.

In 1991, a Local Government Act was passed, which made it mandatory for local governments to consult with faith communities and other minority groups. Consequently, some Local Authorities helped to establish Councils of Faiths to be their pathway into faith communities. It was a positive move but had one disadvantage. Risking generalization, such Councils placed multi faith working – action on issues outside religion such as liaison with the police and social cohesion strategies – above faiths coming to know one another. Dialogue, in some cases, became secondary to local political considerations. Although moves such as this involved more Christians in inter faith encounter, it was at the expense of theological reflection. For one can co-operate with members of other faiths whilst still holding an exclusionary theology.

In 2001/2002 the Church of England initiated a significant project, *Presence and Engagement*, which sought to explore the theological and social responses of Christians living in areas where more than 10% of the population belonged to faiths other than Christianity. Risking generalisation, many responses avoided the theological. Respondents were vocal on practical issues but seemed fearful of engaging with the theological implications of their activities. One of the project recommendations, therefore, was the establishment of educational centres to encourage theological reflection on religious diversity. Three initiatives now function: the St Philip's

Beyond the Dysfunctional Family

Centre in Leicester; Bradford Churches for Dialogue and Diversity; and the Presence and Engagement Network, based at The Contextual Theology Centre at The Royal Foundation of St Katharine in London.

The conviction that Christianity was under threat was multifaceted. The destruction of the twin towers in Manhattan on 11 September 2001 (9/11) and the London bombings of 7 July 2005 contributed to it. Only a few doubted that Muslim terrorists were responsible. Broadly speaking, Christians in Britain reacted in two ways. The first was to assume that terrorism and Islam were so closely interlinked that Islam, as a whole, was a threat to 'civilised' values. Christians who took this view were swayed by writers such as Patrick Sookhdeo, Director of the Barnabas Fund. In 2001, in a popular article, he compared Christianity and Islam, portraying Christianity as superior on every count.[45] He concluded, 'Certainly an aggressive and paranoid approach towards Islam and Muslims is not what God requires of us' but pleaded that a blind eye should not be turned to the differences between the faiths.

The second reaction was that dialogue with Muslims was more important than ever. William Dalrymple might have been an influence here. In a series of talks following 9/11, he stressed a commonality between Christianity and Islam that could be traced to Islam's early centuries, quoting St John of Damascus (d. 749), who believed that Islam was not a new religion but a Judeao-Christian variation.[46] The 'Dalrymplites' stressed that bridges had to be built with Muslim communities, especially in places where white and Asian communities were geographically separated. It was not simply a coincidence, those who took this position argued, that 9/11 had followed a summer of riots between white and Asian gangs in Burnley, Bradford and Oldham.

In the present, this sense of threat is compounded, for some Christians, by the projected numerical decline of Christianity[47] and a perception that 'society' is bent on forbidding Christians to wear religious symbols at work or to celebrate Christmas

How Did the Christian Community Come to Be Where it is Today?

and Easter. In this context, some churches in Britain are more concerned about maintaining identity in a multi faith society than interrogating their theology so that space is made for other religions and the secular. The Church of England, in its membership of the Anglican Communion, and other churches with international partnerships, have also had to listen to Christians overseas, calling them to account for their attitudes to gender, sexuality and inter faith relations.

As I draw this reflection to a close, it is the need for intra-religious dialogue that I would want to stress – a dialogue within Christianity about role, status, identity and theology. It is significant that NIFCON, the Network for Inter Faith Concerns of the Anglican Communion, offered a document to the 2008 Lambeth Conference that called for just such a dialogue on inter faith relations. It began with an affirmation of faith and continued:

> It is not for us to set limits to the work of God, for the energy of the Holy Spirit cannot be confined. 'The tree is known by its fruits', and 'the fruit of the Spirit is love, joy, peace, patience, kindness, generosity, faithfulness, gentleness and self-control.' When we meet these qualities in our encounter with people of other faiths, we must engage joyfully with the Spirit's work in their lives and in their communities.[48]

Expressing an inclusivist theology and echoing *Nostra Aetate*, it called for rigorous theological reflection at a critical time and a spirit of openness rooted in 'hospitality'. The shift to the concept of 'hospitality' as a framework for inter faith relations retained an emphasis on the pastoral which had been a hallmark of Anglican responses since the early 1980s.

CONCLUSION

This reflection has been selective. It has been directed by my life story, which has been driven by a passion for intercultural and interreligious learning and a yearning for justice and peace in the world. I am convinced that retrenchment is not the way

Beyond the Dysfunctional Family

forward for Christians in religiously plural Britain. More than ever before, people from different faiths need not only to work together but to share their wisdoms. They also need to engage positively with secular society and the new forms of spiritual and religious belonging present in the West. If Christians fail to do this, they risk becoming irrelevant.

NOTES

1. The tract claims God does not hear the prayers of Jews, urges that all synagogues should be burnt and refers to the Jews as 'our plague, our pestilence, our misfortune'. It is usually omitted from editions of Luther's work, except for the edition of 1936.

2. See Marcus Braybrooke (1992) *Pilgrimage of Hope: One Hundred Years of Global Interfaith Dialogue.* London: SCM Press. p. 178.

3. Braybrooke (1992) p. 181.

4. Keith Clements (2000) 'Dietrich Bonhoeffer' in Eds. Adrian Hastings, Alistair Mason & Hugh Pyper *The Oxford Companion to Christian Thought.* Oxford: Oxford University Press. p. 79.

5. See for instance, Philip C Almond (1988) *The British Discovery of Buddhism.* Cambridge: Cambridge University Press; Sharada Sugirtharajah (2003) *Imagining Hinduism: a postcolonial* perspective. London & New York: Routledge; Elizabeth J Harris (2006) *Theravāda Buddhism and the British Encounter: Religious, missionary and colonial encounter in nineteenth century Sri Lanka.* London & New York: Routledge; J Jeffrey Franklin (2008) *The Lotus and The Lion: Buddhism and the British Empire.* Cornell University Press.

6. The first British converts to Buddhism came at the end of the nineteenth century. In 1907, The Buddhist Society of Great Britain and Ireland had been formed to greet a Buddhist mission from Burma, led by one of the first British persons to become a Buddhist monk, Ven Ananda Metteyya (Allan Bennett).

7. See Ron Geaves (2010) *Islam in Victorian Britain: The Life and Times of Abdullah Quilliam.* Markfield: Kube Publishing. p. 3.

8. Edwin O James (1938) *Comparative Religion: An Introduction and Historical Study.* London: Methuen; A C Bouquet (1941) *Comparative Religion: A Short Outline.* Harmondsworth: Penguin Books. Bouquet followed this with (1954) *Sacred Books of the World: A Companion Source Book to 'Comparative Religion'.* Penguin.

How Did the Christian Community Come to Be Where it is Today?

9. Kraemer (1888-1965) was a man of many interests – a philologist, an expert on Islam, an opposer of National Socialism, a Director of the World Council of Churches' Ecumenical Institute of Bossey, in Switzerland. He is perhaps most well-known for the book he wrote for the 1938 meeting of the International Missionary Council, *The Christian Message in a Non-Christian World*, which stressed the radical discontinuity of Christianity with all other faiths.

10. Karl Barth (1886-1968) was a Swiss Protestant theologian who stressed that knowledge of God is only given through God's revelation in Jesus Christ and not through 'religion'. Whether this conviction necessarily implied negativity towards other religious traditions is still a matter for academic debate.

11. Herbert W Harris (2005) *This Minister* – unpublished, personal reflection on his life.

12. Not all Christian missionaries in the nineteenth and early twentieth centuries were exclusivists. See, Kenneth Cracknell (1995) *Justice, Courtesy and Love: Theologians and Missionaries Encountering World Religions 1846-1914*. London: Epworth Press.

13. Kenneth Cragg (1956) *The Call of the Minaret*. Oxford: Oxford University Press.

14. Edward G Parrinder (1957) *An Introduction to Asian Religions*. London: SPCK.

15. John A T Robinson (1963) *Honest to God*. London: SCM Press. Robinson was Anglican Bishop of Woolwich.

16. Harvey Gallagher Cox (1965) *The Secular City: secularization and urbanization in theological perspective*. New York: Macmillan.

17. Third World First is now People and Planet (P&P). It claims to be the largest student-based organisation working for world development.

18. It now draws together churches from all the main Christian confessions and denominations except Roman Catholics and Unitarians. See F L Cross & E A Livingstone (1997) *The Oxford Dictionary of the Christian Church*. Oxford: OUP, p. 1765.

19. Ans J Van der Bent & Diane Kessler (2002) 'WCC Assemblies' in Eds. Nicholas Lossky, Jose Miguez Bonino et al. *Dictionary of the Ecumenical Movement*. Geneva: World Council of Churches. p. 1234.

20. Ronald J Sider (1977) *Rich Christians in an Age of Hunger: A Biblical Study*. Intervarsity Press and Paulist Press. An updated edition was printed in 2005.

21. See Frank Whaling (2006) 'A Brief History of the Study of Religion' in *Diskus* Vol 7 (the e-journal of the British Association for the Study of Religion - www.basr.ac.uk/diskus).

22. For information on Parrinder, see Martin Forward (1998) *A Bag of Needments: Geoffrey Parrinder and The Study of Religion*. Bern: Peter Lang.

Beyond the Dysfunctional Family

23. One of Cantwell Smith's most influential books was published in 1963, *The Meaning and End of Religion: A New Approach to the Religious Traditions of Mankind*. New York: Macmillan. For a selection of his writings, see: Ed. Kenneth Cracknell (2001) *Wilfred Cantwell Smith: A Reader*. Oxford: Oneworld.

24. Ninian Smart (1969) *The Religious Experience of Mankind*. New York: Charles Scribner's Sons. Issued by Collins (Fontana Library) in 1971.

25. *The Oxford Dictionary of the Christian Church*. p. 1761.

26. British Council of Churches (1976) *The New Black Presence in Britain: A Christian Scrutiny: A Statement by The British Council of Churches' Working Party on Britain as a Multi-Racial Society*. London: Community and Race Relations Unit of the British Council of Churches.

27. *Ibid.* pp. 18-19.

28. *Ibid.* pp. 33-34.

29. In 1976, Brown wrote *A New Threshold: Guidelines for the Churches in their Relations with Muslim Communities*, published by the BCC and BCMS.

30. The information on the early history of the CRPOF is taken from a history I wrote for the Churches' Commission for Inter Faith Relations (of Churches Together in Britain and Ireland) in 2007: Historical Notes on the Committee for Relations with People of Other Faiths (CRPOF) and the Churches' Commission for Inter Faith Relations (CCIFR) 1977-2003. Compiled by Elizabeth J Harris. It can be found on the website of Churches Together in Britain and Ireland.

31. For instance, Kenneth Cracknell (1980) *Why Dialogue? A first British comment on the WCC Guidelines*. London: British Council of Churches. The World Council of Churches document was: (1979) *Guidelines on Dialogue with People of Living Faiths and Ideologies*, Geneva: World Council of Churches.

32. Cracknell, *Why Dialogue?*. p. 23.

33. (1971) *Together to the Truth* Madras: CLS was among these first publications. (1976) *Faith in Fellowship: A Short History of the World Congress of Faiths*. World Congress of Faiths, was another. A longer version appeared as: (1992) *A Wider Vision: A History of the World Congress of Faiths*. Oxford: Oneworld.

34. See: Ed. Marcus Braybrooke (1992) *Stepping Stones to a Global Ethic*. London: SCM Press; Eds. Peggy Morgan & Marcus Braybrooke. *Testing the Global Ethic*. Oxford: World Congress of Faiths & International Interfaith Centre and Ada: CoNexus Press.

35. British Council of Churches (1981) *Relations with People of Other Faiths: Guidelines for Dialogue in Britain*. London: British Council of Churches. Revised in 1983.

36. Alan Race (1983) *Christians and Religious Pluralism: Patterns in the Christian Theology of Religions*. London: SCM Press. Revised and enlarged 1993.

How Did the Christian Community Come to Be Where it is Today?

37. S Wesley Ariarajah (1985) *The Bible and People of Other Faiths*. Geneva: World Council of Churches.

38. Kenneth Cracknell (1986) *Towards a New Relationship: Christians and People of Other Faiths*. London: Epworth Press.

39. Gavin D'Costa (1986) *Theology and Religious Pluralism: The Challenge of Other Religions*. Oxford: Basil Blackwell.

40. Quoted by Kenneth Cracknell in *Towards a New Relationship*. p. 139.

41. Salman Rushdie (1988) *The Satanic Verses*. Viking Penguin.

42. Ed. David G. Bowen (1992) *The Satanic Verses: Bradford Responds*. Bradford: Bradford and Ilkley Community College.

43. Runnymede Trust (1994) *A Very Light Sleeper: the persistence and dangers of Antisemitism*. London: Runnymede Trust.

44. See for example, Jenny Taylor's chapter (1998) in Eds. Lesslie Newbigin, Lamin Sanneh, Jenny Taylor *Faith and Power: Christianity and Islam in 'Secular' Britain*. London: SPCK.

45. Patrick Sookhdeo (2001) 'A Christian Perspective on Islam' in *Israel and Christians Today*, Winter 2001, p. 6.

46. See printed versions of two talks given by Dalrymple in *Q News*, November 2001 and *The Tablet*, 22-29 December 2001.

47. For example, 'Muslims "will soon outnumber Anglicans"' in *The Sunday Telegraph*, October 28, 2001, p. 6.

48. *Generous Love: The truth of the Gospel and the call to dialogue: an Anglican theology of inter faith relations*. It is available for download from NIFCON's website.

3

How Did the Muslim Community Come to Be Where it is Today?

Dilwar Hussain

Imagine a young man in his twenties – he drifted through school not quite knowing what he would like to be when older, or where he fits into society. He is now unemployed. He didn't perform very well in education, just scraping through. He can't really relate that well to his parents culture – they migrated to Britain from a very different country and still talk of 'home' as somewhere else – but he knows deep down that England is now his home, even if people around him don't think he always fits in. He finds talk of 'immigration' and 'they took our jobs' quite disturbing and, frankly, it makes him feel angry. He lives in a working class area and went to a school that was renowned for performing badly – where he was often bullied for being different and for eating 'smelly food'. That is until the culture of the whole area began to slowly change and the 'local kids' that bullied him gradually became smaller in number, as families migrated away, and the few remaining ones were then bullied themselves for 'being different'! His father is always out working low paid jobs to make ends meet. Mum is always at home struggling to make ends meet and bring up the four kids almost on her own. But they are a proud family, proud of their culture, heritage and religion...and the parents hold out hope that the boys in the family will marry a 'good traditional girl' of their own kind.

One could be excused for thinking that I am describing a typical Muslim youngster growing up in Britain, but this scenario could also be about someone of Polish Catholic

Beyond the Dysfunctional Family

background, or some years ago someone of Italian, African-Caribbean or Irish background, and going back further in the 20th Century, someone of Jewish background...and so on. The experience of migration and subsequent settlement, with all that this entails in terms of the establishment of communities, negotiating new identities, and dealing with poverty, racism and changes in family dynamics, are common threads. I therefore begin this chapter by emphasising that while there are of course specificities to each and every ethnic or religious community, we can also fall into the trap of 'exceptionalising' much of our discussions about Muslims and presenting them in reified religious terms. And whether this occurs because of a strong sense of Muslim identity politics (within Muslim communities), or due to lazy analysis from the outside, we do this to the detriment of a wholesome understanding of the reality of Muslims today.

Looking at 'the Muslim community' must be quite a perplexing task from the outside – a very diverse community of communities, of various ethnic groups, of various different first languages, very traditional and conservative in many senses and yet grappling with modernity, and the modern world, as most 'religious' people are.

We can see the results of that as a tension in the discourses of the first generation who were migrants and the second generation who began to see Britain as their home and many in the third, and now fourth, generations who think that the question of where they belong is itself rather silly (of course they are British). And not only are they British, but also increasingly English (catching up with co-religionists in other parts of isles who have long adopted Scottish and Welsh identities). We can see this tension also in the wide range of views espoused by Muslim organisations ranging from extremists groups who reject all things Western, to liberal/secular groups who resent that Muslims have too much cultural baggage, or would like Islam to undergo a Reformation as Christianity did, or indeed those that wish to be Muslims without being religious.

How Did the Muslim Community Come to Be Where it is Today?

This is without going into details of the post-colonial contexts and origins of many schools of modern Muslim thought, or indeed of classical divisions in theology and religious schools of law that still prevail. But before we go further let us look briefly at the history of the British Muslim presence and think for a moment about how it developed.

HISTORY

The first traceable contact points between the British Isles and Islam go back to the 8th century as shown by the coins minted by King Offa of Mercia (d. 796) that bear Arabic Islamic inscriptions alongside Offa's insignia. Going down the time line somewhat, one finds that Robert of St Alban's married the granddaughter of Salahuddin Ayyubi in the 12th century and that there were contacts between King John and the North African Amir, Muhammad al-Nasir, in the 13th century. Despite this early interaction it was in the 18th century that the first Muslims probably began to settle in Britain. As they were mainly sailors, most of the early communities were formed in areas of the major port cities such as Liverpool, Newcastle and London. Two significant communities sprang up in Woking, where the first purpose built mosque was established in 1896, and Liverpool, identified with Henry William Quilliam (d. 1932) who converted to Islam and was conferred the title of Sheikh al-Islam by the Ottoman Sultan. The Woking community also included leading notables such as Lord Headley Farooq (d. 1935) the first Muslim Peer; Marmaduke Pickthall (d. 1936) and Abdullah Yusuf Ali (d. 1953), the translators of the Qur'an. The early 20th Century also saw figures such as Syed Amir Ali a member of the Privy Council associated with the London Mosque Trust (eventually to be re-named the East London Mosque). These communities were quite small and localised and it was much later, after the Second World War that more significant numbers of Muslims migrated and settled. Of course, Empire was an important consideration in those days and in 1936 Dr. Khalid Sheldrake,

Beyond the Dysfunctional Family

president of the Western Islamic Alliance, stated that King George V had more Muslim subjects than Christian by virtue of the extent of the Empire!

A key reason for migration after World War II was that the post-war economy needed labourers. Additionally, in the recently decolonised regions of the world, economic and educational conditions were not satisfactory. This led to a 'push-pull' effect, which, over two decades, brought a significant number of Muslims to the UK, mostly from the rural areas of West Pakistan and East Pakistan (which became Bangladesh in 1971). Over the years, these communities have been joined by Muslims originating from Africa, Arab countries, Europe and far East-Asia, as well as converts from the UK, to form an ethnically diverse and culturally vibrant community of communities.

This cultural vibrancy has meant that over the last fifty years Muslims have become quite visible, whether through the growth of Indian restaurants (mostly British-Bangladeshi owned), clothing and grocery outlets selling exotic merchandise, buildings with ornate eastern architecture, or the infamous dress of some Muslim women (and indeed men). And then of course there's terrorism. But long before the security challenge, other lesser-hyped issues were paving the way to disenfranchisement. Some of the major challenges for Muslim communities have been education, the maintenance of strong families, identity, discrimination, leadership and representation.

According to the most recent estimates there are around 2 million Muslims living in the UK. Muslim demographics show a very youthful community, about half below the age of 25, most of whom were born in the UK. There is a heightened sense of religious identity – in 2001 96% of people of Pakistani origin and 95% of those of Bengali origin said they were Muslims, compared to 68% in the general white population who said they were Christian. And likewise, many more Muslims think religion says something important about their identity rather than other characteristics such as family, ethnicity or colour.

A MORI poll commissioned by British Asian newspaper, *Eastern Eye* (November 2001) found that 87% of Muslims and

How Did the Muslim Community Come to Be Where it is Today?

90% of Asians say they are 'loyal to Britain'. The Citizenship Survey of 2007 also shows that Pakistani, Bangladeshis and Indians score highly in their sense of belonging to the UK, in fact higher than 'white' people as a category.

My parents came from Bangladesh and I remember vividly in my childhood, growing up in the North of England (Sheffield), how important symbols such as the Royal Family were to us. Broader than that there was also a strong appreciation from my parents that Britain, even if a little strange at times, was a good place to live – a place where we could get a good quality education and a decent job if we worked hard. Even though I was the first person in my family to go beyond compulsory education, and my parents had only a very basic level of education in Bangladesh, the aspirations and expectations were very high. And 'fitting in', having non-Asian friends, speaking English well, were all seen as important dimensions of our education.

So the question of 'being British' was not a major issue for me, but for many Muslims of the second and third generation discussions of identity have been quite vocal debates. Are these Muslims British or Pakistani, Bengali, Gujarati, etc? This evolving debate has seen new twists and turns in the post 9/11 and post 7/7 era. For the vast majority the story has always been of people who saw great opportunities in the UK, people who were born, or at least brought up, here with a sense of pride and belonging – right down to the neighbourhood level and often displayed in the local accents, cultures and customs adopted by Muslims across the country. This process of adoption and adaptation has quite naturally created a gradually developing sense of hyphenated identities such as 'British-Pakistani-Muslim', or later just 'British-Muslim'. It seems that the crux of the matter is how Muslims can become entirely comfortable being British and at the same time remain loyal to their faith. Can this apparently dual sense of loyalty be harmonised?

Some would argue that in fact the problem implicit in the above questions is down to their framing. All citizens have

Beyond the Dysfunctional Family

some 'baggage', be it ideological, religious or moral, which from time to time may need negotiation. And more importantly, people have always juggled multiple identities. The tensions in loyalty, whether the pulls are towards individual interest, family, ideology/belief, nation or the world has always been a negotiated exercise of judgment where a sharp, even if ruthless, sense of justice is a vital yardstick. It is for this reason that the Qur'an instructs, "be just, even if it is against yourself, your parents or kin". Such language identifies that being loyal to one's faith, is ultimately about being a good person, not only in a private context, but also in a public setting, i.e. being a good citizen and one who is working to promote the common good. It is interesting to note that when I began to take religion more seriously, just before going to University, it was actually the teachings about social justice and how this related to my sense of being a responsible citizen that I found most profound about Islam. I was also lucky to meet, in my early journey into Islam, more grounded Muslims that preached the possibility of being British and Muslim at the same time. As strange as it was to some in those days, that was a notion that I latched onto as I read, thought and explored Islam further.

But the religious label accorded to Muslim citizens does now appear to have some problematic dimensions. Increasingly Muslim identity is viewed as reified and exaggerated. If this is true, a number of internal and external factors could be identified as the driving force for shaping this identity. Internally one could point to the desire to create a distinct Muslim identity. The evolving identity politics over the last three decades, particularly, has meant that Muslims themselves emphasised their religious identity in order both to be recognised as having distinct needs (and common rights) while falling through the cracks of old *race* relations legislation which failed to adequately recognise, and therefore deal with, the growing *religiously* motivated hatred against them. But there was also an attempt to transcend ethnic and tribal differences at a grassroots level. Many Muslims growing up in the 1980s of Pakistani,

How Did the Muslim Community Come to Be Where it is Today?

Bangladeshi or Arab descent, born in the UK, having common schooling experiences, and sharing common British culture, found their respective parental heritage and the 'divisions' that created rather bemusing. Emphasising a British and Muslim identity could bring them one step closer to a common citizenry.

On the external level, events such as the Iranian Revolution, the *Satanic Verses* affair, and later 9/11 and 7/7 meant that the public limelight was intensely on the religious dimension of this emerging identity. Together this has created a preoccupation with 'Muslim' identities. A criminal is now a 'Muslim thief', the local GP is a 'Muslim doctor', etc. The trouble with this is twofold: that Muslims cannot be seen simply as human beings, they have to be perceived mainly through a religious prism, and secondly – perhaps more problematic – the identity created is rooted in the politics of defiance, often shaped by major global upheavals. This can all be very confusing: should we refer to Muslims, Asians, Pakistanis, British citizens, or a mixture of the above? Eventually I hope the label can just be British (or English for those of us in England) citizens, but until we get there we may find that people use some or all of the other labels and their different permutations depending on the issue at hand.

In saying this I am not suggesting that Muslims disappear into a secular void, rather that Islam should no longer be an exotic preoccupation; it should become almost banal and ordinary, normal and normalised. We wouldn't feel the need to call, say, Tony Blair or Gordon Brown former 'Christian Prime Ministers', even though Christianity is evidently important to them. It's all about how we choose to define people publicly, and giving them a one-dimensional description, however important, undervalues the complexity of that person. But the current debates seem far from this and the well of victimhood seems to be swelling with Muslim casualties.

Much has been written on the radicalisation of Muslim opinion, and it's not my focus here but it is perhaps worth a fleeting glance at the issue. However small the number of those radicalised, the nature of the threat means that it must be taken seriously.

Beyond the Dysfunctional Family

For a generation of young people who grew up observing the complexity of global politics, with all its double standards and injustices, it is unfortunate that they did not have the leadership and sufficient positive role models to channel their frustration into more positive engagements. Often those frustrations seem largely about foreign affairs, but to blame only foreign affairs for this radicalisation is not nearly enough. Muslims were not able to challenge sufficiently strongly the preachers of hate and the peddlers of simplistic solutions that were able to tap into that frustration. Nor did they create adequate religious institutions that could connect with young people and educate them in an idiom they would understand, something that could have protected them when challenged by extremists. If we can learn from such lessons and move on, perhaps things can be different in the future.

Perhaps the most important challenge faced by British Muslims is in the field of education, particularly for boys. Despite the often strong educational aspirations, the social circumstances and inadequate presence of support mechanisms have often meant that some sectors of the Muslim community are among the weakest performers in educational terms. Largely a function of class rather than ethnicity or religion, this lack of achievement has a devastating consequence on employment, community development, family life and self-esteem.

The impact on self-esteem is clearly not just from education – another key factor is how those around you treat you. I was lucky in that, while I did at times face general verbal abuse on the streets or at school as a child (the usual 'Paki' name calling, etc), I always had many, many other experiences and relationships – with friends, neighbours, teachers, etc – that were positive and this allowed me to see thugs and racists as wholly unrepresentative of where I lived. But perhaps not everyone was as lucky. Among the first generation of Muslims to live in the UK, many faced racist abuse, but more recently that xenophobia seems to have grown, as mentioned above, to become more specific and focus on religion as a marker rather

How Did the Muslim Community Come to Be Where it is Today?

than just the colour of the skin or foreignness of Muslims. This 'Islamophobia' has been written about extensively now, and in a report published by the Runnymede Trust[1] was deemed to be 'a serious issue' for British society in 1997. Post 9/11 the issue became even more serious. Tackling discrimination is something we have done quite well in the UK compared to the rest of Europe, but it has taken some time to even recognise the existence of anti-Muslim prejudice. The legislative framework continues to evolve, bringing in religion as a new dimension to discrimination legislation over successive human rights and equalities Acts in the last decade. With such advances in the legislative arena, the remaining challenge is arguably at the level of culture and how Muslims are seen as 'other', often incompatible with European or British culture and values. But the challenge (mainly for Muslims) is also to be precise about the phenomenon we are describing and not conflate general xenophobia and prejudice of difference with specific anti-Muslim hatred. Furthermore, it can also become easy to dismiss critical remarks about Muslim practice (or often Eastern/Asian cultural practice) as Islamophobia or racism. Rather than stifle debate, we need more debate, but naturally in an atmosphere of decorum and civility.

No doubt a religious identity also raises other questions – should faith not be a private affair? How can we live in a plural society if people publicly bring up contesting ideas that could fragment national solidarity? Is there not an urgent need for integration into a national narrative? Do we not need to go beyond the 'errors of multiculturalism', which placed too much emphasis on difference? Well of course, having an overarching national identity and bringing one's own ideas and values to the table are not mutually exclusive.

INTEGRATION

Looking at the emergence of Islam, one can see that Muhammad, the Prophet, didn't isolate himself from the people around him.

63

Beyond the Dysfunctional Family

He was one of them, he interacted with them, engaged with them, talked to them, lived with them and was seen by most as an important, trusted element of his society, a man who lived with integrity. The verse of the Qur'an: "The food of the people of the Book is lawful unto you and your food is lawful unto them" shows that the world-view of the early Muslim community was not one of isolation. But the word 'integration', in its current usage, often gets a mixed response, usually because it is not defined clearly and because the assumptions behind it can often be ambiguous. Whenever I use this word, it is located somewhere *between* social and cultural segregation and total assimilation. Assimilation would seem to involve one entity dissolving into something else and losing its sense of originality. Sometimes 'integration' seems to be used to mean assimilation and this differential usage can be seen especially in pan-European discussions.

At times the word is used to imply two distinct, essentialised entities coming together and one becoming part of the other, or rather the onus being on one to integrate into the other. I prefer to think of the process of integration as far more complex and fluid, through which a new narrative of the collective 'we' is constantly being re-defined, giving rise to a new vision of being British (and in the context of this discussion new visions of being Muslim naturally should arise).

Sometimes an assumption of the integration discourse is that it will lead to less apparent, less visible minorities, or perhaps less troublesome ones. This may be an unrealistic assumption to make as integration is likely to increase the assertiveness of groups – a natural by-product of an increased sense of ownership of the nation. Whereas immigrant grandparents would pass by racism on the streets with their heads down, teenagers who feel a greater sense of ownership of the space around them and feel they can demand equal treatment may not be as passive. A very useful way of thinking about integration was developed at the Commission for Racial Equality, before it closed down in 2007. Integration was defined as a having three pillars: equality,

How Did the Muslim Community Come to Be Where it is Today?

participation and interaction. Equality in that the playing field needs to be levelled and 'glass ceilings', as barriers to achievement and ambition, need to be removed; a commitment to participating in society and engaging as citizens; and the need for spaces in which different people could interact. Such a vision for integration removes the onus from any single entity or group and talks more about the climate necessary for people to come together and the collective responsibility for making integration work.

A SIGNIFICANT CHANGE FOR EUROPE?

Given that many European nation states historically evolved around tribal or religious boundaries, they were often defined in terms of 'sameness' rather than accommodation of difference. Even in the case of the creation of the French Republic was an attempt to rid Europe of the 'old way', the *Ancien Régime*, and to create a new order based upon individual citizenship, regardless of a person's religious affiliation, or social standing that original egalitarian spirit seems to have turned into a hyper-defensive, secular force that feels very threatened by any form of public display of difference that may fragment republican unity, especialy when it comes to religion. Perhaps we should be less surprised by this, for in fact the notion of citizenship, traced back to Athens, can be shown to be quite exclusive – slaves, foreigners and women, were not part of the privilege for example and one could argue that such notions were deeply embedded in our European conceptions of citizenship. This may explain why it was only in the 20th century that women were granted the vote in Europe, for example. But globalisation has meant that 'foreigners' are not so foreign anymore and it has been a painful experience for European policy makers and thinkers to deal with the diversity that the 20th century brought to this continent. However, that does pose an important question – how can societies, if so diverse, be united enough to be a collective, a nation? How can diversity be respected alongside

Beyond the Dysfunctional Family

unity, solidarity and cohesion? At the same time, how can citizenship be something that is an active socio-political status, with a genuine dissipation of power to the grassroots, and not just an individualised economic function as mere consumerism, for example?

A SIGNIFICANT CHANGE FOR MUSLIMS?

It is not enough to just look at the modern world and the construction of communities. Muslims face a crisis of thought that prevents them from dealing adequately with the challenges they face in the modern world. This crisis of *ijtihad* (independent, creative reasoning) has been written about by many. But to understand the severity of the challenge we also need to reflect on how the context has changed. A number of major events have affected the Muslim world over the last century, of these perhaps the most important were: i) the impact of colonisation – such that by 1920 around 75% of the Muslim world was under European rule, ii) the fall of the Caliphate in 1924, and iii) globalisation with the possibility of mass migration as well as the inter-connectedness of geographical locations in economic, security and other strategic terms. Much of the contemporary discourse around Muslim social justice, social change and activism was developed in the context of anti-colonial struggles and the attempts in the early 20th century to re-establish the Caliphate. But with mass migration we have also seen the withering of the *dar al-Islam* (abode of security and peace) and *dar al-harb* (abode of war) divide, creating a new type of world where one may more safely practice Islam in the heartlands of the West than in traditional Muslim spaces. A large number of Muslims during the 20th century have begun to live as minorities (estimated to be over a third of all Muslims), to whom the idea of the 'old order' of a Caliphate, a *dar al-Islam* (and hence, *dar al-harb*) are meaningless. Furthermore, through migration and settlement in urban environments, the shift from rural to urban lifestyle and the impact of urban living on the family, schooling and the

How Did the Muslim Community Come to Be Where it is Today?

distribution of wealth have had important influences on the lives of these Muslims in the diaspora. Given that our globalised world is highly complex, with international conventions, treaties such as the Universal Declaration of Human Rights, and membership of bodies such as the United Nations, etc., if a nation is to be part of the international community and enjoy the privileges which that membership entails – sharing of trade relations, subsidies, aid, security/intelligence/military resources, etc. – then one cannot lead a life isolated from the international community. And more recently, events such as 9/11, and domestically in a UK context, 7/7, have created a security panic across the world and a mode of important introspection among many Muslim thinkers and activists.

These changes demand a response from Muslim intellectuals that is well beyond the scope of this chapter, and this writer (!), but they are mentioned here to show the magnitude and nature of the challenge to Muslim thought. It is a long-term struggle, nothing short of creating a re-vitalised, re-formed Muslim intellectual paradigm that will allow for a contextual and normalised brand of Islamic practice that – for the purpose of this discussion – is more British/English in its flavour. I am always struck, whenever I travel through the Muslim world, by how different cultures, cuisines, manners and customs are. Just as there are African, Asian, Arab, Bosnian, Turkish expressions of Muslim culture, can there not be European and Western expressions of Islam?

THE NORMALISATION OF ISLAM

Despite the positive times that did exist between Muslims and Christians or Islam and the West/Europe, well documented tensions have built up between Europe and the Muslim world over their thirteen centuries of interaction.[2] This may partly be due to the presence, as mentioned, of Muslims in Spain, Italy, France, Austria and other parts of southern Europe as a very visible 'Other', perceived as conquerors; or the interaction during the crusades for example. The result is a historical legacy

67

Beyond the Dysfunctional Family

that is characterised by suspicion, misinformation and often enmity. Christianity and Judaism (to a lesser degree) are now accepted components of Europe. One can hear people talk of the Judeo-Christian Heritage of Europe or of Judeo-Christian Values. Few would think of Christians and Jews as foreigners to Europe – they have been normalised. Yet Islam remains the other, even though its contribution to European ideas and values are arguably no less significant. And of course all three of the Abrahamic faiths share similar geographic origins, very similar ethical and moral outlooks and have essentially similar religious worldviews.

At a time when intense scrutiny faces Muslims, Islam has become a curious, exotic oddity, the archetypal 'Other'. If Islam is to become a 'normal', perhaps even banal, entity, of course many external conditions need to be suitable, but the internal issues are what concern me here. Faith requires something far more profound than mere rebellious activism, we cannot only be a movement of protest. Faith requires that Muslims live in British society and involve themselves in it fully, that they become of it and own it, that they are *seen* as of it and belonging to it and articulating what they stand *for*, and not just what they are *against*. Muhammad was known as 'the trustworthy', 'the honest', 'the truthful'. How many Muslims in Britain have the same reputation? How can we play our profoundly spiritual melody so that it can rise above the din of the global political debates surrounding us?

But there are a number of opportunities available, not only challenges and obstacles, to this process. These are: the sheer numbers of Muslims resident in Western Europe with 2, 3 or 4 generations present in some countries; the enthusiasm with which many of our youth talk of being both European and Muslim, British and Muslim; the significant contributions that people of Muslim origin have begun to play in the life of Europe, especially Britain – for example within the NHS. On a structural level the potential for Muslim nations to be included in the EU, and broader trade relations with the Muslim world, also pose significant opportunities for enhancing mutual understanding.

As Islam, like Judaism has a strong notion of 'the law', there has been much talk of and debates around the topic of 'a *fiqh* (jurisprudence) of minorities'. The bottom line is, I suppose, that we need a *fiqh* that will deal with the real issues and challenges of Muslims living in Europe and the West and address them in the right spirit – whatever we call this. It will need to be a *fiqh* that is not merely based on the defensive and exceptional position of 'minorityness' (emphasising a begrudging survival in the midst of a 'non-Muslim majority' culture), or temporary hardship and necessity (*darurah*) (in which 'normality' can be suspended to make concessions and compromises), but a *fiqh* that will encourage Muslims to develop confident identities as active participants and citizens and, above all, allow them to live and practice Islam contextually and recognise that they are already 'at home'. *This* is normality now and Muslim thought has to come to grips with it. The recent reports on *Contextualising Islam in Britain*[3] by Cambridge University are a helpful contribution to this process, coming amidst the backdrop of a wider series of debates around how Muslims are challenged by and respond to the impact of modernity.

EMERGING DISCOURSES CONCERNING THE SOCIAL CONTRACT, CITIZENSHIP AND SHARED VALUES

Over the last 20 years we have become accustomed to seeing a visible representation of militant Islam in the media and in public discourse – people expressing frustrations, rage and ultimately engaging in acts of terror. But at the other end of the Muslim spectrum developments have also occurred, albeit of lower profile, which are far more significant to the body of Muslim thought. One can see a gradual emergence of a more liberal frame of thinking on a range of issues. In many ways the development and evolution of Islamic thought in the West, reflects the intellectual journeys of self-discovery of many

Beyond the Dysfunctional Family

individual Muslims in the West. For many of us, Islam was initially read as an Oriental religion, rooted in the cultures of the East. And yet, our lived experiences and cultural familiarity was more Western. Inevitably, and eventually, this led to questions, soul-searching, even doubts, and along with this came a thirst for answers, a search for new and more satisfying ways of tackling un-answered questions – the existence of which only dawns when one develops the maturity and confidence to become self-critical. Again, I feel very lucky – finding myself working at the Islamic Foundation, after graduation, in an environment where I could explore Islamic thought academically and have access to visiting scholars and intellectuals from around the world. Learning from scholars of different faiths and beliefs in an environment removed from the pressures of community activism and constraints of identity politics gave me the space to think about and reflect on a number of issues that seemed pertinent.

One such issue is around the notion of the secular. In recent times Muslims have approached the issue of secularism from a distinctly historical encounter. As seen above, they have often – though not always – taken their point of departure from anti-colonial movements that have placed a high value upon restoring the Caliphate as a symbol of Muslim unity, which looked back to Muslim history for inspiration and which created nostalgic and romanticised associations between state and religious authority. It has been argued that Islam does not recognise a division between the temporal and the transcendental. However a more discerning and critical look at Muslim history could identify clear challenges to this view.

For instance, Muhammad Abduh (d. 1905), the Egyptian reformist thinker, argued that Islam did uphold a clear distinction between the 'religious' and 'worldly'. After all, there has always been a distinction between *din* (religion) and *dawlah* (state), or in *fiqh*, between *ibadat* (worship) and *muamalat* (human interaction), as well as between *hukkam* (rulers) and *ulama* (scholars). One of the key arguments made against this distinction between religion and politics has been the notion of God's sovereignty (*hakimiyah*) over creation, the argument being that if God is the ultimate Sovereign, there can be no real distinction between the affairs of religion and the affairs of the world. This view has partly come about as a result of the early experiences of Islam and more recently can be found most prominently in the ideas of Revivalist[4] thinkers such as Maududi (d. 1979) in the Indian sub-continent and Qutb (d. 1966) in Egypt. Unlike Christianity, which had evolved for some three centuries as the religion of a powerless minority before Constantine and the Nicene era, Islam very quickly acquired state authority and in its formative era came under the protection of the state. As Ernest Gellner[5] observed, Islam had an "absence of accommodation with the temporal power. Being itself Caesar, it had no need to give unto Caesar."

However some contemporary Muslim thinkers have argued that the metaphysical notion of God's sovereignty does not entail the 'rule of God' in the world through some perfect political system. This has been argued even, and indeed mainly, by some intellectuals and political leaders from a more liberal Revivalist background such as Turabi (Sudan) and Ghannouchi (Tunisia)[6] who have urged Muslims to engage in democratic politics. But taking this further it is possible to develop an argument for accepting procedural secularism as a fair way of managing diversity in a plural, multi-faith environment.[7] The Cambridge report[8] affirms support for secularism: *"Secular law in Britain provides for religious freedom and protection against discrimination. History shows that in religious states, the power of religious authority becomes hegemonic"*[9]. This is twinned in the report with a strong appreciation of British society and the *"existence of justice, security and the freedom to practice one's religion. Britain ranks very favourably against these criteria, certainly more so than many Muslim-majority countries"*[10]. Some of Tariq Ramadan's ideas about the relationship of Muslims to European identity are also important in this context. According to Ramadan, Europe embodies important Islamic teachings at its very core.

In addition to this theological debate, the lived Muslim experience of the interaction between religion and politics over

Beyond the Dysfunctional Family

the last century has often been far from pleasant. Olivier Roy's thesis of the 'failure of political Islam'[11] seems to have wind in its sails if we are to consider the situation of despotism and authoritarianism in the Muslim world, not exclusive to, but including, the various states that were created and fashioned in the name of Islam. All of this has meant that while some have strongly advocated a closer and stronger relationship between religion and politics, the Muslim journey for others has been a search for how to limit the power and influence of authoritarian religion. In this context Human Rights has become an important and controversial debate in the Muslim world.

Some Muslim critiques of the Human Rights discourse have asserted that the Universal Declaration of Human Rights (UDHR) does not adequately reflect the cultural and religious needs of Muslims and Muslim states. A range of approaches can be found from strong criticism, particularly from countries such as Saudi Arabia, Iran and Sudan, to those such as Maududi[12], that have argued for a theoretical compatibility of Islam and Universal Human Rights (though Maududi is criticised for adopting a narrow conception of equality and rights in his understanding of the Human Rights discourse), to more recent intellectuals such as Naim[13] in the US, Baderin[14] in the UK and Soroush (Iranian), who have argued for the UDHR to be adopted and embraced by Muslims more fully, as opposed to others that have argued for 'Islamic Declarations' of Human Rights. The key obstacles in terms of application to Muslim nations seem to arise from a mixture of philosophical and practical/cultural positions. Related to the notion of *hakimiyah* (as mentioned before), some Muslims have argued that rights are conferred upon human beings by God and that there are no *a priori* rights of man unless granted by God. This vision sees the world through a specific religious lens and ultimately could undermine the very shared, common and human approach necessary to create a *Universal* declaration of rights. Some of the practical issues include controversies around freedom of religion and apostasy and the rights of women as equals. Baderin has

How Did the Muslim Community Come to Be Where it is Today?

argued that Islamic law can be interpreted in ways that are compatible with the UDHR, while Naim has controversially argued for a radical hermeneutics of the Qur'an based on earlier Qur'anic passages taking precedence over later ones. Soroush has emphasised collective human wisdom and the need for the common heritage and interests of humanity to be recognised by Muslim and Islamic thought.

Some critics of practices in Muslim states, including Human Rights activists have viewed the 'Islamic' objections presented as actually political objections that are presented to mask authoritarian practices in different parts of the developing world. In fact much of the Human Rights debate in the Muslim world, and its spill-over here into the West is reflective of the way in which Muslim notions of the world, the role of the state, the rights of minorities and the issue of pluralism more generally have changed over the last century. As notions of a dichotomous world, divided between *dar al-Islam* and *dar al-harb*, have gradually given way to a more globalised vision of a plural world (these categories were originally challenged by scholars such as Qaradawi and Mawlawi (Lebanese), who argued for a more nuanced understanding of the West in a global era), Muslim thought has been playing catch-up. Intellectuals such as Ayoub[15], Osman[16] and Fadl[17] (see also Affendi[18]) and Soroush have asserted that the sources of Islam can be re-read in more pluralistic terms to accommodate better the rights of minorities and freedom of conscience, religion and belief in a modern setting, both in legal and philosophical terms (including debates around the existence of relative and multiple truths and salvation of non-Muslims).

If one looks at the intellectual trend of the debates presented above, the direction of travel for much of this thought is slowly to evolve a more humanist reading of Islam that can be more at ease with its European and Western cultural milieu. It seems that critical to this is the science of hermeneutics and how one reads ancient religious texts in emerging and new contexts. Already, debates such as the need to adopt more progressive positions

Beyond the Dysfunctional Family

on the rights of people with alternative sexual orientations have begun, as demonstrated in the Cambridge reports, which also contain a very clear and robust line on another controversial subject, freedom of religion. The first report affirms that: *"It is important to say quite simply that people have the freedom to enter the Islamic faith and the freedom to leave it"*[19]. Another important arena of thought is the burgeoning debate around what could be described as an Islamic feminist critique of patriarchy in Muslim history. Scholars such as Barlas[20] and Wadud[21] have argued for a re-reading of Islamic sources to create a more nuanced and equal understanding of gender roles in Islam. The above-mentioned Cambridge report also asserts that:

> Islam forbids abuses and crimes such as forced marriages of men and women, domestic violence, female genital mutilation and so-called "honour killings", and teaches the equality of all human beings regardless of gender. Islam puts no limitations on the roles that women should be able to play in any particular field of employment, for example as government Ministers or in any other arena of leadership.[22]

Debates concerning loyalty have also been at the cutting edge of contemporary Muslim thought. Ramadan[23] was one of the first to argue for and articulate a legal/theological framework for a strongly rooted European Muslim identity. Hussain[24] and others have also addressed a number of socio-political issues central to citizenship in a minority British context, including how Muslims could deal with disagreements with the state, how they conceptualise the territory they live in and should relate to the people around them with a stronger sense of fraternity, as *their* people. It is interesting to note that when the Prophet migrated to Madinah, he set forth a Charter that described all the local residents (Muslims, Jews and Pagans) as one *Ummah* (community). Yet today some Muslims are at such pains to emphasise only the other dimension of this word, that implies a global Muslim fraternity, often in quite exclusive terms. So, our *fiqh* needs a much more sober, honest and nuanced understanding of Islam itself. A number of questions linked with citizenship and the role of Muslims in Europe have also been considered by bodies such as the European Council for Fatwa and Research[25] (ECFR) and in light of important questions that have been raised post-9/11. According to the Council: *"Muslims living in non-Muslim countries are to respect the symbols of those countries such as the national anthem, national flag, etc."*[26] When asked about British Muslims who wanted to go to Afghanistan to fight against British troops, the Leeds based scholar, Abdullah al-Judai, emphasised that the social contract of citizenship was to be considered a legally binding treaty under Islamic law and that:

> ...Muslims are not allowed to take up arms against a party that they are in a treaty with, even when this is to go to the defence of other Muslims, as abiding by agreements and treaties is one of the most crucial aspects and features of Islam. Following this, it is not allowed for British Muslims to go to another country to fight in such a way that British forces would be attacked by Muslims.[27]

Having looked at these emerging ideas, it is fair to say that they represent debates and thoughts at an academic level that are yet to permeate to grassroots Muslim constituencies. At the grassroots level the debates raised by more radical actors tend to create confusion in the minds of lay Muslims who may know through their lived reality that democracy and Islam are compatible or that pluralism, equality and freedom are a force for good – but may also then find it difficult to articulate well grounded arguments against the rejectionist viewpoints that also appear to have a theologically sound veneer. There is therefore an important role in disseminating scholarly debates more widely and in more accessible form, particularly by actors that grassroots constituencies can relate to and trust.

CONCLUSION

The British Muslim experience is a complex one and represents a journey that has some way to go to reach its destination. Its

Beyond the Dysfunctional Family

start (in recent times) is with a strong immigrant base, with migration from East to West, rural to urban, traditional to modern – an experience that has points of intersection with experiences of others in British society, be they Jewish, Irish, African-Caribbean, Indian or Polish communities. Yet each of these communities has its unique and distinctive experiences rooted in history and culture. For Muslims, the way in which globalization has impacted upon diaspora Muslim communities, the influence of the specific post-colonial discourses of the Muslim world and more recently the impact of the evolving political climate post 9/11, create a unique bundle of experiences. The impact of 9/11, 7/7 and the 'war on terror' cannot yet be fully fathomed, but there are signs of polarization within Muslim opinion, with a worrying sense of victimhood developing in some quarters. There is also the sad reality of a new generation growing up in a post-9/11 world, with an intense scrutiny of all things Islam and Muslim, and the possible psycho-social impact of this upon on them.

New Labour under Tony Blair (Prime Minister from 1997 - 2007) made significant strides in engaging Muslim communities (and faith communities more generally) by funding Muslim schools, opening up access to Whitehall where there previously was very little meaningful contact, placing Muslims into the House of Lords, etc. These were significant steps for their time, sadly overshadowed by the War on Terror. For some, Gordon Brown (Prime Minister from 2007 - 2010) showed a more nuanced understanding of the tensions in engaging with Muslims in a post-7/7 world. The term 'war on terror' for example was dropped, but much of this period was under the cloud of Counter Terrorism measures that led to great strains between Muslims and the government. The change in government in 2010 and the arrival of the Conservative-Lib Dem coalition provided an opportunity to recast some of that negative cloud, as important moves were made in terms of reducing stop and search powers of the police, recasting the controversial Preventing Violent Extremism programme and creating greater space for civil liberties by rolling back other counter terrorism legislation. However, there was also a stronger challenge by the coalition government in other areas such as conservative Muslim preachers, integration and values. Looking forward there is a need for a real attempt to recognise the contributions of Muslims to British society, appreciate the serious tensions of leadership among Muslims and to empower (all) citizens through enhanced opportunities for education and economic empowerment. This must go hand in hand with willingness from citizens to participate and avail of opportunities as they present themselves and to think self-critically about their traditions. Government 'engagement with Muslims' must be broader in terms of partnerships, and also broader in terms of issues. Counter terrorism and security, or even integration and cohesion, cannot be the main prisms for addressing citizens of Muslim background, or we risk sending the message that Muslims are all potential terrorists or misfits. And there is a need for a real debate around how we now risk exceptionalising Muslims and consequently reifying their identities further by treating them as a distinct body even when the subjects under consideration whether security, unemployment, economic empowerment, etc, apply equally to all other citizens.

There is clearly a long way to go, but perhaps the starting point for Muslims is to give a greater sense of importance to the nation (to the local as opposed to the global). This is not to say that the global is not important, but the UK is where around 2 million Muslim citizens (and nearly 60 million fellow citizens) experience life, day in, day out. Moreover, there is also the need to elaborate a new contextual theology and *fiqh* of Islam that is firmly rooted in Muslim sources and tradition, but is read and expressed in ways which deal with the challenges of the new contexts that Muslims face. Among these challenges a key issue is to resolve the inequalities in gender relations found in some misogynistic Muslim cultures. Furthermore, for a religion that developed much of its worldview and theology in a context of being the majority there is a need to develop ideas in relation to its diasporic and minority status, particularly in the context of living in a

Beyond the Dysfunctional Family

plural, secular space. Can Islam develop a British/European/ Western flavour? I would ague that it can and must.

For the nation, the starting point could be to see that Muslims, as citizens, can contribute something of value to British life. More broadly, Europe has to come to terms with its fear of 'difference', particularly the Oriental 'other'. This is not about a clash of civilisations or even a clash of values; after all, much of what we all aspire to are human needs and desires. Think of freedom, equality, justice, accountable governance, rule of law, prosperity, education, charity, protection of rights, etc – such values, aspirations and ideas have no single creed, no specific culture, and no particular civilisation. They are now truly universal and human aspirations. Such shifts among Muslims and the wider European landscape will obviously not come easily, or quickly, but our role in meeting these challenges can be to create a vision for the next generation – to inspire them with hope for the change that can come.

NOTES

1. Runneymede Trust (1997) *Islamophobia: A Challenge for us All*. London: Runneymede Trust.

2. See for example, Norman Daniels (1997) *Islam and the West: the Making of an Image*. Oxford: Oneworld Books, and Edward Said (1978) *Orientalism*. London: Routledge.

3. Yasir Suleiman (2009) *Contextualising Islam in Britain: Exploratory Perspectives*, Cambridge: Alwaleed Bin Talal Centre of Islamic Studies, University of Cambridge and Yasir Suleiman (2012) *Contextualising Islam in Britain II*, Cambridge: Alwaleed Bin Talal Centre of Islamic Studies, University of Cambridge.

4. Often the terms 'Political Islam' or 'Islamist' are also used.

5. Ernest Gellner (1976) 'A Pendulum Swing Theory of Islam', in Robertson, R. (ed.) *Sociology of Religion*, London: Penguin.

6. Rachid el-Ghannouchi (1993) 'The Participation of Islamists in a non-Islamic Government', in Ed. Azzam Tamimi, *Power Sharing Islam?* London: Liberty.

How Did the Muslim Community Come to Be Where it is Today?

7. See for example, Eds. Yahya Birt, Dilwar Hussain and Ataullah Siddiqui (2010) *British Secularism and Religion: Islam, Society and the State.* Leicestershire: Kube Publishing.

8. Yasir Suleiman (2009) *Op. Cit.*

9. *Ibid.* p. 28.

10. *Ibid.* p. 36.

11. Olivier Roy (1994) *The Failure of Political Islam.* London: I.B. Tauris.

12. Abul A'la Maududi (1976). *Human Rights in Islam.* Leicester: The Islamic Foundation.

13. Abdullahi an-Naim (1996) *Towards an Islamic Reformation: Civil Liberties, Human Rights and International Law.* Syracuse University Press.

14. Mashood Baderin. (2005) *International Human Rights and Islamic Law.* Oxford: OUP.

15. Mahmud Ayoub (1997) "Islam and Pluralism" in *Encounters: Journal of Inter-Cultural Perspectives.* Vol. 3.

16. Fathi Osman (1996) *The Children of Adam: An Islamic Perspective on Pluralism.* Washington: Center for Muslim-Christian Understanding.

17. Khaled Abou El Fadl (2007) *The Great Theft: Wrestling Islam from the Extremists.* San Francisco: Harper.

18. Abdelwahhab el-Affendi (2001) *Rethinking Islam and Modernity: Essays in Honour of Fathi Osman.* Leicester: Islamic Foundation.

19. Yasir Suleiman (2009) *Op. Cit.* p. 75.

20. Asma Barlas (2002) *Believing Women in Islam: Unreading Patriarchal Interpretations of the Qur'an.* University of Texas Press.

21. Amina Wadud (1999) *Qur'an and Woman: Re-Reading the Sacred Text from a Woman's Perspective.* OUP.

22. Yasir Suleiman (2009) *Op. Cit.* p. 75.

23. Tariq Ramadan (1999) *To be a European Muslim.* Leicester: The Islamic Foundation.

24. Dilwar Hussain (2005) 'Can Islam Make us British?' in Ed. Madeleine Bunting, *Islam, Race and Being British,* London: Guardian Publications.

25. Established in 1997, the Council is based in Dublin and chaired by Dr Yusuf al-Qaradawi.

26. Date of *fatwa*: October 2002.

27. Date of *fatwa*: November 2001.

PART TWO

Encounters in Dialogue

4

Jewish-Christian Dialogue

(a)

A Jewish Reflection on Relations with Christians and Christianity

Rachel Benjamin

'Fraught with background' is how Erich Auerbach[1] describes the biblical narrative that tells the story of Isaac in Genesis chapters 21 and 22. It is a fitting phrase to appropriate in describing Jewish relations with Christians and Christianity. The long and difficult history that has characterised the relationship between Jews and Christians is indeed 'fraught with background'.

For centuries, many Jews knew only too well what it was like to be on the receiving end of suspicion, persecution and hostility. The unspeakable tragedy of the Holocaust, perhaps a dire consequence of this history, led to changes of attitude not only outside the Jewish community, but within it, too. Sympathy was expressed from outside it, as Michael Hilton has mentioned, as well as guilt and soul-searching. From within, there arose a determination never to allow such things to happen again to the Jewish people, of which the establishment of the State of Israel was such a tangible symbol.

The Holocaust is still too recent history for it not to continue to touch sensibilities deeply. The continual discovery of new information about events that took place during that period leaves wounds open, and the prospect of the Vatican finally opening its archives from those years, though one to be welcomed of course, is anticipated with considerable trepidation and concern over what will be revealed there.

The soul-searching that took place after the Holocaust led to re-evaluations of the relationship between Judaism and Christianity, and to many positive moves to change prevailing

85

Beyond the Dysfunctional Family

attitudes and perceptions, to build bridges and to heal. The Vatican II document, *Nostra Aetate*, in 1965 marked a turning point in Jewish-Catholic relations. *Dabru Emet: A Jewish Statement on Christians and Christianity* in 2000, acknowledged the remorse expressed by an increasing number of both Roman Catholic and Protestant church bodies, and their recognition of the need to reform Christian preaching and teaching 'so that they acknowledge God's enduring covenant with the Jewish people and celebrate the contribution of Judaism to world civilization and to Christian faith itself'.

While great strides have been made in positively developing the relationship between Jews and Christians, there are still a number of areas that challenge us. Supersession is an obvious example, as are some textual, liturgical and theological difficulties in Christianity that make uncomfortable reading for Jews, and which point to areas of irreconcilable difference. While Christians can be quite comfortable in Jewish services, it is not so the other way round. Shared worship requires sensitivity to Jewish feelings. I remember, as a child, attending assemblies in school, which included Christian prayers, when I would say the words that were theologically acceptable to me, and omit those which were not. As a Rabbi, participating in Remembrance Day services, for instance, might require delicate handling.

All this highlights an imbalance, a certain 'lop-sidedness' about the Jewish-Christian relationship. Instead of meeting in the middle, there has been a view that Christianity has to go further towards Judaism than Judaism has to go towards Christianity, and I imagine this could be a cause of resentment. This stems also from the perception that, while Judaism does not *need* Christianity in order fully to understand itself, Christianity *has* an essential need to understand Judaism, for *its* self-understanding. Statements such as *Dabru Emet*, and books such as Hilton's *The Christian Effect on Jewish Life* point the way to a more reciprocal relationship, which still needs to be much more fully explored.

The nature of, and the diminishing size of the Jewish community in Britain are factors in Jewish-Christian relations.

A Jewish Reflection on Relations with Christians and Christianity

Lack of self-confidence, as well as elements of suspicion, perhaps, the legacy of the past two millennia, play their part, and feed into the fear that Jewish practice might be weakened as a result of dialogue, leading to assimilation, intermarriage and an increase in Christian missionary activity. Despite concerns about our numbers, there is a growing confidence within the Jewish community, and that will contribute to healthy dialogue. As the seventh of *Dabru Emet's* eight statements points out, 'We respect Christianity as a faith that originated within Judaism and that still has significant contacts with it. We do not see it as an extension of Judaism. Only if we cherish our own traditions can we pursue this relationship with integrity.' We need to be confident in, and love, our own heritage and tradition, in order to effectively engage in dialogue. Then, in learning more about each other, we learn more about ourselves.

Another area of challenge is simply a general lack of knowledge or understanding – about who or what Jews are and Judaism is, and about issues that affect the Jewish community. In the large metropolitan areas where there is a concentration of Jews, we might be less likely to encounter this, but in far-flung provincial areas, we still come up against an astounding degree of ignorance, which leads to attitudes that appear anti-Semitic, such as the perpetuation of old and negative Jewish stereotypes. In some areas, Jews are afraid to show that they are wearing a Magen David (Star of David) around their neck, or to put a *mezuzah* up on the doorpost of their house, or to wear a *kippah* in public.

Also to be found is the perception of Judaism as a somewhat 'quaint', ancient religion, not in tune with the modern world. There is often a lack of understanding that there is more than one type of Jew, and that Judaism is a contemporary, dynamic religion – albeit its adherents are very small in numbers – encompassing the full range of denominations from traditional/ orthodox (with its many shades) to progressive (with its variations) to secular, engaged with the modern world, and facing the same struggles as others. Just like other religions, a range of attitudes can be found among adherents of Judaism –

Beyond the Dysfunctional Family

there are those who embrace modernity, those who reject it, and others who attempt to find a balance between tradition and modernity.

A further complication is the 'otherness' of Jews that is not widely acknowledged by Christians. There is a feeling of familiarity with Jews, and a sense of understanding Judaism, because of the Bible that we share. However, as Jonathan Magonet put it to me in conversation, Judaism is unique to itself and therefore different in unexpected ways. Such uniqueness and 'alien-ness' is somehow assumed with regard to Islam and Muslims, simply because of unfamiliarity, but is not always recognised with regard to Jews and Judaism. There are, for example, two factors which contribute to making Judaism alien to Christianity: 1) because Christians see Judaism through the lens of the New Testament and later Christian thinking, projecting that onto Judaism, and 2) because Judaism today is not *biblical* Judaism; it grew out of *rabbinic* Judaism, and studying the Hebrew Bible through Jewish eyes, with the rabbinic texts, is quite different. Unfamiliar and unexpected to Christians, for example, are Jewish concepts such as putting practice before dogma, and the plurality of interpretation. I taught Jewish Interpretation of the *Tanakh* (Hebrew Bible) at Heythrop College for a couple of years. In talking about the multiplicity and diversity of interpretations of the text, the most difficult concept for the students (mostly ministers, pastors or other professional Christian community workers) to grasp was the idea that, far from this plurality representing inconvenient complications to our finding the 'truth', they are of the essence of that 'truth'. Judaism teaches that all interpretations were known at Sinai and intended by God. Indeed, the more interpretations that emerge, the greater God must be. Our task is to find strategies for living with this plurality.

Clearly, much more needs to be done to educate and engage each other in dialogue. Where lies the responsibility for that? I suspect it lies with both the Christian and Jewish communities. To what extent should the churches be doing more, we might

A Jewish Reflection on Relations with Christians and Christianity

ask, and how can the Jewish community, small as it is, most effectively contribute? These are questions that we need to address in order to move forward.

The trend towards traditionalism is another worrying challenge that we all face. Raymond Apple recalls how 'Jonathan Sacks found himself in trouble a few years ago with his book *The Dignity of Difference: How to Avoid the Clash of Civilisations.* (The phrase, 'the clash of civilisations', is from the political scientist Samuel P. Huntington who argues that cultural and religious identities are increasingly our main source of conflict). Sacks' thesis that there is truth in other religions and not just in Judaism led to other rabbis accusing him of blatant heresy. How can a Jew not see, demanded the critics, that it is Judaism which is truth? That is the gist of the accusations that Sacks faced. A new edition of the book calmed things down when he softened his language and spoke of wisdom in other religions. This is one way of reducing the problem, but it does not make the moot point go away.'[2]

There is some concern in the Jewish world that more traditional voices are coming out of Rome, too, and worry about what that might mean for the future.[3] So much has been achieved since 1965. Positive statements have been made, and 'centres for the study and teaching of Jewish-Catholic relations are flourishing in a number of Catholic environments in North America and Europe'.[4] It would be dreadful if that progress were to grind to a halt, or worse.

What place can interfaith dialogue have in an increasingly conservative and traditionalist religious world? It is hard to see how it can flourish where any one particular group claims a monopoly on 'the truth'. How much more important is it, then, that the moderate, pluralist voice be heard.

Another challenge to the Jewish-Christian relationship is the situation in the Middle East and, of course, concern for Christians living in the region. Across the spectrum of the Jewish community itself, attitudes and feelings about the Israeli-Palestinian conflict vary broadly. The situation is a source of

Beyond the Dysfunctional Family

great anguish and pain, and feelings of protectiveness, love for and loyalty to the State of Israel exist alongside concern about actions taken by its government and military. While attitudes might be driven by the wish to see justice and peace prevail in the region, opinions as to how that can best be achieved differ widely.

Opinions about Israel are complex. Puzzlingly, the State of Israel appears to be held to standards different from those of other nations, and a balanced perspective is hard to find. Where there is greatest Christian support for Israel, it comes mainly from evangelical Christians. On the other hand, the attitude of the World Council of Churches is hostile. Viewing the Israelis as the *only* perpetrators of violence, and the Palestinians as the *only* victims of the Middle East conflict is problematic in the arena of Jewish-Christian dialogue.

Not enough is heard or made of the dialogue that is taking place in Israel, or of the extraordinary work of organisations such as Rabbis for Human Rights, Physicians for Human Rights, or the Interreligious Coordinating Council in Israel. Many Jews support the Palestinian cause, as well as the right of Israelis to live in peace and security. Uncritical support of either side is unhelpful. Perhaps the question that needs to be asked is: Is there a role that Christians can play that will be helpful in resolving the conflict?

In conclusion, there are many things that Jews and Christians share – a biblical text, and the general morals and principles that arise from it. There are also many teachings and attitudes that we do not – and cannot – share. However, we do not have to agree on everything. Indeed, we cannot agree on everything. What is important is to continue the dialogue, to be open, respectful and humble in our approach to our traditions and each other. There are forces that threaten both our communities, indeed all communities, in particular the growing trends towards traditionalism, on the one hand, and secularism, on the other. It is not only in dialogue that the way forward lies, or in learning about and learning from each other, but it is in acting together in the cause of justice and peace, working together to combat social injustice, intolerance and hatred. More important than what divides us, is what we share, and what we can achieve together, as God's partners, to bring about the day on which, as the prophet Malachi taught, 'the sun of righteousness will rise with healing in its wings' (Malachi 3:20).

NOTES

1. Erich Auerbach (2003, 1953) *Mimesis: The Representation of Reality in Western Literature*. Princeton and Oxford: Princeton University Press. p. 12.

2. 'Healing Rifts Between Religions', Keynote Address by Rabbi Raymond Apple AO RFD, International Conference, ICCJ, Sydney, 9th July 2007. http://www.jcrelations.net/en/?item=2874.

3. See Edward Kessler (2007) 'A Deafening Silence'. The Tablet Publishing Company. (http://www.thetablet.co.uk), in http://www.jcrelations. net/en/?item=2820.

4. *Ibid.*

(b)

A Christian Reflection on Relations with Jews and Judaism

Jane Clements

A Christian priest participated in a seminar organised by Yad Vashem, the Holocaust remembrance and education centre in Jerusalem and in his concluding report he wrote about:

> the painful estrangement between the two peoples of faith and the deep, deep roots of anti-Semitism which go back to the early Church Fathers. This leaves us with the bitter question: 'How could this have happened in Christian Europe where the perpetrators and bystanders were often in the majority of cases baptised Christians?'[1]

It was understandable that the shock of Christian complicity should dominate our approaches to Judaism in the latter half of the twentieth century. There was an acceptance – we would say fortunately – of culpability at some level, even allowing for individual acts of heroism and insight. Nazism was not Christian, but the centuries of anti-Judaism perpetrated by the Church as a whole provided an intellectual and emotional background for such terrible antisemitism to take root. The term 'anti-Judaism' used here refers to a denigration of the practices and institutions of Judaism, as distinct from social or racial prejudice against Jews *per se*.

The overwhelming sense of guilt felt by Christians after the Shoah was coupled with the recognition that, through its theologies no less than its practices, Christianity had in some way betrayed Christ himself. Scholars and church leaders, as well as many individual Christians, acknowledged the pressing

Beyond the Dysfunctional Family

need to address the relationship with Judaism; the work of those such as James Parkes and Henry Cargas laid the foundation for 'post-Auschwitz Christianity'. The impact of this sea-change in Christian attitudes continues to be felt, especially at the highest levels within the churches.

In terms of theology, things have undoubtedly moved on; some of this is deliberately driven by the need to address anti-Judaic concepts such as supersessionism. Of particular significance have been the statements by the churches, beginning with the Catholic document *Nostra Aetate* in 1965. These have been highly regarded more for the spirit of openness to Judaism (and other faiths) which they embodied than for the wording itself. Likewise, the response of Jewish scholars in *Dabru Emet*[2], was welcomed as an act of reconciliation and appreciation expressed for Christian efforts. Overwhelmingly, each of these statements and pronouncements highlighted the desire of many Christians and Jews to build and maintain positive and creative relationships in the face of so terrible a history.

The dialogue opportunities that have arisen subsequently have been profound. Of course, Christians have long found that a clearer understanding of the traditions and perceptions which lie at the heart of Christian liturgical and textual practice is both inspiring and invigorating. But beyond that the exploration of texts, first of all those we share, and then those which we do not, have opened up the possibility of spiritual growth within our own traditions. For a Christian, the opportunity to see how a rabbi or other learned Jew might approach a well-known Biblical passage remains as popular and as exciting as ever. Traditionally, Christians have been taught to look for the answers in texts; if these are not obvious, there will usually be someone at hand to provide them. From Jews we have learnt to ask questions – perhaps the answers will be there, but not necessarily. This Jewish interrogative approach to text is seen as creative and, in some indefinable and seductive sense, a little dangerous.

What Christians have received from engagement with Jews and Judaism in recent decades is immeasurable – new

A Christian Reflection on Relations with Jews and Judaism

and deeper understandings of Jesus as itinerant rabbi, of the Eucharist, of the Hebrew Bible. By contrast, however, when one looks at some of the letters pages of today's Christian press, sometimes it is difficult to see what Jews have gained from the process. As ground-breaking as the post-war developments have been, the task is by no means finished. Not only has much of the constructive work largely failed to impact on the average worshipper in the pew, but there is also a sense that, for the many steps taken forward, there are also quite a few taken back. Sadly, it would appear that reports of the death of anti-Judaism in the churches were, to paraphrase Mark Twain, a little premature.

One reason for this sense of retreat may be that, having for centuries been the default position of most people in Britain, Christianity now finds itself with an identity crisis. Not only must it compete with a rapid secularisation of society, but it must also stand its corner alongside other faith communities. This crisis of confidence has led to a sense of 're-affirmation' of Christian identity in recent years. One of the casualties of this process has been the removal of any sense of collective guilt for centuries of anti-Judaic teachings. Guilt is not, of course, a healthy basis for productive inter faith dialogue, let alone one's own theology. However, the memory of this guilt has prompted Christians to recognise and value Judaism and to engage in productive self-examination.

A second source of concern is found in the general trend towards conservatism in religious life, as is the case most mainstream faith communities. This has resulted in the desire for many burgeoning Christian groups to embrace a basic evangelicalism, with a theology that does not challenge or question and which is rigid and formulaic. The fastest growing churches in Britain are the 'free evangelical' congregations with their emphasis on personal salvation, simple teaching and ecstatic worship. Orthodox Christianity is also attracting significant numbers of converts from other mainstream denominations. Polarisation inevitably results.

Beyond the Dysfunctional Family

Nowhere is this more apparent than within the Anglican Communion, but it is true almost universally. It may also be possible to observe an emphasis on 'toeing the party line'. This means that many individual churchgoers are unclear about what may be expected of them with respect to Jews. Notwithstanding the work of senior figures and academics, individual Christians have often learned to accept and affirm the integrity of Judaism and to respect Jews as individuals somewhat in opposition to their traditional understanding of theology.

An unpublished survey, carried out by the Council of Christians and Jews in 2008, asked a cross section of active Church of England members about their attitudes towards Jews and Jewish issues. The overwhelming majority were clearly well disposed towards Jewish neighbours and individuals, abhorring antisemitism and believing firmly that God loves and values every person equally. However, when it came to bringing their theology to this point, they stumbled. Faced with the statement 'I find it hard to understand how Jews do not accept Jesus as Messiah', most respondents ticked the box marked 'strongly agree'. Furthermore, many respondents saw a need to bring Jews into the Christian fold – the dreaded issue of conversion. This was not from a desire to eradicate Judaism but the reverse – namely, to ensure that Jews are included in the eternal Kingdom which, they believe, is available exclusively to those who have accepted Christ.

If one needed an illustration of this, it was found in the reactions of Christians throughout the world to Mel Gibson's film 'The Passion of the Christ', released in 2004. This comprised an extended graphic portrayal of the doctrine of 'penal substitution' – the tortuous death of the Son of God as a payment or natural penalty for the sins of the world. The blood and pain shown to be at the core of this teaching shocked Christians as well as others. For thousands of churchgoers, however, across the world, it reflected their understanding and teaching of the Christian gospel and they were affirmed by it. Such reactions show the gulfs which dialogue must bridge, not just between Jews and Christians, but within the Church herself.

A Christian Reflection on Relations with Jews and Judaism

Christian-Jewish dialogue has rightly been seen as the template for developing skills and approaches in all our relationships with other faiths. The health of this dynamic provides a useful gauge for plotting the progress of others. Furthermore, such dialogue is not simply an academic exercise; it has far wider implications. The recent CCJ survey highlighted another stumbling block. As expected, the Israeli Palestinian conflict was cited as a source of misunderstanding, pain and anger which threatens Christian Jewish relations. In fact, there are a good many voices in both communities which take very similar views towards the situation now facing people of the Holy Land, but these are largely overshadowed by the stridency of others. The overwhelming problem in addressing this emotive issue comes not, essentially, from disagreement about the history or even about contemporary events – although these are difficult enough – but from the inability of many Christians and Jews both to comprehend the baggage which we each carry and to be willing to consider what is involved in carrying it.

The difficulty of cutting loose from our terrible history is compounded by the fact that Christians are obliged to develop some sort of approach towards Jews. While it is perfectly possible, and indeed almost certainly much easier, to be a Jew without any reference to the Christian presence whatsoever, the reverse cannot be said for Christians. Through our scriptures and in our heritage, Christians are obliged to recall that our understanding of God includes that of the Jews, and that the passages of sacred text which we read each week are drenched in the language, liturgy and socio-political history of pre-rabbinic Judaism. In short, Christians cannot be neutral. The consequences of getting it wrong are before us.

For the process between us to be positive, both Jews and Christians must remain engaged, open and welcoming to dialogue. However, there are Christian voices which ask: but where is the reciprocity? If I am required to address my theology, my liturgy, my textual interpretation, where is the corresponding drive from my Jewish counterparts? The response to this must

Beyond the Dysfunctional Family

be to acknowledge the enormity of this task for Jews. Many have managed to get beyond the barriers of bloody, alien imagery of Christianity, but it cannot be easy. When Jews actively seek to engage with a Christian agenda and to seek to learn from the process, this is a significant step.

Certainly, there were some less helpful post-Shoah attempts to address problems of theology. The desire to eradicate any sense of Christian superiority led in some quarters to a tendency to hide Christ away, lest his presence be the cause of offence. Now, however, Jews can acknowledge the centrality of Jesus for Christians, and encourage a greater understanding of his place within the Jewish world of the Second Temple period. Whether or not we regard the teachings of Judaism and Christianity to be either mutually exclusive or mutually resonant, in order to be real dialogue partners we are each required to hold in tension our own tradition and the recognition of the integrity of the other.

Such a tension, however, can encourage and promote creative and liberating thought. And indeed, the reverse may also be true. So, for example, recent theological work on Christian approaches to 'atonement' can help to provide more open and inclusive ways of considering the Divine relationship with all people of faith. Furthermore, a liberal theological approach to problematic texts is not enough; we must continue to work on the development of a pro-Judaic discourse in interpretation, using the text as it stands. This is important not just in terms of improving Christian-Jewish relations but also because this will contribute to Christian life and understanding. Those Christians who are committed to dialogue with Jews must continue to address these issues, and be movers in our own worlds to produce clearer theological models and insights.

It may be impossible, certainly in the short term, for Jews and Christians to approach each other as they might dialogue partners from another faith. But we are both people who speak about a Covenant relationship with the God of Israel, however we may argue about our perceptions of the Divine. In seeking

A Christian Reflection on Relations with Jews and Judaism

to love and obey God, it is part of our joyful religious duty to pursue reconciliation with Jews and to co-operate as partners in fulfilling our shared prophetic imperative to 'mend the world'.

NOTES

1. Terranova, R: Yad Vashem/CCJ clergy seminar 2009; unpublished reflections.
2. (2000) 'Dabru Emet: A Jewish Statement on Christians and Christianity, *New York Times*, September.

(c)

A Muslim Eavesdropper on Jewish-Christian Dialogue

Humera Khan

A common response to dealing with traumas, conflicts and grief is to say that 'time heals'. The essays between Jane Clements and Rabbi Rachel Benjamin are a testimony that indeed time can begin to heal once there is honesty, transparency and effort. The Shoah is symbolic in our modern times, that from trauma can come new beginnings; as the Qur'an says, *"And Who brings forth the living from the dead, and brings forth the dead from the living?"* (Qur'an 10:31)

I have not always found it easy being on the outside of Jewish-Christian dialogue, primarily because it is not directly part of my personal history nor is it central to my sense of self. I have said in many dialogue groups, as a second generation British Muslim of Pakistani heritage, I struggle with my own history so do not always have the space to immerse myself in someone else's.

But it has been through dialogue that I have come to understand much about the historical relationships between Jews and Christians, in particular the effect of the Shoah. My first experience of dialogue was at the JCM conference in Bendorf in 1987. I travelled to Germany in a group made up mainly of Jews and Muslims. Once we arrived in Germany we travelled by coach along the Rhine to our destination. It was on this coach that suddenly the sound of sobbing could be heard. A Jewish woman in our group was travelling to Germany for the first time since the Shoah and every mile on the journey was difficult for her, as was the conference itself. It was my first awareness of how the past continues to live in the present.

Beyond the Dysfunctional Family

Since that first experience I have been part of many dialogues where issues related to the Shoah have been a recurring theme. The essays by Jane and Rachel reflect the core essence of the dialogue which from what I have understood revolves around Christian guilt and accountability and Jewish self determination. But as a Muslim, eavesdropping on this conversation, my response varies between empathy and frustration.

I am a Muslim but have not been brought up to think of Judaism and Jewish people other than as People of the Book and as people with whom we not only share a religious heritage but also a migration experience. My family, like many generations of Jews before, came to Britain via the East End of London. With Christians, Muslims have also shared a chequered history from the Crusades to colonialism, the latter being the cause of why we migrated to Britain in such large numbers. But, as Muslims, we also have our own distinct and complex history, which has become lost or distorted through the centuries, and is usually projected on to us through the prism of other people's perspectives and idiosyncrasies. We have become and are still a war-torn, displaced people struggling to come to terms with ourselves and modernity. It is a story that few wish to tell truthfully let alone find meaningful solutions. This is a present reality not a reality we are having to come to terms with from the past.

From this point of view I can empathise with Jewish people because I know what it feels like to reclaim ownership of my own history and the need for self determination. If I am frustrated it is because Jewish-Christian dialogue can also become extremely insular where the two groups, having developed a shared language, can make others feel excluded. This is highlighted in Jane's comment that 'Christian-Jewish dialogue has rightly been seen as the template for developing skills and approaches in all our relationships with other faiths'. I am not sure if I agree with her that this is a good thing.

I was also surprised that Rachel, quoting Rabbi Jonathan Magonet, considers Judaism to be 'alien to Christianity, just as

A Muslim Eavesdropper on Jewish-Christian Dialogue

is Islam' and she further comments that 'there is no problem in acknowledging that 'alien-ness' with regard to Muslims'. Reading this statement made me stop in my tracks and my first reaction was once again of feeling excluded and separate. How can we say we are from the Abrahamic family and then say that our faiths are 'alien' to each other? Since Rachel didn't expand on the conversation she had with Jonathan it is difficult to know what else went with this statement. After some contemplation I came to two interpretations. The first more constructive interpretation would be that Judaism as the first revealed scripture doesn't directly refer to people as 'Christians' or 'Muslims' and so in that sense the statement is true. The second interpretation is that it projects a sense of separateness, difference and unwillingness to share. If the premise of this statement is the latter then I am very confused. Yes, there are different tangents to our scriptural stories and each story can be considered to be unique in themselves, but isn't there a connection between us all? Don't we at a basic level share a transcendent experience of the Divine? Don't we share many concepts and beliefs? To call the relationship between our three faiths 'alien' is something I find difficult to comprehend at any level. Our specific experiences may be personal and therefore unique but we should be able to share the universal lessons within it.

Then there is Jane's comment that 'Nazism was not Christian, but the centuries of anti-Judaism perpetrated by the Church as a whole provided an intellectual and emotional background for such terrible anti-Semitism to take root'. My first response to this was, 'Yes, you're right!' My second response was then why can't you try to understand the difference between anti-Islamism and Islamophobia? Christians eager to disassociate themselves from the intellectual and theological background that justified the treatment of Jews can be slow to acknowledge the same with regard to Islam and Muslims. On the other hand, I find Jews can be reluctant to share grief and pain and acknowledge that other people's history can also have the same tragic consequences as

Beyond the Dysfunctional Family

that of the Shoah. Acknowledging this doesn't take away from it.

Rachel then quoted Rabbi Jonathan Sacks when he said that 'there is truth in other religions and not just in Judaism' – a brave statement and one that can arouse much tension in relations with believers from our own community who are less sympathetic to dialogue. The fact that he had to later soften the language to 'wisdom' perhaps reflects the reality we all face that being truly open and brave in dialogue is not easy. It is within our own faiths that insecurity to share still remains deeply embedded. In this instance I believe the challenge is universal.

As a Muslim I know I have learnt a lot through the encounter between Jews and Christians, but my concerns have always been that this dialogue shouldn't be the template for other experiences, that there shouldn't be a hierarchy in personal tragedy and that we should all be allowed to be tell our own stories, in our own way, using our own language.

In conclusion, I find that dialogue can often confuse the meanings we bring to the table. I believe our stories reflect not just our spirituality or scriptures but also our sense of tribes, nations, history and politics. Our faith is sometimes at the centre of this discourse and sometimes it is on the periphery and more often than not the critical action is for us first to negotiate and become aware of these varied experiences amongst our own faiths in an open manner. Dialogue, as Jane and Rachel's essays reflect, can only be meaningful when we come to the table as equals.

5

Christian-Muslim Dialogue

(a)

A Christian Reflection on Relations with Muslims and Islam

Shanthikumar Hettiarachchi

I was raised in an orthodox Roman Catholic family, learned Dutch catechism as the basic Christian foundation during my primary school education period and in adult life was trained in western Christian philosophy and theology. Regarding other religions, neighbourly relations particularly with Buddhism existed in my part of the world, but in terms of a Catholic theological scheme of thought the religions were considered to be 'far other'. Buddhism was accepted as the religion of Sri Lanka, a nation which seemed to have absorbed it as a central element in its national identity. A kind of mythic union between being both Sinhalese and Buddhist existed, especially in the nation's post colonial political arrangement. Hindus, being the largest minority, were also predominantly ethnically Tamil. Generally however, no Tamil on the island was Buddhist, and neither was a Sinhalese a Hindu. Religious allegiance was determined along ethnocentric lines.

Muslims were yet another minority, scattered both in the Sinhala and Tamil speaking areas all over the country but existing in small pockets. To Christians the Muslims seemed the 'farthest other', as their origins were remote in the Moorish and Malay heritages from the pre-colonial history of Sri Lanka, and in spite of the belief that both Christians and Muslims share a common root in the figure of Abraham. Compared to Muslims the Sinhala Christians maintained better relations with Sinhalese Buddhists. Hence, my exposure to Islam was unusually strange, as my association with Islam was made initially without meeting a single Muslim in person but came

Beyond the Dysfunctional Family

through a French Catholic priest-teacher of Islam and later through the writings of the celebrated Afghani scholar-teacher, Jalal ad-Din Muhammad Rumi.

Since those early impressions I have encountered and worked with many Muslims, as both a community organizer and a theologian. There are four basic issues or areas which occupy the core of my Christian response to Islam and Muslims as a result of these experiences and my wider exposure to the world of Islam and Muslims. These can be listed as: the Qur'an, the meaning of the Prophet of Islam as the 'seal of prophets', the value and discipline of prayer, and the impact of Islam in secular society.

QUR'AN AND REVELATION

First, the role of the Qur'an in Islam as text seems less straightforward to me than it first appears. Intellectually, Islam seems straightforward to grasp, as it does not concentrate on complex doctrinal formulae as part of its belief system. It is a faith that requires loyalty or obedience to the divine command as postulated in the Qur'an and the practice of the Prophet (*ahadith*). What is permissible (*halal*) and what is non permissible (*haram*) are clearly stipulated, such that the touchstone whether one is or is not regarded as a 'good Muslim' becomes heavily reliant on the observance of rules. This Islamic position was very puzzling to me as I could not conceive of a God whose relationship to human beings would be concealed simply within a text. Was this the way to truly understand God's interaction with his created world? It seemed to limit unduly the omnipotence of God. How could God's final act of revelation find its terminus in a text? Surely the divine capability, productivity, immensity and transcendence could not be confined definitively and finally in the text of the Qur'an, no matter how 'holy' Islam deemed that to be? If Allah is to be Allah, then the reality of God's omniscient nature must extend beyond our human grasp of that nature and therefore beyond a mere written text. The eternal nature of Allah must be such that the divine reality exceeds all textual portrayals of it – a point which deserves also to be addressed to both Judaism and Christianity.

The Islamic prominence and insistence on the revealed word in the Qur'an as a text is so emphasized in Islam that the text becomes an idealized object and is thereby elevated to a sacrosanct position. Further, this idealization has led to an implicit association of the Qur'an with Transcendence, an association which comes close to compromising the real core of Islam which is the belief in the utter oneness of God (*tawhid*) with no associates of any kind or type. Christians have the same issue over the person of Jesus, who was similarly elevated to divine status in the tradition. Muslims are troubled by this association of Jesus with his heavenly Father, as are some Christians. But whether they see the same issue in the elevation of the Qur'an to an almost divine status is a matter needing greater investigation.

SEAL OF THE PROPHETS

Second, a closely related issue to the elevation of the Qur'an to an infallible state is linked to the notion of Muhammad as 'seal of the prophets'. This concept of the seal of the Prophet of Islam within Islamic theology functions in a comparable way to the New Testament belief in the 'fulfilment' of the Jewish Law and the Prophets by the impact of Jesus (a belief which was later transformed into the doctrine of the incarnation). The upshot is that nothing which historically postdates either Jesus (for Christianity) or Muhammad (for Islam) can be tolerated as revelatory in any significant sense. My position in both cases, therefore, is theologically simple. As monotheistic religions, Islam and Christianity hold the concept of 'Allah/God' as inviolable, self-existent and foundational. This entails that anything which remains subordinate or dependent on Allah/God is necessarily subject to historical change and contingency. And this must include the notion of 'finality' as it is embodied in the belief in Muhammad as 'seal of the prophets'. All peoples, cultures and religions are fallible by definition. Even the theological notion of

Beyond the Dysfunctional Family

revelation operates under historical contingency. How can it be that the meaning of the whole is wholly represented, contained or reflected solely in one moment of historical vulnerability? This evaluation of course applies also to other representations of revealed sanctity with other religions.

It follows that the eternity of Allah/God's being cannot be corralled in a fixed boundary, for this would not only be intellectually futile but also spiritually unsustainable. Moreover, one can notice that this position is retained even among Muslims and Christians who wish to remain faithful to their traditions but who have also absorbed this element of critical thinking. If one were to scrutinise the history of conflicts between Islam and Christianity, to a great extent they have been the result of theo-political superiority (finality) married to hegemonic power arrangements and the failure to adhere to the basic teachings of both of them. A close look at the two traditions as practised by certain sections of their global communities indicate a complete abandonment of that peace, justice, mercy and forgiveness which is integral to their very nature. They thrive on self-righteous hypocrisy as they compete with each other, shamefully betraying both spiritual traditions in irreparable ways.

PRAYER AND THE KA'BA

My third area concerns how I have been edified by the meticulous discipline of prayer within the Islamic tradition. This 'ritual' of prayer in fact is what binds all Muslims together, even though the performance of this very ritual prayer may vary from culture to culture. The prayers that Muslims fervently offer are directed to Allah alone, with the example of the Prophet and the Qur'an as the inspirational means and reason for Muslims to offer their obligatory supplications. However, it is interesting to notice that even though Muslims detest any physical object as a focus for prayer – seeking in the process to safeguard the transcendence of Allah – their physical prostration is directed towards Mecca where the Ka'ba is erected, and hence they seem deeply attached

110

to an iconic form of the sacred in terms of the Ka'ba itself. This prayerful prostration of Muslims in the direction of the Ka'ba suggests to me an utter need in the human consciousness for tangibility in order to sense even the divine presence not just in 'heaven' but in the midst on the real earth.

All prophets and sages engaged in prayer, mediation or in stillness have maintained a definitive 'one pointedness'. For a devout Muslim it has to be the place where his/her prophet made his home. Therefore, the physical directing of one's thoughts and body movements towards Mecca indicates a certain willingness to emulate ideals of holiness which are pleasing to Allah, who is thereby honoured in all history. Hence, all Muslims turning towards the Ka'ba in prayerful prostration, might be said to be involved paradoxically in the most iconic of religious rituals that we are able to identify in any single religious tradition. Muslims will no doubt disagree with this assessment, but it is the most plausible explanation if one were to listen carefully to the individual promptings of the devotees engaged in this prayerful ritual. My sense prompts me to say further that, even if they were sympathetic to my view at this point, Muslims need not have any doubts about being unislamic in their prayerful prostration towards the direction of the Ka'ba, as all prophets whom they believe to be messengers of Allah did the same in their prayerful orientatation towards Allah/God. The people will always need symbols, for without symbols we stumble. The motor traffic signs in themselves may not make sense unless they are posted in the right place and as such will direct our journey to safety. Hence, the prayerful prostration towards the Ka'ba is a ritual of great importance, as Muslims too need a symbolism, 'a one pointedness', in order to praise the mercy of Allah and offer complete submission the divine will.

BEYOND TERROR

My fourth area of interest in the Christian response to Islam enters perhaps one of the most controversial issues in contemporary

Beyond the Dysfunctional Family

society, an issue also which contemporary Islamic scholars have found most difficult to handle. The difficulty concerns how some Muslims groups have very successfully attempted to interpret, teach and persuade young men and women to take up arms to 'defend' Islam from infidels (*kuffar*). This issue is also coupled with the spectre of several imams across the nation unreservedly and openly preaching what is embarrassing to mainstream Islam and its impact in the public sphere. It is a fact that recent acts of violence in different parts of the world have been perpetrated by self proclaimed jihadists who have continued to claim Islamic religio-political justification for their use of terror tactics to achieve their goals. The challenges for the Muslims are many, even though such groups are not globally or regionally a homogenous entity. It is because of this very diversity in the appropriation of the tradition for extremist violent ends that the theological interpretation of Islamic texts and jurisprudence which have been so abused needs to be urgently addressed in contemporary Muslim self-understanding.

Ever since the time of the Prophet of Islam a subtle combination of religious leadership and political arrangement has operated in Islam. This Islamo-theological union in contemporary understanding can be described as theocracy. The Iranian revolution in 1979, for example, depicts a model which some Islamic countries wholeheartedly admire, even though some schools of thought disowned it altogether. However, in a sociological sense, it was a clear sign of change from a US backed regime – that of the Shah – to an indigenous (Shi'a) Islam-led socio-political transformation of Iran. This Islamic revolution of Iran has formed the most formidable political force from Morocco to Malaysia in the Islamic world since the defeat of the Ottomans in Europe. Its influence and effects are still felt across the Islamic world, even though it has been derailed by Al Qaeda led mayhem in several parts of the world. Such terror-induced chaos has undermined the very Islamic way of life for many younger generations of Muslims, especially in the Western world. Muslims in the West are continually challenged by sheer

A Christian Reflection on Relations with Muslims and Islam

circumstances to portray themselves as responsible citizens and to re-stage Islam as a religion of peace by confronting its association with terror and violence in the minds of the general population. However, many western Muslims remain trapped in an 'in-between' situation – hovering between their own allegiance to the theological axiom of the house of Islam (Ummah) and certain Muslim groups who are seeking to redress Muslim grievances with the use of terror tactics, which for the vast majority of ordinary Muslims is an abomination, a violation of *Sharia* and the will of Allah.

Fighting a so-called 'war on terror' and the media's generally negative approach to Islam and Muslims have rendered all parties impotent. Some Muslim groups are under the impression that the West is all corrupt and godless, little realizing that nearly twenty five million Muslims live believing in Islam but belonging to the West (Europe and North America). Some in the West think that everything of Islam is to be feared, without weighing up any historical or contemporary knowledge. Even if one does not know anything about Islam, it is possible to meet Muslims and then try to see the world as they see it. Such an endeavour would be transformative.

Muslims and non-Muslims have irritably and unfortunately failed to keep their religious or other convictions in decent conversations with one another. These failures have snowballed profusely causing permanent damage to communities. Opportunities for the healing of wounds, truth-telling and reconciliation have always been there, and various initiatives for dialogue and peace-building have enabled warring parties to meet and converse about their differences. In this way, dialogue is a path to healing. It happens at many levels, global and local. The initiative that runs in this book, for example, indicates hope for a future in which all might have a stake. Moreover, these challenges are not just for Muslims, but also for all groups who desire a just and peaceful future.

(b)

A Muslim Reflection on Relations with Christians and Christianity

Sughra Ahmed

As a young British Muslim growing up in the northern mill towns of England I learned first-hand to understand various manifestations of religious and cultural identities from those around me. This included those I attended school with, as well as those living in the same or surrounding neighbourhoods. It is here that I first became aware of Christianity, with concepts such as the Trinity and events such as the crucifixion. Looking back, it is perhaps this close adolescent encounter with Christianity which provided the impetus to learn more about it during my adult years.

My sense of affinity with practising Christians at the time was further based mainly on my family's acceptance that theologically we have a lot in common with both Jews and Christians and that we shared a substantial legacy through Prophet Abraham. As a young adult, I often thought about whether such feelings were reciprocated; after all, if I felt a love for Jesus and believed in some of his teachings then what would prevent Christians from sharing a comparable affinity towards Islam as a religion. I later realised that for a Muslim Christianity formed part of the history of Islam, but for many Christians Islam was a step too far.

In retrospect, many of those who 'looked' Christian were probably what is sometimes known as 'nominal Christians' or of no faith at all. A judgement had been made on my part on the basis of appearances as to which faith community they may belong to. As the years have passed, I have come to see

Beyond the Dysfunctional Family

that Christianity is more complex in its organisational and denominational structures and, more theologically, reflective thinking concerning the role of Jesus and his position in the conscious life of Christians can vary between Christian individuals or from one denomination to the next. At times discussions with some Christians have left me confused about the role of historical Christian teachings and their place in the life of Christians today. Have Christian teachings 'evolved' over time because Christians have learned to understand the faith better or, as some ask, has Christianity been made subject to the intellectual wilfulness of its followers rather than the other way around? Whatever the answer to such questions, it is becoming increasingly important for Muslims to understand how many Christians are trying to grapple with the meaning of its faith in changing cultural contexts.

Christianity as practised through the Church of England played a significant role in my early years; it enabled me to understand that simple acts of worship and contemplation such as joining hands together in prayer before school lunch was a way in which I could appreciate life's many blessings. It also allowed me to comprehend the role of religious expression through biblical readings, poetry and music, though carols and hymns were sang most often. I later realised that my love for God and his creation could be expressed in a similar fashion as a Muslim. So I now find spiritual encouragement through classical poetry, especially through renowned poets such as Rumi and Gibran, but also through modern day artists, such as Dawud Wharnsby and others who write and sing about many aspects of religious awareness, including peace and 'spirituality' – however we may choose to understand that word.

Having worked with many Christians, and gained a broader understanding of the history of Christianity and its interpretation through some of the main denominations, I am no longer limited to anecdotal learning but am able to embrace more discursive and meaningful discussions. This leads me to make the following two simple observations:

116

A Muslim Reflection on Relations with Christians and Christianity

First, it is interesting to know that other faith communities also have complexities which are similar to the groupings within Sunni and Shi'a Muslim communities. Second, there must obviously be some differences between the denominations, but for Muslims it is a major challenge to understand the ways in which they work and the relationships that they may or may not have with one another. This can often distract Muslims from the wider picture of a belief in one God, the shared concepts of messengers, the hereafter and so on.

Christianity in my childhood was one of regularity through timetables of choir practice, singing and attending Mass. The act of collective prayer brought a deeper understanding of faith for Christians, with the oft quoted love that is particularly prominent in Christian theology and thinking. These reflections would not be complete without the mention of divine love that many Christians hold on to as the foundation of faith and on which other layers in life are built – everything is centred on Jesus' agape love for his followers. This love stems from biblical parables which portray Jesus as one who demonstrated love to others through his actions and teachings, later written down by his followers. For Muslims the Bible is important, in that they believe it to have been once divinely inspired, though they remain troubled by the absence of an original version, the reliance on translations and what strikes many Muslims as a rather cavalier attitude on the part of some Christians in respect of what the Bible appears to teach, especially in the areas of belief and ethics.

Key aspects of Christianity, such as the love of Christ manifested through his coming on earth, his suffering and death and the saving of his followers through his love for them, are the foundations upon which Christ's followers base their devotion to him. As one of the New Testament Epistles says, 'Whoever does not love does not know God, because God is love' (1 John 4:7-12). Love is at the heart of Jesus' teachings for Christians and many express this allegiance to him through the symbols of Christianity such as the cross, fish and the dove.

Beyond the Dysfunctional Family

Muslims are unclear as to the way in which Prophet Muhammad is understood by the Church. Is it in a confessional way or is it by an appreciation of his life as a human being, a human being who changed the course of history and warrants respect and admiration as a genuine man? A statement to begin this dialogue is necessary for the future relations between many Christians and Muslims. A reluctance to address this would amount to turning a blind eye to the 'white elephant' in the room. For Muslims prophecy is one of the many shared aspects of religion between Christianity and Islam. Other key similarities include the virginal conception and the divinley inspired life of Jesus a shared history since the first man, Adam, and his wife Eve, with the deepest connection of all perhaps being the shared understanding of life after death and a judgement day for all.

In order to understand oneself one must understand others first. Spending time with others becomes an essential aspect of learning and knowing oneself. Becoming familiar with Christians for me is part of a wider process which enables me to learn more about myself and my own identity as a British Muslim woman. Thus I have learnt (long before I realised I was learning) that my encounters with Christianity, both at an institutional level as well as through personal friendships, have been an important part of my journey of self discovery.

Some may feel that encountering other religions makes them vulnerable to ideas and ideologies with which they feel uncomfortable. Interfaith dialogue in its present form is a relatively modern phenomenon for some and can therefore arouse misgivings. However, for Islam, interfaith friendship has a historical precedent in so far as it was anticipated by Prophet Muhammad when he shared food with non-Muslims and gave permission for marriage among people of the book (Jewish, Christian and Muslim). For Christianity interfaith dialogue is a relatively contemporary and modern concept which the Church is often seen to be leading, particularly in Britain.

Interfaith dialogue creates opportunities for exposure to people, groups and faith communities – and especially for me,

A Muslim Reflection on Relations with Christians and Christianity

a revisit to Christianity, which I have used in exploration not only of my own beliefs but also those of others. Particularly challenging has been the closeness in relationship of the three Abrahamic faiths, the complexities within them and the way they relate to each other.

A combination of schooling and teaching in the home entails that a Muslims' understanding of Jesus in Islam and a Christian's understanding of Jesus in Christianity is bound to differ. At times some Muslims may feel they understand the role of Jesus without taking a moment to understand who Jesus is for those of the Christian faith. Do Muslims understand Jesus as a prophet of Islam or as Christians understand him as 'the Christ' in Christian thought? Do I understand what it means to be you, a Christian, or do I see Jesus only through the lens of my own religious identity?

Muslims often understand Christian and Jewish traditions through Islamic texts and scriptures, stories and tales of times gone by which describe key events in the Judaic and Christian calendars – for example the story of Moses and Pharaoh, Abraham and his families, with Sarah and Hagar as well as the lesser known traditions of Jonah and the whale. Islam talks of such times extensively and for many Muslims this is the point of access to Christianity. Naturally, many Muslims may then only understand people of the Christian tradition not for who they are or how they see themselves, but instead as they are viewed through the lens of Islam.

There is a great need in British society for education about religious pluralism so that others may see Christianity (and other faiths) for what it is and not for what they believe it should be. Moreover, by understanding and de-mystifying the 'other' we do not thereby make ourselves vulnerable to the path of conversion. Given the reputation of evangelism in both Christianity and Islam, there is a genuine need to appreciate that understanding the 'other' for who they are makes us better adherents of our chosen religion. This is pertinent at a time where some faith groups are demonised through myths and the

Beyond the Dysfunctional Family

actions of fanatics; so perhaps at these points we are called to work harder and to remember the affection and respect Islam has for Christianity and their shared theology.

Commonly known as the religion of love, Christianity is also of course a faith with many concepts and complexities, which often remain inconsistent in light of simplistic notions of love and the absolution of sins through Jesus Christ. For example, many people find it difficult to understand the teachings of Jesus when they learn of key events in history such as the Crusades and their battles in the Middle East. Similarly, many find it difficult to appreciate the division between the peaceful teachings of Prophet Muhammad and the actions of those few who choose a violent means to advertise their cause.

Religions often find themselves betrayed by the very people who claim most vociferously that they follow the faith in truth and are the closest to the teachings of the Prophets who bring messages of love, mercy, honour and justice. This is the challenge many people of faith find themselves faced with from those who choose not to profess a religion, arguments for and against both religion and secularism rage among us and debates on the benefits and challenges of both find merit. Religion is facing its greatest challenge not from within – as in the books of history – but from the voices of secularism which often portray religion as a threat to the well being of wider society, as exclusive clubs to which, should you wish to belong to, means obedience and submission.

Through my school years Christianity exposed me to formal worship in Church and informal prayer before taking meals, and this was further developed through the formal prayers in Islam as well as the conversations with God that Muslims are taught to have. This regular communication with God led to a curiosity about forms of worship and in particular the role of songs/hymns in Christian worship.

It is interesting to note that my introduction to Christianity came through the choir. Christian hymns and songs about harvest time and Christmas formed a strong part of my learning

A Muslim Reflection on Relations with Christians and Christianity

encounter with the Christian faith. As a result, today I feel a closeness to Christian faith, more than perhaps some would expect. So when I see Church steeples across the landscape in Britain and hear the bells ringing on Sunday mornings, I understand this to be the outward call of Christian faith leaders to remind their followers of a long held tradition in this Christian land – and it is a Christian land, despite the debates around secularism and the possible absence of religious influence in the political domain. We have a relationship between the State and the Church which has come neatly together in the figure of the monarchy as we know it today. In the face of an increasingly secular society, a post-secular understanding of British politics and religion in the 21st century needs to be developed. Both secularity and religion need to be part of a vibrant debate on the future of a post-secular, modern Britain today.

(c)

A Jewish Eavesdropper on Christian-Muslim Dialogue

Miriam Berger

We bring so much of ourselves to our encounter with the other. We seem unable, as human beings, to separate ourselves and our own experiences from the immediate value judgements we make on others. We experience the other from a perspective of what we already think we know about them and what makes them similar or different to us.

The Muslim or Jew who has always lived in England will feel she or he has a good knowledge of Christianity, for we believe we live in a Christian country. Yet for most Christians, the idea that today's British melting pot of cultures and religions is still Christian is problematic. As Sughra Ahmed shows, the Muslim in Britain, like the Jew, begins any encounter with Christianity with the experiences of their British upbringing – the nativity play, the portrayal of Christianity on the television and, perhaps most unhelpfully, the need to make sense of the other by comparison to one's own religion. The initial encounter is therefore likely to be flawed by an over-confidence in one's knowledge of the other laced with over-hasty comparisons.

But what of knowledge based on the theoretical, without any personal encounter at all? As flawed as an encounter based on the personal knowledge of your Christian next door neighbour may be, just as flawed is knowledge of the Muslim abroad about whom you have learnt so much from reading texts and books but have never met at all.

Sughra accepts her initial misinterpretations of Christianity based on observing from outside how it appears to play out

Beyond the Dysfunctional Family

in people's lives. Shanthikumar Hettiarachchi realises that the religion that one constructs through an understanding of text is not the same religion that is practiced after generations of interpretation and development.

A religion, as we see it set out in the foundational texts and by subsequent scholars, fails time and again to equate to the religion as it is practiced by its believers today. The 'stubborn and rebellious son' as described in the Torah in Deuteronomy 21:18 is the best example of this from the Jewish tradition. The Torah permits the stoning to death of such a boy outside the city walls. Yet the space devoted in the Talmud to defining such a child out of existence – so that the stoning of such a child can never take place – allows us to understand that there have always been statements in our foundational texts which have long since, perhaps never, represented the view of that faith community. This verse in the Torah would never reveal to an other thousands of miles from any Jew, the importance of justice and the centrality of family in Jewish tradition.

Although Sughra and Shanthi recognise the traps, it takes a great deal to start again and not allow past misconceptions to prejudice later encounters.

For instance, it seems to me that Shanthi overstates the elevation of the Qur'an in Islam. Religions that do not make idols or graven images of the Divine create instead tangible manifestations of the Divine will. Manifestations of the Divine are vastly different from manifestations of the Divine will. In order to understand a religion, one may focus on two things: practice and place. The place of the Qur'an and the Ka'ba in Islam seems to parallel the place of the Torah and Jerusalem in Judaism. However, again, we find ourselves only being able to understand concepts within other religions through reference to our own.

These references we make back to our own religion when encountering the other two Abrahamic faiths can be problematic. Sughra understands that Islam includes its own interpretations of some Jewish and Christian traditions and

124

A Jewish Eavesdropper on a Christian-Muslim Dialogue

therefore feels a comfortable affinity with the older religions which Islam has drawn on. Yet, because of the chronology, the threat of supersessionism is felt by Judaism and Christianity. This manifests itself clearly in Shanthi's impression of Islam's 'Seal of the Prophet' as offering an authority over and above that of Jesus. As a Jew it is easy to recognise this sensitivity of Christianity towards Islam, as it is experienced by Jews in respect of Christianity.

Shanthi opens up a vital question as to the place of Islam in modern day society and the combination of the religious and political responses to the world made by Islamists. The challenging aspect of introducing such a perception of Islam in this kind of forum is the lack of agreed definition of what makes a Muslim a Muslim. Just because someone professes to be acting in the name of Islam does not mean that they hold a definition of Islam acceptable to mainstream Muslims. In fact, it seems unfair to include these people in a reflection on the Christian response to Islam. Sughra seems to pre-empt this issue by highlighting the difficulty of responding to 'Christianity' which too is an umbrella term for many groups of people without an over-arching, accepted definition. Both identify what they see as the threat to religion. Sughra identifies the voices of secularism who portray religion as a threat to society and Shanthi identifies the terrorist acts being carried out in the name of Islam. Both these accusations – religion as a threat to society and religion as violent extremism – cannot validly be levelled against mainstream religion but are made against the periphery, the elements of our own faiths that we know threatens our own place in society. Is it fair, as representatives of the mainstream of our religions, to include in our perceptions of the other those who would not fit within our own understanding of our faith either?

Sughra feels that to some extent Christianity has defined her as a person. Though she is a practicing Muslim, by living in England she couldn't fail to be influenced by Christian society in some way. Shanthi speaks of Islam as a remote entity, only something which impacted on his life outside of the academic

Beyond the Dysfunctional Family

world through the media's very negative perception of Islam. One cannot fail to listen to this conversation and not understand the importance of face to face encounters between people of different faiths.

When individuals can be completely committed to their own religion yet acknowledge that their rounded character and view of the world is influenced by their relationships and encounters with people of other faiths, their practices and values, then communities will be able to live in peace with one another. To live with one another, we have truly to know one another. Knowing is not a comparison but an acknowledgement that the other's very being will have some kind of influence on oneself. And then one should do everything one can to see the world through their eyes; working at standing in their shoes; taking the risk of being changed through the encounter and trusting that the change will be for the better for all concerned.

6

Muslim-Jewish Dialogue

(a)

A Muslim Reflection on Relations with Jews and Judaism[1]

Abdul Jalil Sajid

It needs to be acknowledged at the outset that one of the main barriers to honest dialogue between Jews and Muslims at the present time is the conflict in the region of the Middle East. This conflict, however, is due to the different presuppositions which lie behind the two versions of its history, leading to mutually exclusive perspectives. The Jewish reading of history assumes that after many centuries of Diaspora the Jewish people have been able to return to their God-given 'homeland'. In the creation of that homeland the violence that occurred was the result of obdurate Arabs who have never accepted a peaceful settlement whereby Jews could live among them, and so they have remained hostile to their very existence. The Jews as a people and a nation would like to live in peace; it is the Arabs who need to understand the aspirations of a people who need a homeland.

On the other hand, Arabs view the creation of the state of Israel as a blow to the integrity of their own existence. They see the insertion of Israel in the Arab heartland as a new method of proxy colonialism, thereby furthering control over the Arabs. They blame the Jews, who with the help of the Western powers, brought about the displacement of a huge resident population from their homes through violence. The expansion and retention of the ownership of land has only been possible for the Jewish state because of Western financial and military support.

In this conflict what is lost is the basic recognition that there is a great deal of commonality between the two communities. The

Beyond the Dysfunctional Family

basic building materials for mutual acceptance are still available if the two communities wish to build together. These materials provided much support over the centuries for a proposal to live side-by-side. The current conflict has meant that both communities have lost the larger framework of understanding.

This larger framework of understanding requires the recognition that each community has to acknowledge that their history is much broader than the present day conflict. However, the history is not always rosy. Today, with the interpretation of history provided through the lens of the present conflict, it is far more difficult to capture the real essence of the relationship.

The context has to be looked at against the historical backdrop of Jewish-Roman and Jewish-Christian relations. The Romans made a special effort to accommodate the Jews within their legal and social context and exempted them from the requirement to honour the divinity of the Roman Emperor and make sacrifices to the pagan deities. The Edict of Caracalla (212 CE) granted free men within the empire full Roman citizenship, although Jews were required to pay the special tax instituted by Vespasian. There were times when Jews lived in Palestine in relative peace and prosperity, yet the yoke of Rome lay heavily upon them and oppressive acts led them to full-scale rebellion in 66-70 CE and again in 131-35 CE. Judaism was nevertheless a permitted religion, unlike Christianity which was banned under Roman law, so that Christians were for a time persecuted on account of their religion.

However, Jews were never persecuted during the three hundred years of the Common Era. As I have mentioned, Jews lived in Palestine in relative peace and prosperity and they were tolerated far more compared to the Christians. The situation drastically changed, however, when the Roman Emperor Constantine declared Christianity a licit religion. His Edict of Toleration (315 CE) proved to be the most intolerant act. All non-Christians gradually lost their citizenship, and the Jews became a particular target. The Edict was not enough; a further series of enactments, deliberately designed to curtail Jewish influence in

A Muslim Reflection on Relations with Jews and Judaism

the society, were issued and vigorously implemented. Buried anti-Jewish feeling, which hardly showed during the pagan Roman Empire when Christianity was a persecuted religion, rose again after the Emporer's conversion. Judaism, which was generally accepted within the Roman Empire as a respectable faith, was now referred to as a 'nefarious sect'. The persecuted yet highly educated and business-minded Jewish population fled from Palestine and began to settle outside Roman jurisdiction. Jewish people also settled in the Arabian peninsula and near Yethrab (Madinah) and its surrounding area. They were innovative, particularly in agriculture and irrigation, and through their business acumen contributed much to the local economy. This sense of self-sufficiency also created a feeling of pre-eminence.

It was against this backdrop that the Prophet Muhammad was received by the local Arab tribes who converted to Islam in relatively large numbers and over a very short time period. One of the reasons for the rapid influence of Islam amongst the Madinian tribes was that they heard from their Jewish neighbours that the arrival of a messiah in the region was imminent. When they heard of Prophet Muhammad they thought that this must be the one whom the Jews talked about. In Palestine the conflict between Jews and Christians and the hope of a messiah turning up at any moment amongst the Jews clashed with the idea of a Prophet arriving amongst the Arabs in Madinah. The image of the Prophet thus increasingly became a derogatory one. The 'madman' (as they were to call him in later writings) and his increasing success created a psychological resentment.

Against this background Prophet Muhammad called for an agreement known as the Covenant of Madinah. This was a historic event both in the history of Islam and the Arab lives of the peninsula. Prophet Muhammad arrived in Madinah in 622 CE, and at his earliest opportunity he brought together all the leaders of the inhabitants of the city and its surroundings. He proposed the idea of a covenant where the relationship between people would not be determined by tribal allegiances which were responsible for long tribal feuds and bloodshed. The

Beyond the Dysfunctional Family

Covenant demanded a new paradigm of social engagement. The native tribes and the Jewish community, along with the migrant refugees from Makkah, were asked to create new bonds and new connections. Identity was now forged along the lines of faith, and not by tribes or tribal loyalties. This in itself was something unheard of. The people of the city of Madinah were now defined as 'one community' (*ummah*) to the exclusion of others. The city would now be a sanctuary for all members of all communities.

The right to seek justice had moved from an individual and tribal arena to a centrally accountable authority, and the society was collectively responsible for the city's welfare. The Covenant was pitched against the *mushrikin* (polytheists of Makkah) with a clear intention to protect the newly established community of Madinah from any foreign attack and any interference to divide the community. It stated that:

> And verily the Jews shall bear their expenses (of war) and the Muslims shall bear their expenses; and verily there shall be aid between them as against those who fight the parties (*ahl*) to this document (*sahifah*), and there shall be sincere counsel and well-wishing between them; and there shall be fulfilment (of pledge) and not violation.
> And verily no one violates the pledge of his ally (*halif*); and verily help shall be given in favour of the oppressed.
> And verily the Jews bear (their) expenditure along with the Believers so long as they fight in conjunction.
> And verily the valley (*jawaf*) of Yathrib shall constitute an inviolable territory for the parties to this document (*sahifah*)

Furthermore after some more detailed clauses between the parties it states:

> ...the Quraish shall be given no protection nor those who help them

and it emphasises that:

> ...there shall be aid between them (i.e. the Muslims and the Jews) against those who invade Yathrib.[2]

A Muslim Reflection on Relations with Jews and Judaism

By entering into this binding agreement, the Jewish community had secured a future, both individually and collectively. However they were obliged to pay a tax, as they did with the Romans, levied upon able bodied male members of the community, in lieu of participation in war, though they were welcome to join the war of protection of Madinah if they wished to do so.

Prophet Muhammad hoped that the Jews would be more welcoming as they shared the same belief in One God and the Jewish prophets, and their message was part of his own. But for the Jews the idea of a stranger from the south of the peninsula arriving and taking control of their surroundings provoked an active resentment and a hostile attitude to the Prophet and Islam. This hostility resulted in the constant breaking of the Covenant, which eventually resulted in the dispersal of Jewish tribes from *jawaf*, the surroundings of Madinah. One of the Jewish groups was fined, and another group was later found to be guilty of a greater degree of offense by helping the Quraish against the Madinans. But the most severe consequences were felt by the Banu Qurayza who sided openly against the Prophet and the people of Madinah when the city was attacked unsuccessfully by the Quraish. Unlike the other two Jewish tribes who asked for the Prophet to be the arbitrator, this tribe asked Sad bin Mu'adh, a member of the Awas tribe and allies of Banu Qurayza, to be the arbitrator. The number of people put to death varies from 400 to 900 and 960.

This high number of killings was disputed by the Arab historians and biographers of the Prophet. A detailed discussion on the subject can be found in Arafat's article.[3] What his interesting thesis suggests is that the most widely quoted source of the Prophet's biography, *Sira* by Ibn Ishaq, which details some of these events, had already been denounced by contemporary jurists like Imam Malik, who called the biographer 'an imposter' who just transmits the stories without proper evidence. It is well known that amongst Islamic scholars the biographers of the Prophet were very lax about their sources compared to

133

Beyond the Dysfunctional Family

those who compiled the *ahadith*. They did not always provide the chain of transmitters of the story and largely relied on Jewish sources for Jewish stories or Christian sources for Christian stories, disseminated by the converts amongst the Muslims. Arafat suggests that the mass killing of the tribe has a remarkable similarity to the incident between the Masada and Banu Qurayza. The numbers, he argues, are particularly significant: those who died in Masada at the end were 960 and the hot-headed *sicarii* also killed 600 people. It is also reported that 'at the point of despair they were addressed by their leader Eleazar (precisely as Ka'b b. Asad addressed the Banu Qurayza), who suggested to them the killing of their women and children.' He further remarks that not only 'are the suggestions of mass suicide similar but even the numbers are almost the same.' He finds even that the same names occur in both accounts.[4]

This story may be disputed, but what is perhaps not disputed is that it was not directed against a people but against guilty individuals. Even after Banu Qurayza's event, the fall of Khyber, the residents, who excessively abused the Prophet and were openly hostile to Islam, were treated fairly and the Prophet only rebuked them verbally.

When Islam expanded into northern Arabia, Syria, Egypt and Palestine, where a large number of Jewish population lived, they were treated as innocent Jewish *ummah*. Perhaps for the first time in Jewish history, after the fall of the Babylonian invasion in 586 BCE, they could model their life according to the teachings of the Torah and be supported by the public laws. For the first time they could defend their Jewish identity. They saw Islam and Muslims as their liberators. A Jewish mystic writing under the pseudonym Simon bar Yohai, at the time of the Muslim conquest of Palestine, surprisingly states that Umar, the second caliph, was a 'lover of Israel who repaired their breaches' and comforted the community that 'The Holy One, blessed be He, is only bringing the kingdom of Ishmael in order to help you [the Jews] from the wicked one.' Furthermore

A Muslim Reflection on Relations with Jews and Judaism

highlighting the similarities between the two faiths, he pointed out that 'of all the seventy nations that the Holy one, blessed be He, created in His world, He placed his name, El, only on Israel and Ishmael'.[5]

As far as Islam's relations with the Jews were concerned, its political relation was largely tamed by the defined and secure position it has within Islam. The political domination of the state was curtailed by a vigilant presence of *ulama* over the centuries. It has consistently defended Jewish life and its presence amongst Muslims as part of Islam. But over the past 200 years the Muslim world has consistently defined itself against the dominance and control of the Western powers. The state of Israel in particular and Jews in general are defined against this backdrop. This fear factor of political domination has now exhausted its appeal. Perhaps it has very little to offer to both Muslims and Jews. There is still some basic material available to develop a sensible 'hospitable theology' which may define its relationship afresh. If the Romans could find a way of accommodating the stranger, and Islam could define Jews and Muslims as one *ummah* (community), and the Second Vatican Council could speak of 'rays of light' in other traditions, then there is still hope for a 'hospitable theology' that will not look at Jews and Muslims only through political lenses. For decades Arabs and Israelis have searched for an agreeable border where we all agree that religion and politics is intrinsically linked, but using the religious aspect of relations to resolve the issue has hardly been approached. In the absence of such an important dimension of their relationship, each side has the tendency to magnify its victim status and not to see the other as their 'faithful' partner.

As far as my own long involvement in Jewish-Christian-Muslim dialogue is concerned I arrived at a conclusion that the European socio-political and historical memories fuel prejudice against Islam and Judaism. I strongly believe that the struggle against anti-Semitism and Islamophobia is a common struggle and requires a common stand. While the dark shadows of the

Beyond the Dysfunctional Family

Middle East will overshadow us for some time to come, it should not discourage us from engaging in an honest and a fruitful conversation and working together for the common good of all. [6]

NOTES

1. I am grateful to Dr Ataullah Siddiqui for responding to the original draft of this paper by providing substantial modifications and references.
2. Muhammad Hamidullah (1975) *The First Written Constitution in the World*. Lahore: Sh. Muhammad Ashraf.
3. W N Arafat (1976) 'New Light on the Story of Banu Qurayza and the Jews of Medina'. *Journal of the Royal Asiatic Society of Great Britain and Ireland*. pp. 100-107.
4. *Ibid*. p. 6.
5. Salo Wittmeyer Baron (1957) *A Social and Religious History of the Jews, Vol 3*. New York: Columbia University Press. p. 93. (The real Simon bar Yohai lived five hundred years earlier).
6. Islamophobia analysed by Imam Sajid in the *Jewish Chronicle* on 18 June 2004 at: http://website.thejc.com/home.aspx?AId=31049&AType Id=1&search=true2&srchstr=imam%20Sajid&srchtxt=0&srchhead=1& srchauthor=0&srchsandp=0&scsrch=0.

(b)

A Jewish Reflection on Relations with Muslims and Islam

Norman Solomon

No 'official' statement of Jewish doctrine on Islam is possible; the Bible and the Talmud, the foundational works of Judaism, were compiled before the time of Muḥammad and are therefore silent on the subject. However, ever since Islam began there have been Jews living in Muslim lands. Over the centuries both Judaism and Islam have developed in response to changes in the world order and the expansion of knowledge; they have taken on a variety of forms, often interacting with one another. There have been good times and bad, and Jewish attitudes to Islam and to Muslims have ebbed and flowed with the changing conditions. My own attitude – if I can be said to have one, seeing that I prefer to be open to people as individuals rather than as flag-wavers – has been formed partly by reading history, but rather more by meeting Muslims and by meeting Jews who have left Muslim countries to settle here or in Israel.

BEGINNINGS

There were several Jewish tribes in Arabia in Muhammad's time. Some Jews were among his earliest followers, and during his period in Madinah following the *hijra*, Jews were numbered as allies of one of the eight clans who supported him. However, others were neutral or opposed him, and there were occasions when he and his followers fought against them and slaughtered them, such as the Battle of Trench against the Banu Quraiza (Sura 33:9-27);[1] he took captive at least two Jewish wives, Rihana

Beyond the Dysfunctional Family

bint Zaid and Safya bint Huyay. It is likely that the survivors of this defeat and their sympathizers would not have been well-disposed toward the new faith and its Prophet, but this is no more than speculation; information about this early period comes to us mainly from Muslim sources, not from contemporary Jews.

Some sources suggest that other Jews reacted positively. A Jewish apocalyptic tract composed not long after the conquest of Jerusalem by Caliph Omar in 637 has this to say:

> When he[2] beheld the kingdom of Ishmael come he began to say, 'Is not what the wicked kingdom of Esau has done to us sufficient, that the kingdom of Ishmael comes too?' The angel Metatron at once answered him, 'Fear not, O son of man! The Holy One, blessed be He, brings the kingdom of Ishmael only to save you from this wicked one (Rome). He will send a prophet to them and conquer the Land [of Israel] ...
> And the second king who arises from Ishmael will love [the people of] Israel and conquer all the kingdoms. And he will come to Jerusalem and he will repair its breaches and the breaches of the Temple and hew out Mount Moriah and build there a place to bow down at the *even ha-shetiya* (foundation stone).[3]

'Esau' stands for Rome (Byzantium), or Christendom, and 'Ishmael' for the Muslims; *Nistarot* places the Muslim conquests in an eschatological context, and implies that Muḥammad had a positive role to play in the messianic process.

Pirqei d'Rabbi Eliezer, a Hebrew composition originating in early eighth-century Palestine just prior to the fall of the Omayyads, also places the rise of Islam in an eschatological context, but negatively; it looks forward to the downfall of the Omayyad caliphate as an omen of the end of the (Jewish) exile.

At about the same time Isaac ben Jacob of Isfahan, known as Abu 'Isa, proclaimed himself a prophet, led a revolt against the Muslims, and was killed when the rebellion was suppressed. His followers did not believe that he was dead but rather that he had entered a cave and disappeared; the 'Isawiya or Isfahanian sect continued for some centuries. Abu 'Isa taught that five prophets, of whom he was the last, preceded the coming of the true Messiah and that the missions of Jesus and Muḥammad were restricted to their respective communities. His notion of the 'hidden prophet' is close to the Shi'ite concept of *ghaiba*, or 'occultation', of the Imams.[4]

It was also during this early period that the Arabic collections of mainly Jewish material known as Israeliyyat were made. This may indicate a closer relationship or better understanding between Muslims and Jews, it may represent the input of converts to Islam, or it may simply be that Muslims wanted to collect all available information.

THE ERA OF SYMBIOSIS

The early years of Muslim rule were unsettled, but under strong rulers such as the Abbasids in Iraq (749-1258), the Fatimids in Egypt (907-1171) and the Western Caliphate in Spain, periods of relative peace and stability ensued. Jews adapted themselves to the new situation, adopted Arabic rather than Aramaic as their vernacular, and participated in the general cultural development including science, linguistics and the composition of poetry. Classical philosophy, revived by the Syrian Church in the sixth and seventh centuries, was translated from Syriac into Arabic and greatly influenced the kalam, or philosophical exposition of Islam, as well as Jewish philosophers; together with commitment to the Unity of God, belief in prophecy and revealed law, all these shaped a culture shared by Jews and Muslims.

Many rulers encouraged free and open debate among representatives of different religions, whether in the hope of conversions, as genuine scientific enquiry, or for entertainment. These *majalis*, or open debating sessions, took place typically in the court of a caliph or emir, providing a forum in which Jews, Christians, Zoroastrians and occasionally even free-thinkers could express their views on Muhammad and Islam as well as on each other's faiths. Unfortunately, the reports of these meetings are notoriously unreliable; it is likely that

Beyond the Dysfunctional Family

Jews remained prudently circumspect despite the promise of open debate.[5]

Jews certainly discussed the new religion among themselves. Anan ben David, the eighth-century founder of Karaite Judaism,[6] acknowledged the prophetic missions of Jesus and Muhammad, but another Karaite, Jacob al-Kirkisani (tenth century), wrote a tract *Kitab fi'Ifsad Nubuwat Muhammad* in refutation of Muhammad's claim to prophecy. Rabbanites likewise firmly rejected claims of prophetic inspiration made for any text other than the Bible; their emphasis on the uniqueness and permanence of Moses' prophecy is a central theme of Jewish religious philosophy from Saadia to Maimonides.

Our sources tell us something about relationships among the intelligentsia and the ruling classes in the mediaeval Islamic world, but not much about the lower echelons. Ordinary Jews and Muslims engaged in commerce, frequented the same markets, spoke the same language, wore similar (though not identical) clothes, practised male circumcision (if at different ages); none of them ate the meat of pigs; they had similar culinary traditions, though Jews had additional dietary restrictions and Muslims abstained from alcohol; Jews observed a strict Sabbath, when they would have been absent from market; Jews prayed three times a day facing Jerusalem, Muslims five times facing Mecca. Religious leaders on both sides discouraged social relationships across the divide, but we do not and probably cannot know what happened in actual fact.

The *dhimmi* ('protected') status accorded to non-Muslims under the Pact of Omar falls far short of modern standards of human rights, and would now be regarded as institutionalized discrimination; but in the mediaeval world it would have been accepted as confirming the right of a dissident minority to live in peace and under legal protection provided they remained subservient, paid a special tax (*jizya*) and took care not to cause offence.

Later in the Middle Ages several Jewish philosophers in Muslim lands, including Judah Halevi and Moses Maimonides,

A Jewish Reflection on Relations with Muslims and Islam

acknowledged Islam and Christianity as stages in the messianic process, the former for spreading belief in the pure unity of God, the latter for spreading knowledge of the scriptures; however, most of them would have regarded Jesus as a blasphemer and Muhammad as an impostor.

On the other hand, the Yemenite Jewish communal leader and philosopher Nethanel ibn Fayyumi, in 1164, wrote a book called *Bustan el-'Uqul* ('The Garden of Intellects'),[7] in which he asserted the authenticity of the prophecy of Muhammad as revealed in the Qur'an, and at least the possibility that there were additional authentic revelations (he does not mention Christianity). He writes that 'Mohammed was a prophet to them but not to those who preceded (sc. were prior to) them in the knowledge of God'; God 'sends a prophet to every people according to their language,' and 'permitted to every people something He forbade to others'[8]; the specific commands of Torah and Qur'an differ because the people to whom they are addressed are at different stages of spiritual development. Nethanel's synthesizes the contemporary culture – in this case the world-view represented by the *Rasa'il Ikhwan el-Safa* – with Judaism, while strongly defending the latter.

Despite the intellectual and spiritual closeness with Islam, the *Bustan* indicates a strong degree of Muslim-Jewish tension. Nethanel refers to 'what they assert because of the power they exercise over us, because of our weakness in their eyes, and because our succor has been cut off', and declares, 'The nations do revile us, treat us contemptuously and turn their hands against us, so that we stand among them in speechless terror as the sheep before the shearer'; he amplifies the theme of Jewish suffering under Muslim rule to the extent of citing swathes of Hebrew laments by Solomon ibn Gabirol and Judah Halevi.[9] His forebodings were well-founded, for shortly after his death the Jews of Yemen were subjected to severe persecution.

In general, prior to the era of European domination, where there was firm and enlightened rule, as under the Abbasids and the Fatimids, or later under the Turkish Sultanate, Jews

141

Beyond the Dysfunctional Family

were often able to flourish, prosper and contribute to the wider society in which they lived; in Egypt, in Iraq, and eventually under the millet system in Turkey, they were allowed a considerable measure of self-government, though always ultimately answerable to the ruling power. But during the numerous episodes of religious fanaticism which affected the Islamic world, such as the Almohad incursions in Spain, they – as well as more enlightened Muslims – were vulnerable to suffering and persecution.

RECENT TIMES

Commenting on the degrading status of the Jews he came across in Egypt in 1833-1835, Edward William Lane wrote:

> At present, they are less oppressed: but still they scarcely ever dare to utter a word of abuse when reviled or beaten unjustly by the meanest Arab or Turk: for many a Jew has been put to death upon a false or malicious accusation of uttering disrespectful words against the Kur-án or the Prophet.[10]

However, in the course of the nineteenth century in the Islamic world as well as in Europe there were attempts to 'modernize', and to create more egalitarian societies. In 1839 the Sultan Abdülmecid I (ruled 1839–61) introduced the first of the 'Tanzimat' reforms in the Ottoman Empire, which then ruled much of the Middle East excluding Egypt, guaranteeing justice to all with respect to life, honour and property, and stipulating that its provisions extended to all subjects irrespective of religion or sect. The tentative progress of Ottoman reform cannot be followed here, as it was in any case complicated by European interference, the rising tide of nationalism and the demise of the Empire. Factors affecting the position of Jews in Muslim countries in the twentieth century were the collapse of Western imperialism, the establishment of the state of Israel, increased participation of Islamic countries in world politics, and the growth of fundamentalism; whereas Iraq, Egypt and Syria still

A Jewish Reflection on Relations with Muslims and Islam

boasted significant Jewish communities at the beginning of the twentieth century, only Morocco, Turkey and Iran retain viable communities, while about half of Israel's Jewish population originates in Muslim lands.

Modern Jewish interest in Islam and its Prophet arose in the West in a scholarly rather than a theological context, as the following makes clear:

> In the development of Islamic studies in European and, later, American universities, Jews ... play an altogether disproportionate role ... not only in the advancement of scholarship but also in the enrichment of the Western view of Oriental religion, literature, and history, by the substitution of knowledge and understanding for prejudice and ignorance.[11]

The best scholars rejected the so-called 'Orientalist' ideology of difference and supremacy' and laid foundations for the modern scientific study of Islam.[12] More romantic notions led the early Zionists to dream that a much rosier future awaited them among their Arab cousins than on the hostile soil of Christian Europe. No-one foresaw the traumatic events of the twentieth century in Europe and the Middle East, or the technological developments which would by the twenty-first century bring the whole world much closer together and interdependent, rendering past models of relationships among Jews, Christians and Muslims largely irrelevant.

How do the historical and theological factors affect my own relationship with Muslims in Britain today? On a day to day level, very little, other than if we happen to get into a conversation on the Middle East, when our perceptions – conditioned by our respective histories – sometimes seem so far apart that I wonder whether we are talking about the same part of the world; but this is surely a challenge to both of us to distance ourselves from our inherited perspectives and look afresh at current realities.

Like most thinking Jews today I recognize the vast range of thought that exists within each faith, and the considerable

Beyond the Dysfunctional Family

overlap between them. Historical understanding and philosophical critique lead me to take a softer line on doctrinal definition than tradition suggests, while not abandoning my tradition, and to be more open to the notion that absolute religious truth cannot be wholly captured in language; the great faiths, including those from further East, all have something of value to contribute to human understanding of the infinite. God cannot be tied to one human being, to one scripture, or within the bounds of an exclusive tradition; Islam should be seen not as a rival or usurper with a competing claim to exclusive truth, but as another manifestation of the infinite self-revelation of God.

NOTES

1. There are many accounts of this battle and its causes. I am not concerned to accuse or justify either side, but only to point out that the losers, who no doubt thought their cause justified, would have been aggrieved.

2. That is, the second-century sage Shim'on bar Yoḥai, in a vision of the future.

3. *The Nistarot of Rabbi Shim'on bar Yohai*, edited by Adolf Jellinek, *Bet Ha-Midrash* 3:78, 79. See also Gordon D Newby (2000) 'Jewish-Muslim Relations 632-750 CE' in Eds. Benjamin H Hary, John L Hayes and Fred Astren *Judaism and Islam: Boundaries, Communication and Interaction: Essays in Honour of William M Brinner*. Leiden: E J Brill. pp. 83-96.

4. On Abu 'Isa and his followers see Israel Friedlander (1910/11) 'Jewish-Arabic Studies' in *Jewish Quarterly Review* N S I (1910/11) pp. 183-215; II (1911/12) pp. 481-517; III (1912/13) pp. 235-300, and Newby, *Op. Cit.* Friedlander *Op. Cit.* II: 482f. compares docetism, occultation, *ghaiba*, and Raj'a.

5. Several studies of these meetings are collected in Ed. Hava Lazarus-Yaffe, Mark R Cohen, Sasson Somekh and Sidney H Griffith (1999) *The Majlis*. Wiesbaden: Harrassowitz Verlag.

6. A major schism within mediaeval Jewry, especially in the Near East, centred on the teaching ascribed to Anan ben David, who rejected rabbinic interpretation of scripture. His followers were known as Karaites ('scripturalists'); those Jews who continued to follow rabbinic teaching were called 'Rabbanites'. Some scholars, such as Leon Nemoy, think there is no foundation for the claim that Anan acknowledged the prophetic missions of Jesus and Muhammad.

A Jewish Reflection on Relations with Muslims and Islam

7. David Levine (1908) *The Garden of Wisdom*. New York: Gorgias Press (reprinted 1966), an English translation of Natanaël Ibn al-Fayyumi's *The Bustan al-Ukul*.

8. *Ibid*. pp. 103-109. Compare Qur'an 5:48 and 14:4. For Natanaël, as for most medievals, 'older' equals 'better'.

9. *Ibid*. p. 105.

10. Edward William Lane (1871) *An Account of the Manners and Customs of the Modern Egyptian*. Ed. Edward Stanley Poole, 5th Edition, London: John Murray, Vol. 2, p. 305.

11. Bernard Lewis (1993, rev. edition) 'The Pro-Islamic Jews' in *Islam in History: Ideas, People, and Events in the Middle East*. Chicago: Open Court. pp. 142-144.

12. Ed. Martin Kramer (1999) in *The Jewish Discovery of Islam*. Tel Aviv: Tel Aviv University. p. viii. Nineteenth-century Jewish scholars of Islam include Abraham Geiger, Salomon Munk, Moritz Steinschneider and Ignaz Goldziher; Shlomo Dov Goitein and Georges Vajda in the twentieth century inspired or taught many of the scholars who are with us today.

145

(c)

A Christian Eavesdropper on
Muslim-Jewish Dialogue

Marcus Braybrooke

Loves and hates are thrust
Upon me by the acrimonious dead,
The buried thesis, long since rusted knife,
Revengeful dust…
How can I here remake what there made me
And makes and remakes me still?
Set a new mark? Circumvent history?[1]

The question that the poet Edwin Muir asked in the midst of the Second World War is the question, tinged with hope, that all who pray for peace of Jerusalem ask themselves: can we circumvent history?

Jewish-Muslim relations are embittered by the continuing hostility between Israelis and Palestinians and between the state of Israel and surrounding Arab nations. Honest dialogue has to acknowledge this just as Christian acknowledgment of centuries of anti-Jewish teaching has been a necessary precursor of Jewish-Christian dialogue and apology for the Crusades and Western imperialism is required of Christians before they come close to Muslims.

Sadly, as Abdul Jalil Sajid reminds us, Arab and Israeli perspectives on events in the Middle East during the last century are so far apart that, as Norman Solomon says, they seem to be talking about different parts of the world. At least both contributors avoid offering the instant solutions from outside, such as Christian delegations are often tempted to produce.

Beyond the Dysfunctional Family

The current conflict is also the lens through which the past is viewed, for example in the continuing arguments about the Prophet Muhammad's treatment of the Banu Quraiza. Yet, viewing the past from this perspective, as Abdul Jalil says, means that 'the basic recognition that there is a great deal of commonality between the two communities' has been lost. Both authors try to correct the misreading of history by pointing to times when members of the two religions co-existed in peace and mutually enriched each other's culture and scholarship.

Even more important than recalling such happier times is the task of developing a 'hospitable theology' that will not look at Jews and Muslims only through political lenses. As Norman says, 'Islam should not be seen as a rival or usurper with a competing claim to exclusive truth, but as another manifestation of the infinite self-revelation of God.' Abdul Jalil says that Jews and Muslims should see each other as 'faithful partners.' Indeed, long ago, the great Jewish thinker, Moses Maimonides, suggested that the only truly monotheistic religions were those that practised circumcision, namely Judaism and Islam. 'According to me,' he wrote, 'circumcision has another very important meaning, namely, that all people professing this opinion – that is those who believe in the unity of God – should have a bodily sign uniting them… It is well known what degree of mutual love and mutual help exists between people who all bear the same sign.'[2]

Recognition of the Oneness of God by Abraham, who has an honoured place in both religions, and of the fact that Isaac and Ishmael were brothers, may encourage such 'mutual love. It is interesting that for at least two centuries Muslim scholars were unsure whether it was Isaac or Ishmael that Abraham intended to sacrifice. Tabari, who died in 923, preferred Isaac and as the Islamic scholar, Tim Winter says, 'there is no strong reason why this would damage Ishmael's claim to prophetic and patriarchal status; Ishmael, after all, was sentenced to a near-certain death by his expulsion into the wilderness as a child. Exploiting the story to give categoric preference to one son over the other was therefore not attempted.'[3] In the Qur'an the emphasis is on the obedient surrender of both father and son.

> And when he was of an age to walk with him, (Abraham) said, 'O my dear son, I have seen in a dream that I must sacrifice you; so look what do you think?'
> He replied, 'My father, do as you are commanded. God willing, you will find me to be steadfast.'
> Then, when they had both surrendered unto God, and he had cast him down upon his face,
> We called unto him, 'Abraham!
> You have made the vision true. Thus do we reward the doers of good.'[4]

In the Biblical tradition, Isaac is the chosen son, but Abraham clearly loved his elder son, Ishamel. Abraham and Ishmael were circumcised on the same day. The Bible says that when Sarah insisted that Hagar and her child were to be driven away, 'this greatly distressed Abraham because the slave girl's child too was his son.'[5] God comforted Abraham by promising that Ishmael too would be a father of a great nation. Whatever their differences, Isaac and Ishmael came together to bury their father in the cave of Machpelah.[6]

There is a Midrash where Abraham once again argues with God:

> God said: take your son.
> *I have two sons*
> Your only one.
> *Each is the only one of his mother*
> Whom you love.
> *I love them both*
> Isaac!'[7] – God insisted, but surely God Himself does not have to choose.

For both Jews and Muslims, Abraham is the first monotheist. In the Midrash there is this passage:

> Abraham wondered in his heart, 'Who created heaven and earth and me?' All that day he prayed to the sun. In the

Beyond the Dysfunctional Family

evening the sun set in the west and the moon rose in the east. Upon seeing the moon and the stars around it, he said 'This one must have created heaven and earth and me – these stars must be the moon's princes and courtiers.' So all night long he stood in prayer to the moon. In the morning the moon sank in the west and the sun rose in the East. Then he said, 'There is no might in either of these. There must be a higher Lord over them – to Him I will pray, and before Him I will prostrate myself.'[8]

Similarly, in the Qur'an there are these verses:

When the night grew dark upon Abraham he saw a star. He said, 'This is my Lord! But when it set, he said I love not things that set.'
And when he saw the moon rising in splendour, he said, 'This is my Lord.' But when it set, he said, 'Unless my Lord guide me, I surely shall join the ones who are astray.'
And when Abraham saw the sun rising in splendour, he cried: 'This is my Lord! This is greater.' And when it set he exclaimed, 'O my people, I am free from all that I associate with Him.
Assuredly I have turned my face toward Him who created the heavens and the earth, as one by nature upright, and I am not one of the polytheists.'[9]

Both passages remind me of the Christian hymn:

O Lord, my God,
When I in awesome wonder
Consider all the works
Thy hand has made,
I see the stars,
I hear the rolling thunder,
Thy pow'r throughout
The Universe displayed.

In both Jewish and Muslim traditions, there are stories of the young Abraham arguing with his father, who was a maker of idols, and smashing them. Perhaps today, all who in different ways look to Abraham as the father of the faithful, need together

150

A Christian Eavesdropper on Muslim-Jewish Dialogue

to shatter the religious ideologies, which would divide his descendants. And I cannot resist interrupting the conversation, to which I have been privileged to listen, by quoting the words of Pope John Paul II, 'Your God and ours is the same, and we are brothers and sisters in the faith of Abraham.'[10]

The God in whom Jews, Muslims and Christians believe is a God of justice and of mercy. Edwin Muir's only hope that we might circumvent history was if 'a grace comes of itself to wrap our souls in peace.' If in their dialogue Jews, Christians and Muslims find their souls wrapped in peace, then they can offer to others the hope that the future need not be the prisoner of the past.

NOTES

1. Edwin Muir in Ed. William Muir (1960) *Collected Poems*. Oxford: Oxford University Press.

2. Moses Maimonides (1963) *The Guide for the Perplexed*. University of Chicago Press, trans. Shlomo Pines, Pt. III, Ch. 49. p. 609.

3. Tim Winter in Eds. Norman Solomon, Richard Harries and Tim Winter (2005) *Abraham's Children*. London: T & T Clark. p. 32.

4. Qur'an, 37: 102-6.

5. Genesis 21.11 (Jerusalem Bible).

6. Genesis 25.9. This passage was referred to by President Clinton at the funeral of Yitzhak Rabin in 1997.

7. Sanhedrin, 89b.

8. This passage is based on Genesis Rabba 42.8 in W G Braude's translation of N Bialik and C Ravinsky (1992) *Sefer ha-Aggada*. New York: Schocken Books. p. 31. Quoted by Sybil Sheridan in *Abraham's Children*, p. 10.

9. Qur'an, 6: 75-79.

10. Quoted by Tim Winter in *Abraham's Children*, p. 35.

PART THREE

Sharpening Dialogue through Critical Thinking

7

Me, My Jewishness, Modernity and Other Faiths

Tony Bayfield

INTRODUCTION

All of today's Jewish denominations – Orthodox, Reform, Liberal, Conservative – emerged with German Jewry as it was allowed out of the ghettos and entered the modern world at the beginning of the 19th century. Whilst 'Orthodoxy' is applied to those most resistant to change, 'Reform' was the label for those more open to modernity, including historical scholarship. I am a Reform Jew. I therefore come out of two centuries of Judaism which is fully engaged with the modern world. I approach the Judaism that went before the Enlightenment with humility and respect. It is, after all, the God-inspired product of three thousand years of fine minds and remarkable experiences. But nothing is beyond questioning. I regard myself as a faithful Jew but a spiritually and intellectually restless one.

In one of his many persuasive books, Rabbi Jonathan Sacks tackles the question as to whether his Orthodoxy can find a way of still including me and my Reform tradition within the Jewish world.[1] He cites a passage from the Talmud which refers to *tinok shenishba*, a child who has been brought up by idolaters and therefore believes and does that which transgresses Jewish law. The child may still be included and, by analogy, so may Reform Jews because modernity, like idolatry, has blinded us and we cannot be expected to be other than we are.[2] 'Father, forgive them for they know not what they do'. I hold a very different view of modernity from Rabbi Sacks.

Beyond the Dysfunctional Family

EVEN A RUBBISH TIP?

Classical Jewish Bible commentary is called *midrash* (inquiry). One particular *midrash* poses a most unlikely question of the story of Moses and the burning bush. 'Why did God speak to Moses out of a thorn bush?' The answer is less obscure: 'To teach us that there is no place devoid of the Divine Presence, not even a thorn bush.'[3] I discovered that the same is true of a rubbish tip.

I was in Israel for a conference. One afternoon was taken up with field trips. I was uninspired by the choices but one of the conference organisers took me aside and said that she was concerned because they had accepted sponsorship funding for one of the trips but not many people had booked in. Would I make up the numbers? Which is how I ended up on an ecology field trip to Tel Aviv's rubbish dump.

The Hiriya land-fill site had developed into a 200 foot mountain of rubbish which spread smell, pollution and disease to the poorer suburbs of Tel Aviv. Out of this had come a plan to create a huge green 'lung' for the coastal towns. The rubbish mountain had been earthed over and seeded. Work on creating an ecology park that would benefit local people and show Israel at its best was already well under way.

First, we visited the new recycling plant at the foot of the mountain. It is relatively low tech, using water extracted from the rubbish itself. The model is being exported all over the world. It recycles 80% of Tel Aviv's rubbish and is a net generator of power.

We then went up by coach to the top of the former rubbish heap and looked out over the Ariel Sharon Park. We stood on top of the heap-become-green-mountain and looked across the huge site (2000 acres) to the distant suburbs of Tel Aviv now largely rid of smell, pollution and rubbish-generated disease.

The head of the project pointed to the opposite corner of the park. One could just make out, in the distance, some ruins. They were, said the Chief Executive, the ruins of an Arab village called Hiriyah from which the inhabitants had fled in 1948. I experienced instant painful, conflicted feelings.[4] He added

Me, My Jewishness, Modernity and Other Faiths

that the village itself had been built on the ruins of an ancient Jewish site – B'nei Brak. The complex feelings of inspiration and belonging that Israel evokes in Jews swept over me.

I was back in the world of the Hagaddah, that curious anthology of symbols, anecdotes, exegesis and Psalms which Jews read on the first evening of Passover when we explore the Exodus from Egypt. Five great Rabbis of Roman-occupied Judea in the early second century CE are so absorbed by the relevance of the journey from slavery to freedom that they stay up all night discussing their own situation. The location for the discussion was B'nei Brak.

Gradually, I sensed that this field trip was going to feature in my thinking and writing and was grateful to the conference organiser who had pressed me into accepting the hospitality of the Tel Aviv tourist authority. Over the next few weeks I thought about the experience a lot. It occurred to me that explaining my reactions would be a good way of responding to the questions this Chapter is meant to address: the impact of modernity on me and shared causes for despair and hope in the future.

Since I have already referred to the Hagaddah and the five Rabbis, let me take that framework one step further. The whole evening of explanation is triggered by four questions. Let me pose four questions that I have been asking myself over the weeks since I stood on Tel Aviv's mountain of rubbish.

WHAT IS MY RELATIONSHIP TO ISRAEL (AND BRITAIN)?

I realise it is significant that I chose to start at this point. Alan Race says that Israel has become more prominent in my thinking over the years that he and I have been in dialogue. I suspect that is true for many liberal Jews. It is something that makes me different from both Christians and Muslims.[5] Certainly the multiple identities which we now recognise produce different configurations. The assertion that Judaism has a geography as well as a history (some would say too little geography and too much history!) is a theological as well as political statement for me.[6] B'nei Brak carries very strong resonances.

Beyond the Dysfunctional Family

Israel and the Jewish future

My ancestors rebelled against Rome three times. The first revolt began in 66 CE and led to the destruction of the Temple and to the mass suicide at Masada. A second rebellion occurred between 115 and 117 CE. In 132 CE the final revolt took place led by Simeon bar Kochba and it was whether to join or oppose that revolt that the five Rabbis of the Hagaddah may well have been debating in B'nei Brak. By and large the rebellions were lead by Zealots[7] (with echoes of contemporary religious fundamentalists) rather than by supporters of Pharisaic/Rabbinic Judaism. They were not a success, condemning Jews to more than 1800 years of exile. The decisions, however, were largely taken in Israel/Judea and not in the Diaspora – in Alexandria or Babylon.[8]

There are 14 million Jews in the world of whom 5 million live in Israel. Demographers suggest that in two generations time – if Israel survives that long[9] – the majority of world Jewry will live in Israel. The future of Jews and Judaism rests with Israel. That is a contentious observation but one about which I am convinced. At times I have a real sense of missing out, of being in the wrong place, of living in a Jewish backwater.

Israel and British Jewry

It is clear that what goes on in Israel has a profound effect on Jews in Britain. It affects how we are perceived. It contributes to people's 'image' of the Jew. Today, more than forty years on from 1967, Israelis are no longer David but Goliath. Israelis are no longer led by heroes like Moshe Dayan and Yitzhak Rabin but by ambiguous politicians like Bibi Netanyahu and Avigdor Lieberman. We are no longer gallant freedom fighters but intransigent occupiers, western cultural imperialists rather than the romantic revivers of biblical culture. I say 'we' because the image of the Israeli impacts on the image of the British Jew. It affects how we feel about ourselves. It affects our security. It affects our relationship with other faith communities.

I have no complaint about this. It is how things are. It is part of my lot. But it is hugely significant for British Jewry. It

Me, My Jewishness, Modernity and Other Faiths

polarises us, producing, at the extremes, Jews who believe that everything that the Government of Israel does is right and who seize on every scrap of evidence (of which there is quite a lot) to prove that Israel is regularly traduced in the media. At the other extreme it brings out ambiguities about being Jewish in Jews who cannot cope with certain other Jews – those in Israel who struggle with the exercise of power and fall short of the values of the Torah and the Prophets. Which, in turn, have so influenced Christianity, Islam and the modern, western world. Which judges us.

In the middle are Jews who feel increasingly compelled to raise agonised questions from their perspective in the Diaspora but are afraid to voice them in public lest they be used by the enemies of Israel.

All of which makes the British Jew particularly difficult to engage with. We see in all criticism of Israel an attack on ourselves. We are prone to paranoia but then 'just because we are paranoid doesn't mean that you – everyone else – aren't out to get us.'[10] Our existential commitment to Israel which was, of course, re-born in 1948 actually makes it harder to move on from the trauma of the preceding fifteen years, since the rise of Hitler.

Victimhood

The dominant self-perception of the British Jewish community is one of victimhood. We are profoundly scarred by the Holocaust and cannot escape the long history of anti-Judaism in both Christian and Arab lands.[11] It is infuriating for all who want to engage seriously with Jews but a moment's reflection will tell you that the past cannot be undone or erased in one or two generations.

The Jewish sense of victimhood is understandable and greatly exacerbated by the widely articulated view that Israel alone holds the key to world peace; by the implications of the attack on the Chabad Centre in Mumbai in 2008; by the need for constant synagogue security throughout Britain. Anti-Semitism is on the rise again. Yet, somehow, we Jews have to find a way to contain

Beyond the Dysfunctional Family

our existential fears and sense of victimhood. Not everyone is an enemy and even if they were, we cannot give our Jewish identity meaning and purpose if we live as perpetual victims. It hasn't always been like this and mustn't stay like this.

What follows is a quotation from a lecture I heard three years ago by the European intellectual Jewish historian, Diana Pinto. The quote is a long one, but I make no apology because what she has to say is so important:

> ...Those Jews who wish to stress Jewish 'difference' have found support inside Europe's pluralist democracies who seek to strengthen the notion of the Jew as someone who is visibly 'Jewish' in religious/ethnic terms, for their own (positive) pluralist needs. For the only way physically to show (for television or the press) that one is dialoguing with the 'other' is to have the 'other' look different. This can be seen in the tendency for Europe's political representatives to prefer being seen in the company of a Lubavitch for the annual public lighting of Chanukkah candles than, say, with a completely 'invisible' Jewish woman community representative. There is a danger in such a practice, mainly that the Jewish narrative that is integrated in the national narrative will remain that of a people that was fundamentally 'different'...
>
> ...As a result, 'Jews' are increasingly associated with victims, with immigrants and with poor historical marginal figures. This vision is taking over the older vision of the Jews as members of the intellectual and cultural elites, who 'belonged'...
>
> ...Jews should stop thinking of themselves as the victims of the Holocaust and of anti-Semitism, and consider themselves as the full-fledged, integrated and positive actors they are across Europe.
>
> The time has come to restore the image of the humanist Jew fighting for universal causes beyond his group's own interests ...
>
> ...Jews, on the basis of their iconic value, are in the best position for the rewriting of a *res publica* contract, which can balance identity needs with shared universal principles in the creation of an open tolerant but value-laden space.
>
> Jews know what they need, in terms of cultural and religious spaces and respect for multiple identities, in order

Me, My Jewishness, Modernity and Other Faiths

to be able to live as fulfilled citizens in their respective countries. Their needs should set the standards for the needs of others. The most important lesson for the future is that democracies can only exist and prosper if they contain citizens, not a collection of competing victims. [12]

Pinto's reference to a collection of competing victims is a reference to Muslims as well as Jews. The understandable sense of victimhood felt by British Muslims is strikingly illustrated by Sughra Ahmed's earlier contribution.[13]

Role modelling

I believe passionately in the biblical injunction that Jews should be a blessing to all the families of the earth.[14] I believe in the deep significance of the phrase '*tikkun olam*' – Jews are required to be partners with others in the 'repair of the world'.[15] I also share Diana Pinto's conviction that Jews have to model for others (with less experience) multiple-identity citizenship in modern democratic societies. I hope that is not arrogant or misunderstood as exclusive. I am delighted that Ataullah Siddiqui has indicated strong approval.

Which brings me back to the top of the Tel Aviv rubbish dump, looking with deep pain at the ruins of Hiriya and with profound connection at the site of B'nei Brak, at the sense of Israel as 'where it's at' for Jews and of living in a backwater. I don't take that back but what I have just said balances the picture. Whatever the lessons of history, I enjoy being British and rejoice in its multifaceted cultural traditions. I couldn't actually live easily anywhere else. As a British *Jew*, I feel that I am the heir to another valuable and influential tradition. Not the best tradition. Not the only valuable or influential tradition. But a tradition which bears the fingerprint of God, with a part to play in British society: Judaism.

The place of Israel in contemporary Jewish theology has become more and more important to me in recent years. I acknowledge that is true and believe it to be the result of the growing isolation of Israel in international politics and the re-opening of the question of Israel's right to exist.

Beyond the Dysfunctional Family

I sense that some Christians are now impatient with my Zionism – seeing it as a distraction from the theological dialogue they wish to engage in, an inhibition to making common cause in furthering universal values and a throwback to something that was once part of Christian thought but has now been outgrown.

I sense that some radical Muslims would like to disown the doctrine of the Caliphate and the absolutism of many Arab countries, preferring to make common cause with Diaspora Jews as minority citizens of Europe. My Zionism makes me a highly problematic colleague. Yet an enthusiastic one.

There are only 270,000 Jews in Britain today. Back in the 1950s we were the largest religious minority, probably equal to the sum of all the others. We have fallen to fourth in the religious minorities list and live with a perpetual sense of being an endangered species. There aren't many advantages to our paucity of numbers. The obsession with survival is often a dead hand. But there is one positive note to strike: it makes some of us aware that we cannot be a blessing to all the families of the earth alone. We cannot repair the world on our own. We cannot restore the good name of religion and its values within British society on our own. We cannot establish an appropriate model of citizenship on our own. We can only do these things in partnership with others.

For as long as there are British Jews, we have a role. The future of Judaism may well be decided in Israel but, come what may, it is clear what we must do, must engage in, here in Britain today.

WHAT IS MY RELATIONSHIP TO MODERNITY?

The view from the top of the rubbish heap was not a bad one for surveying the modern, western world – the skyline of a modern, secular city with its tower blocks; the more squalid areas mutely underlining the scandalous gap between rich and poor; the park reflecting a newly discovered concern for the environment and the globe; ruins from a past both disturbing and inspiring.

Me, My Jewishness, Modernity and Other Faiths

The fourth dialogue partner

It was Norman Solomon who first helped me to understand that when a Jew engages in dialogue with a Christian, a third dialogue partner is always present – modernity, post-modernity, the secular western world.[16] For European Muslims, that same dialogue partner is also present. Our feelings towards modernity, the west, will be different. The responses to it that we make will vary. But it asks the same questions – about our relationship to the state, about the kind of society we wish to live in, about our values and about our fundamental beliefs.

Defining modernity; identifying the characteristics that separate the modern from the post-modern; analysing what the term 'the west' stands for; relating each term to the concept of secularity are as important as they are challenging. Fortunately such an exercise is far outside the scope of this particular chapter. However, let me be self-indulgent and use the terms 'modern', 'secular' and 'western' more or less interchangeably to describe the dominant voices and values of the society within which so many Jews, Christians and Muslims live today – in London or Manchester, Berlin or Rome, New York or Tel Aviv.

Don Cupitt, in his book, *The Meaning of the West*, defines the modern western world as the secular climax of Christianity.[17] That seems to me to be a skewing reflected in his subtitle (and personal 'theological' agenda) 'An Apologia for Secular Christianity'. But he is right to say that Christianity has contributed significantly to western values – as has Judaism and, *pace* Cupitt, as has Islam. But so too have Greek and Roman cultures – to philosophy and rationalism; to democracy, political science and concepts of citizenship; and to legal and educational systems.

There is absolutely no doubt that my upbringing and education in 1960s Britain has played a significant part in who I am and how I think – the legacies of Kant and Freud, Darwin and Einstein feel inescapable but I would not want to run away from them even if I could.

Yet I know that I am a religious Jew, a link in an immensely long chain of tradition, the heir to a culture of great value and

Beyond the Dysfunctional Family

vitality. Despite the seductions of secular hedonism and the cold, self-focused despair of secular reasoning, my trust in the God of Abraham, Isaac and Jacob, Sarah, Rebecca, Rachel and Leah will not leave me. So, modernity continues to shine a challenging and disturbing light on the richness – and dross – of my tradition, on the nature of religious authority, on sacred texts, on prayer and liturgy and on the mystery of God, God's self.

All in the same boat

Living in the west is challenging, liberating, disturbing and exhilarating. One of its most remarkable features is that my Christian and Muslim neighbours have reached the same place by radically different routes. Our origins are inextricably interwoven but our subsequent journeys have been markedly different (and conflictual). But now we find ourselves in the same boat. I am reminded of a *midrash* by a second century Jewish mystic, Shimon bar Yochai. 'It [he was referring to sin] is like a group of people in a boat. One person takes a drill and begins to bore a hole under his own seat.' 'What are you doing?'they say. 'Mind your own business,' he replies, 'I'm boring under my own seat.' 'It is our business,', they say, 'because if water comes into the boat from under your seat, we'll all drown.'[18]

Let me move into the second half of this section by exploring three dimensions of the west we share: capitalism, liberal democracy and the secular state.

Back to the rubbish heap! A couple of sentences early on in the tour had been revealing. The Chief Executive 'admitted' that the motivation for the project had been neither a commitment to ecology nor to the disadvantaged residents of eastern Tel Aviv. The rubbish heap had become a magnet for flocks of migrating birds, thus imperilling the passengers and freight flying in and out of nearby Ben Gurion Airport. The decision had been economic, pragmatic not ecological or ethical.

In other words, Israel is typical of modern western states in which the market, democracy and a governing secularity are the overriding hallmarks. Once again, we come to subjects that

Me, My Jewishness, Modernity and Other Faiths

merit chapters if not books in themselves, but it is important at least to offer a few pointers to essential in-depth discussions.

The Free Market

Neither the bible nor rabbinic tradition indicate a particular economic ideology. Over the last 150 years, many Jews have been enthusiastic about socialism, Marxism and communism and Jews have contributed to the development of these ideologies.[19] However, Thatcherism and Reaganomics also had their appeal to middle class Jews who felt that they had got to where they were by dint of their own hard work, pulling themselves up by their bootstraps. The shift in Israel from the kibbutz as the ideal to fully embracing free market economics over a period of sixty years is not unrepresentative even if I, who could never endure kibbutz life, feel sad.

The biblical concept of the Jubilee[20] – whether it was ever implemented or not – does indicate a strong sense of the individual's economic dignity and of the need to intervene to prevent economic life degenerating towards extremes. The unfailing prophetic emphasis on provision for the poor, the needy, the orphan, the widow and the immigrant; the stress on divine revulsion at religious rites unaccompanied by economic justice; the protests at the building of great wealth at the expense of the poor; Isaiah's remarkable definition of the (Yom Kippur) Fast as freeing the oppressed and dealing one's bread to the hungry – all point to a theology and ethic of economic justice[21] rather than the endorsement of a transcendental economic system.

I am therefore a pragmatist. I recognise that the free market system seems to work better than its alternatives. But it is not a theological principle and the 2008/9 banking crisis and recession indicate that free markets unregulated by values are hell rather than heaven.

As a Jew, I do not advocate poverty and come from a tradition in which material benefits are a sign of blessing. Rabbi Ignaz Maybaum, a German Jewish refugee to this country and one of the few genuine theologians that British Jewry has ever hosted,

165

Beyond the Dysfunctional Family

described Abraham in positive terms as a bourgeois, blessed by God with children, with grandchildren and the good life.[22] As an aside, the biblical metaphor for reward is 'plenty'. In the light of the contemporary environmental crisis the metaphor needs to change to 'sufficiency'. Nevertheless, prophetic Judaism sees no contradiction between this affirmation of the material world on the one hand, and its bias towards the poor, the needy, the widow, the orphan and the immigrant, the profound sense that extremes of wealth and poverty are scandalous, on the other. Neither do I.

Democracy

The religious right in Israel, though it takes advantage of Israeli democracy to win financial support for its people and institutions, is often heard to voice dislike of democracy. Democracy is seen as 'of Athens', threatening the absolutist authority of the contemporary rabbinic sage who is truly 'of Jerusalem'. However, Rabbi David Rosen, in an article in *Religions in Dialogue: from Theocracy to Democracy*,[23] argues that Judaism is essentially pro-democracy having early on developed strong consultative processes.[24]

Whilst it seems to me that Rosen offers much the more cogent argument, this is another case where Jewish tradition does not clearly endorse a pillar of modernity, in this instance a particular political system. But it is without doubt that Jews and Judaism fare best in democratic rather than totalitarian societies and the values of democratic societies are much closer than those of dictatorship. In the mid-1960s there was an American television series called Slattery's People which began with a deep and sonorous voice-over, paraphrasing Churchill, declaring democracy to be 'a very poor form of government but all the rest are so much worse'. That seems to me to be precisely the Jewish experience. We did not create democracy. But our values are strongly supported by it. It is a feature of modernity/the west which we embrace and defend enthusiastically, in Israel as well as in Britain.

166

The secular state

The modern western state has liberated itself from religious control. In a masterly article, John Bowden traces the process over many centuries by reference to the universities.[25] Given the iniquities that were and still are performed within theocracies, this is no bad thing. Religion is too powerful a matter to be combined with state power. In any event, the secular state is our reality and poses a number of questions.

First, what is the role of religion within a secular state? In an excellent essay in *Religions in Dialogue*,[26] Alan Race argues that the concept of the Kingdom of God, which relies much on its Hebrew legacy, provides both support for democracy and the critique of its realities. In other words, religions have a dual task: both to work with the democratically-elected government for social justice, consensus ethics, and a value-laden society, and also to point out the short-comings, to press for progress and, above all, to challenge abuses of power. Race goes on to argue that what is required is a 'public square' at the heart of secularised democracies – a place, an institution or institutions, where religions can collaborate, participate and challenge.

There are, of course, important questions as to what happens when the faiths cannot agree on a shared ethic or where the faiths themselves are divided. Many Catholics, Evangelical Christians and Orthodox Jews interpret the concept of the sanctity of life to mean that God is utterly opposed to assisted dying. Exponents of modern faith are sceptical of such 'hot-line' absolutism. However, secularism asserts the primacy of personal autonomy, the right of the individual to make the choices that seem best for them. Exponents of modern religion recognise that the individual does not live in a vacuum but lives in the context of family, community and society which also have rights. So religious moderates have a triple function: first, to mediate between the two extremes; second, to ask questions about the extent to which secular society has the right to impose its values on faith communities; third, at least as important, to question the extent to which faith communities have the right

Beyond the Dysfunctional Family

to impose deep and sincere convictions on others beyond their own communities.

This is such a difficult area but one which we must address if we are to achieve the kind of society in which the faiths can flourish and play a progressive role.

In short, I have no doubt that the role of the faiths in a modern, western, secular democracy is one of both participation and challenge, offering both critical solidarity and prophetic challenge. The American Jewish theologian, Eugene B Borowitz, coined the phrase 'creative maladjustment'. As a Jew, that is how I choose to live in the secular state – as an integrated member of society who resists assimilation; as a passionate contributor through the creative maladjustment generated by the best of my tradition and what I learn from others.

Majority and minority religions within the state

Which brings me to one final topic in response to the second question – the place of the majority religious tradition within the secular state.

Others find it hard to understand just how much Jews yearn (even if they don't live in Israel) for a place where the culture, the rhythm of life, is Jewish.[27] It comes from nearly 1900 years of living within another culture and according to someone else's rhythm. Christians find it hard to understand emotionally because they are more aware of what they have lost in the modern western state than of what they still have. Muslims should understand but Israel exists within the Muslim world and Muslims react as if an otherwise legitimate aspiration is being satisfied at their expense and within their hegemony. Israel is seen as a project of (western) modernity, as a Trojan horse of American imperialism, not as the legitimate realisation of Judaism's two millennial yearning.

Israel's declaration of independence owes quite a bit to the American declaration of independence, but it also owes a lot to the Jewish prophetic tradition. It embodies both the best of the western values of democracy, pluralism and tolerance and also the best of Jewish values embodied in the phrase 'social justice'.

Me, My Jewishness, Modernity and Other Faiths

At its best, Israel aspires to be 'a Jewish state and a state for all its citizens'.[28] I believe that is possible and it is not just possible but essential to achieving a balance between blinkered secularity and oppressive theocracy. A state should reflect the best of the faith tradition which moulded it, shaped its people, institutions and landscape whilst at the same time respecting, being sensitive to, leaving appropriate space for its various minorities.[29] That space has to be determined by negotiation with the minorities themselves, not imposed by the majority as a pseudo-democratic dictat.

Britain owes much to Christianity and it would be an act of barbarism, sheer Luddite folly to obliterate the Christian landscape. As a beneficiary of another, hard-won part of Britain's tradition, giving full rights to minorities, I will insist on my full equality and my rights of equal participation but I am positively happy that the rhythm of life remains a Christian one – providing only that I can continue to live according to the rhythm of Judaism. Respect and tolerance does not, must not imply the eradication of all signs of faith.

It is very noticeable how Christians, Jews and Muslims are each troubled by issues of power and authority in the modern western state – but differently. In Britain today, Christians need to deal with issues around their loss of power, Jews with the exercise of power (in Israel with its implications for Jews everywhere). Muslims need to confront diminished power i.e. living as a minority in the west and in a global culture which is sceptical of the theocratic state.

WHAT IS MY RELATIONSHIP TO OTHER FAITHS?

When Esau and Jacob are reconciled, the Bible tells us that 'He kissed him and they wept.'[30] But if we read on, we discover that the two soon part to live their own separate lives. One of the characteristics that distinguishes the modern world from the past is that separate existence is no longer possible. Because of globalisation and migration, the major faiths of the world live side by side, sharing a global village.

Beyond the Dysfunctional Family

Authenticity depends on relating

I am convinced that the pragmatic discloses the theological. The revelation of modernity is that religions can no longer validly exist as islands with echoing straits thrown between them. Faiths can only exist authentically in relationship to one another. If they strive for separation or pay only lip service to collaboration, they fail humanity both spiritually and ethically.

This applies to all of the major faiths. I am not a relativist who believes that all opinions are equally valid and that any credulous nonsense is entitled to respect. But I do believe that religion is provisional and that faiths contain only fragments of Truth. In fact, it is absurd to believe that any one group of people have a complete understanding of God and unbelievably arrogant to think that God would entrust the whole of God's Truth to any one group of people at any one time. There is incalculable value in the Christian story, the Hindu story, the Muslim story, the Sikh story. Faiths are not in competition with each other for the title of 'the best'. But every faith must constantly submit its teachings to ethical scrutiny. Which is why I, as a Jew, find the theology of Abraham Joshua Heschel (with its emphasis on righteousness) more sympathetic than that of Kierkegaard (with its emphasis on a leap of faith which goes beyond, and even contradicts, the ethical).

I want to make clear at this point that, though I have made a speciality of Jewish-Christian-Muslim dialogue, I don't regard it as any more important or of greater merit than, say, Jewish-Hindu dialogue. In fact, in some ways, I have more to learn from the Indic family because it embraces a quite different experience from the Jewish experience. My concentration on Jewish-Christian-Muslim dialogue has to do with the complex inter-relatedness of our respective revelations, sacred scriptures, traditions and histories. I regard us as a family and the most dysfunctional family at that. Our three faiths are espoused by more than 50% of the population of the globe and are implicated in many of the world's trouble spots. To a significant extent we hold the reputation of religion in our collective hands and I am fearful for the outcome.

Me, My Jewishness, Modernity and Other Faiths

The tragedy of our dysfunctionality

Looking out on Hiriya, the Arab village whose residents fled in 1948, makes me despair. The story of Israel sometimes feels to me like a Greek tragedy which begins with those revolts against Rome nearly two millennia ago, to expulsion and wandering, to the inability of both Christian and Muslim societies to cope with their Jewish minorities. The narrative that Jews always fared well in Muslim societies and it was only the re-establishment of the Jewish State in 1948 that brought about tension is, sadly, a myth.[31] Both in the Christian and Muslim worlds, Jews have rubbed along when times were good but suffered terribly when times were difficult. Interpretations both of the New Testament and of the Qur'an, have played a full part in Jewish suffering. Which is not, of course, to say that Christians or Muslims would not have fared as badly at the hands of Jews if the balance of society had been different. Who knows? But it doesn't ease my fear of a Greek tragedy. The inability to find a formula by which to share the land; the Jewish part in creating and maintaining (along with others) a new victim, the Palestinians; the seeming hopelessness of the present situation; the possibility of another Masada[32] – all make me tremble.

Healing through a partnership of the moderates

Yet as I looked out over Hiriya at the poor and once polluted suburbs of Tel Aviv and the inventiveness of the recycling plant, I was reminded that Judaism, Christianity and Islam share at their very core a commitment to social justice and to human rights and duties. We share responsibility for the globe: 'The Holy One Blessed Be He kept creating worlds and destroying them until he created this world …… do not corrupt and desolate my world for if you corrupt it, there is no one to set it right after you.'[33] We share a remarkable inventiveness manifested in the contributions of Muslim, Christian and Jewish societies of the past.

A reconciliation of the dysfunctional family is still possible. Working together can still provide hope. A partnership between

Beyond the Dysfunctional Family

the three Abrahamic faiths can avert another Masada and, more importantly, the serious threat to the good name of religion and, most important of all, impending global disaster.

What is it that in this modern world of interdependence and much greater awareness of the other drives us still further apart?

Back once again to the rubbish tip and to the site of ancient B'nei Brak where those five rabbis of the Hagaddah considered the meaning of slavery and freedom in second century Judea. There is a second resonance to B'nei Brak. Seven kilometres away from the site of the old B'nei Brak lies B'nei Brak New Town – an expanding conurbation of *charedi*/ultra-orthodox/ fundamentalist Jews living life as dynamic, urban Amish without the phobia of technology.

Although I understand intellectually the rise and rise of religious fundamentalism since the 1960s, I still find it emotionally incomprehensible. If we define religious fundamentalism as a negative reaction to modernity; a response to the shaking of the old truths of faith to the roots; a reassertion of those truths in an unsubtle and crude form; the insistence that those truths are the only truths; a desire to impose those truths on others whether they like it or not; a preparedness to subvert democracy to gain the power to impose truths on others – we identify a phenomenon that has undermined the good name of religion. It affects not only Judaism, Christianity and Islam but Hinduism and Sikhism as well. It may not be the cause of all the troubles in the world but it is inextricably bound up with many of them.

We know how the unsubtle spokespersons for secular fundamentalism – Richard Dawkins and Christopher Hitchens – exploit this fearful perversion of religion to discredit all religion in a crude and blatant way. But listen to the same questioning in more measured terms from the philosopher A C Grayling:

> What kind of ethics would be imposed by, say, a fundamentalist Christian government in the United States, if such came to pass? The world has seen Taliban rule in Afghanistan, where music was banned and women had to walk about covered completely from head to foot, two facts

Me, My Jewishness, Modernity and Other Faiths

quite staggering in their meaning when one contemplates them. And of course the whole of history is an object lesson in this regard. From it one knows that *a religious morality imposed by enthusiasts for their faith would controvert almost every tenet of liberal views about tolerance, openness, personal autonomy and choice, and would impose instead a harsh and limiting uniformity on behaviour and opinion, and doubtless even on dress and recreation. It would be done in the name of a God, in the alleged interests of our souls;* and it would not reflect or accommodate much in the way of facts about human nature and human occupancy of a natural physical world.[34] [Italics are mine].

A huge difficulty is presented by the bifurcation of the Israeli and Palestinian narratives to the point of total disconnection. I believe that this is just one of the pernicious effects of the ideology of religious fundamentalism (allied with right-wing secular nationalism)[35] that has prevented a just solution to the Israel/Palestine situation so far. It is religious fundamentalism which rears its ugly head in many of the world's trouble spots. It is religious fundamentalism that drives the three Abrahamic faiths apart. The mainstream of our three faiths has done all too little to combat it. As a result the good name of religion has been severely damaged and a secular fundamentalist backlash has ensued. It is the most urgent of imperatives that both locally and globally, the moderate majority re-assert themselves – together.

WHAT IS MY RELATIONSHIP TO MY IDENTITY AS A PROGRESSIVE JEW?

I may be a religious leader but I confess to being a pretty ordinary human being. I believe in God but doubts and uncertainty litter my life. I may lay great stress on the ethical but my failings and stupidities cause me to bury my head in the pillow in shame before I fall asleep at night. I try to follow the Jewish injunction to carry two pieces of paper, one in each pocket, one saying 'for my sake the world was created' and the other saying 'remember

Beyond the Dysfunctional Family

you are but dust and ashes'[36] but extremes of self-importance and insignificance are the source of many of my inner conflicts and anxieties.

Nevertheless, I am an enthusiastic, religious Jew, just as enthusiastic and religious as the chaps and chapesses who wander round B'nei Brak New Town dressed as if they were living in late 18th century Poland.

We shall not be marginalised

That comment reflects British-Jewish neuroses. In America, Reform and Conservative Jews have been the majority for more than a century. But that is not true in Britain where Orthodoxy has held sway with institutions which, in some respect, parallel those of the established Church. My late mother-in-law was once overheard participating in the following conversation: 'What does your son-in-law do?' 'He's a rabbi.' 'Oh, he must be very religious then.' 'No, he's Reform.' In Israel there is the same exclusive equation of traditional observance with religiosity. Thus one is either *dati* (religious, strictly observant) or *chiloni* (secular). As recently as 2004, research revealed that the British-Jewish community is obsessed with authenticity defined as the Judaism of the synagogue that my father or grandfather didn't go to! This is not said in anger or bitterness (well, not much anyway) but to emphasise the importance of what we – the authors of this book – share.

I often refer to myself and my dialogue partners as liberals, but it's a risky term in the sense that it has acquired a particular definition in political philosophy. I would call us moderates but moderation sounds dull and lacking in passion. Middle of the road? The Chasidic leader Menachem Mendel of Kotsk famously declared 'the middle of the road is for horses'. Perhaps progressive gets us a little closer but as a term it also has its problems, certainly within the Jewish world. Perhaps critical mainstream?

In any event, what I am trying to say is that all the contributors to this book are at the cutting edge of the encounter between the

Me, My Jewishness, Modernity and Other Faiths

three Abrahamic faiths and the modern or post-modern western world. We are right at the exciting and challenging point where religion engages with secularity, where faith grapples with the world of the 21st century, where religious traditions are confronted by the crises of contemporary life, where faith is required to offer meaning and purpose in a world where many struggle to find meaning and purpose. It's a terrifying and wonderful place to be.

We are where it's at. We are where the world needs us to be. We have to show the courage to assert ourselves, to take the moral and spiritual high ground. We can only do what needs to be done together – we religious progressives, we members of the critical mainstream or whatever term we choose to share.

I want finally to answer three questions that I have raised during this chapter but not answered sufficiently.

1. Will faith and the faiths survive?

This is, of course, a peculiarly Jewish question and stems from our tiny numbers and our dependence upon the future of the experiment of return to the Land. As far as Jews are concerned, I genuinely do not know. The odds are probably against us but we have defied the odds before.

I am sure that the world, Christianity and Islam can survive without Judaism – though you would miss us, as one always does when it's too late! But I pose the question because I really do think that religion – spiritually and ethically – is in crisis and the danger to Islam and Christianity, as well as Judaism, is far greater than most people realise.

2. In what form should we seek to survive and thrive?

I am going to rely on two rather trite and superficial metaphors to make my point. I believe passionately in the retention of different identities – a patchwork of gardens not a single, uniform park. What should characterise us is that we regularly visit each other's gardens, enjoy them and learn more about gardens and gardening from them. Not only will we return to

Beyond the Dysfunctional Family

our own garden enriched, but we will be better able to spot the many weeds.

Some years ago there were riots in certain northern cities and a report on the riots referred to people living 'parallel lives'. I coined the risible metaphor of the salad bowl. What is required is not a blending of the constituents into an ultimately tasteless soup. Nor is it desirable to have a scattering of isolated vegetables. But rather what society requires is a salad bowl in which the various faith and ethnic communities retain their distinctive shape and texture but harmonise within the salad bowl of society to form a tasty, nourishing salad. I made the dubious remark that Jews are the garlic in the salad – small but decidedly pungent! Most Jews winced! They are, of course, inadequate metaphors but I hope they convey the kind of society in which, I envisage, we can not only survive and thrive but contribute to progress.

I want to mention faith schools at this point. I believe in faith schools if they root their pupils in their respective faith traditions so that they are knowledgeable, confident and secure, so that they are motivated to go out and partner others in the building of a society based upon those values which are conducive to the good of society and the globe. I suspect that the modern democratic state must allow those who wish to remain in their own garden or live parallel lives as isolated vegetables to do so. But I am clear that the state should not be financing schools and other institutions which take the separatist position.

Diana Pinto referred to the 're-writing of a *res publica* contract, which can balance identity needs with shared universal principles in the creation of an open, tolerant but value-laden space.' I think that we should be developing such a contract. What I have in mind is that the faiths would commit to democracy; to playing the role of fully engaged citizens committed to the good of British society; to respect for the traditions and culture of the UK; to genuine and meaningful partnership with others; to working for social justice, consensus ethics and global, environmental values. Government would commit to allowing the faiths their own space; keeping citizens secure from racism and religious hatred; encouraging community formation and maintenance; allowing minorities to live according to their own religious rhythms; and providing an effective 'public square' where the faiths can make a full and positive contribution to the building of British society.[37]

3. What are the criteria for working together?

I hope I have largely answered this question but let me try to summarise. I believe that the ground rules require, first, a preparedness to look at our sacred texts and stop blaming God for their all too human failings. Second comes a preparedness to acknowledge that we are siblings but not identical triplets and to engage with and accept the value of otherness as well as sameness. Third, there is an overriding need for deep self-criticism and a humility which leads to a radical moderation of our respective truth claims, so they do not invalidate or condescend to others. Fourthly we need a willingness to engage not just socially or ethically but also theologically, so that we can come a little closer to 'understanding the heart of the stranger', grasp the deep sense of the relatedness and inter-relatedness of Judaism, Christianity and Islam and acknowledge our individual incompleteness. Finally, we must commit to engaging with the fourth dialogue partner, learning as well as rejecting and thus moving forward on our respective and collective journeys.

Modernity has thrown down one challenge that is greater than all of the rest. It is the challenge to faith itself.[38] Here in Britain we are not adequately meeting the challenge and the responses of religious fundamentalism do not help us at all. Is faith possible and expressible in a form that is consonant with 21st century experience rather than as a reassertion of old truths that do not work for most people? Is faith possible without retreat into a full blown ghetto or at least a mental ghetto – a compartment of the mind reserved for the irrational and absurd? Which brings me back – as you might have guessed – to Hiriya, the rubbish heap and the *midrash* with which I began.

Beyond the Dysfunctional Family

The 19th century English poet Elizabeth Barrett Browning wrote in her greatest work, Aurora Leigh: 'Earth's crammed with heaven, and every common bush afire with God; But only he who sees, takes off his shoes.'[39] The reference is to Moses' thorn bush – and to my rubbish heap. Did I take off my shoes? Am I still able, despite my exposure to modernity, to affirm God in the commonplaces and challenges of the world?

Was that a religious experience on Ariel Sharon's tip? Did I encounter God? I say: 'It certainly provoked a whole range of interesting intellectual questions and ideas.' God says: 'If that's how it works for you, sonny, don't knock it.' I feel the faintest touch of an encouraging arm round my shoulder. 'Ridiculous? Fevered imagination? Self-delusion? Wishful thinking?' What is that I think I heard? 'There is no place where God is not, even …'

For the faiths in Britain today, there is still no more chilling poem than Matthew Arnold's 'Dover Beach'. Can we together halt the 'Melancholy, long, withdrawing roar?'[40]

NOTES

1. Jonathan Sacks (1993) *One People? Tradition, Modernity and Jewish Unity*. London Littman Library of Jewish Civilization.

2. *Ibid.* pp. 133-4: 'excusable ignorance … Deviant belief is to be attributed to the impact of secularizing culture'.

3. Exodus, Rabbah II.5.

4. Michael Hilton asked me to explain my conflicted feelings. On the one hand, I have no doubt that Israel was right to fight the invading Arab armies in Israel's War of Independence. On the other hand, there is no doubt that many Palestinians suffered as a consequence. It reminds me of a profoundly important *midrash* commenting on the rejoicing after escaping from Egypt in Exodus Ch 15. The Talmud places in God's mouth the astonishing words, 'The work of My hands is drowning in the sea and you want to sing songs of rejoicing!' Babylonian Talmud Megillah 10b; Sanhedrin 39b.

5. The difference in attitude to land is probably the feature that makes me most 'other' for a number of my dialogue partners in this book. However, there are Christians for whom land is still important – see for instance, Walter Brueggemann (1982) *The Land*. Philadelphia: Fortress

Me, My Jewishness, Modernity and Other Faiths

Press. The Muslim concept of an Islamic world, of the Caliphate and the status of Arab lands and Muslim holy sites remained largely undiscussed by our group.

6. See for instance Tony Bayfield (2008) 'Happy Birthday Israel? Dialogue and the Dysfunctional Family Sixty Years On' in *Contemporary Church History*, Vol 21, Issue 1.

7. The first century of the Common Era was a period in which there were many groups and sects within the Jewish world. There were revolutionaries – Zealots and Sicarii (knife-men). Most, except for the Pharisees (founders of rabbinic Judaism) and the Christians disappeared with the destruction of the Temple. Louis M Feldman, 'Palestinian and Diaspora Judaism in the First Century', in Ed. Hershel Shanks (1993) *Christianity and Rabbinic Judaism*. London: SPCK. p. 13.

8. This is less true of the second rebellion which took place largely in Egypt and Cyrenaica. But the revolt which led to the destruction of the Temple in 70 CE and the Bar Kochba rebellion of 132-5 CE were the most significant for the future of Judaism.

9. I, like most Jews both inside and outside the State, take both the naked military threats and the attempts at political de-legitimising with the utmost seriousness.

10. A number of members of the group, Ataullah in particular, find this sad and disturbing. I share those feelings but need to reassert that they are real. Large numbers of British Jews believe that British Jewry has many enemies and that much anti-Israel feeling is an excuse for anti-Semitism. Whilst there are those in the community who consciously or subconsciously use Jewish paranoia to extract communal loyalty, the police-verified need for security and the number of recorded attacks on Jews and Jewish institutions ground Jewish fears in reality. A millennium or more of trauma is constantly reinforced. Many Jews are therefore suspicious of the hand of friendship.

11. See Martin Gilbert (2010) *In Ishmael's House: A History of Jews in Muslim Lands*. London: Yale University Press.

12. Diana Pinto (2006) 'Are there Jewish Answers to Europe's Questions?' in *European Judaism*, Vol. 39, No. 2, pp. 47-57.

13. See pp. 115-121.

14. Genesis 12:3, which refers to all Abram's descendants i.e. Christians and Muslims as well as Jews.

15. The phrase *'tikkun olam'* – repair or mend the world – became widely used in the 20th century as synonymous with the pursuit of social justice. The idea of pragmatic acts of repair to create or restore more just situations resonates with Amartya Sen's critique of John Rawl's pursuit of the ideal of justice. Sen calls for a 'realization-focussed' approach making what is manifestly unjust a little less unjust or a little more just. Amartya Sen (2009) *The Idea of Justice*. London: Allen Lane.

Beyond the Dysfunctional Family

16. Norman Solomon (1992) 'The Third Presence', in Eds. A Bayfield and M Braybrooke *Dialogue with a Difference*. London: SCM Press. pp. 147-162.

17. Don Cupitt (2008) *The Meaning of the West*. London: SCM Press.

18. Midrash Rabbah Vayikra 4:6.

19. To a significant extent I became a rabbi because I saw in the Jewish prophetic tradition the source of my 'left of centre' political views.

20. Leviticus 25 vv 10-13.

21. See Fn 15 and my sympathies with Amartya Sen's endorsement of Adam Smith, *Op. Cit.* p. 50.

22. A frequent theme of Maybaum's writing. See, for instance, (1960) 'The Bourgeois, the Citizen and the Jew' in *Jewish Existence*. London: Vallentine Mitchell.

23. Eds. Alan Race and Ingrid Shafer (2002) *Religions in Dialogue: From Theocracy to Democracy*. Basingstoke: Ashgate.

24. The profound definition of democracy as 'government by discussion' goes back to Walter Bagehot.

25. John Bowden (2002) 'Secular Values and the Process of Secularisation' in *Encounters,* Vol 8, No 1, March, pp. 29-43.

26. Eds. Alan Race and Ingrid Shafer (2002), *Op. Cit.* pp. 73-82.

27. This is true of some of our group.

28. This is the phrase that the Movement for Reform Judaism uses in its statement of Zionist commitment on its website www.reformjudaism. org.uk. We learned it from a remarkable Israeli Muslim, Mohammad Darawshe of the Abraham Fund, which seeks to raise the *de facto* position of Israeli Palestinians to where *de jure* it should be.

29. The 16th century Mughal emperor Akbar is totally remarkable. 'Taking note of the religious diversity of his people, Akbar laid the foundations of secularism and religious neutrality of the state in a variety of ways; the secular constitution that India adopted in 1949, after independence from British rule, has many features already championed by Akbar in the 1590s. The shared elements include interpreting secularism as the requirement that the state be equidistant from different religions and must not treat any religion with special favour.' Sen, *The Idea of Justice*, p. 37. I gladly adopt that view save for the fact that if there is one faith that has already played a formative role in a particular society, if there is a clear majority faith, it should receive public recognition and play a part in the calendar and rhythm of that country. Its values should carry a certain weight (which is not the same as 'specially favoured').

30. Gen 33 v4. It is also the title of a book, Eds. A Bayfield, S Brichto and E Fisher (2001) *He Kissed Him and They Wept*. London: SCM Press.

31. See Gilbert, *In Ishmael's House*.

Me, My Jewishness, Modernity and Other Faiths

32. A Herodian palace on a cliff overlooking the Dead Sea where the last Jewish forces in the revolt of 66 CE were besieged and committed suicide rather than submit to Rome.

33. Genesis, Rabbah IX.2; Ecclesiastes, Rabbah vii 29.

34. A C Grayling (2009) *Ideas that Matter*. London: Weidenfeld & Nicolson. pp. 158-9.

35. Michael Hilton makes the point that religious fundamentalism in Israel, if equated with the Settlers, is less of a problem than the secular fundamentalism of right-wing Governments. This is an important point, though it should be stressed that all recent Israeli Governments have included fundamentalist religious parties in an often unholy alliance. There are constant critiques of the Israeli democratic system which allows minorities such power. But why has this not been changed and why does the Israeli electorate allow religious-secular fundamentalism to flourish? Could it be that they express the paranoia and promise the security that the mainstream would prefer not to articulate themselves?

36. Attributed to the Hasidic Rabbi Simhah Bunem of Przysucha (1765-1827).

37. I had a first attempt at this in Ed. Alex Bigham 'The Jewish Experience in Britain in Having Faith in *Foreign Policy*. London: Foreign Policy Centre.

38. Responding particularly to Michael Hilton: 'We miss the point if we think of ourselves as a bunch of liberals gathering together to point out how different we are from religious fundamentalists.' Indeed. We also need to address secular fundamentalists and ask, 'How can our dialogue engage with those who reject all faiths?'

39. Aurora Leigh Bk vii.

40. Dover Beach, 3rd stanza, line 5.

8

Religious Absolutism, Violence and the Public Square

Alan Race

A PARABLE

I once invited a rabbi from the reform tradition to address a group of students who were training for Christian ministry. The rabbi informed the group that he had scrapped his synagogue sermon on the previous Friday evening and asked the congregation what they would like him to say to the Christian seminarians. He reported that overwhelmingly they had said, quite simply: 'Tell them, we're alright!' There was a quizzical silence among the seminarians.

What could such a message mean? Surely Christians didn't feel that Jews were not alright? Further discussion revealed the following. The Jewish congregation wanted to convey that they did not feel 'unfulfilled' or 'deficient' in their Judaism; there was no need for any 'Christian extra'. God had called the Jewish people into being and this congregation were part of a long line of tradition, existing in the present no doubt with its own mix of proud achievements and lamentable failings, but in this respect they were no different from devout believers of any other tradition. 'Please hear us,' they urged, 'for sooner or later you will start getting at us with your "good news". Only for us it will be bad news, because we know where it leads. We're alright. Christians, get over it.'

It was an important lesson for the ministers in training to learn. It has been an important lesson for the churches to learn, though it has not yet been absorbed fully by all churches.

Beyond the Dysfunctional Family

How others see us is hugely significant. Where Christians want to offer saving grace; others may experience intrusion, may be even aggression. Why is it that after five minutes in conversation with Muslims the accusation of the Crusades is slapped on to the table as though they happened only yesterday and as though I could be blamed for them so many centuries later? Why can we not lay the ghosts of the religious past to rest? Their present haunting is tellingly illustrated by Akbar Ahmed's fascinating anthropological travelogue, *Journey Into Islam*[1]. Taking postgraduate students with him across the Muslim world, he discovered the bottom-line question which preoccupied the vast majority of his fellow believers: 'Why do they want to destroy our Islam?' It was not Afghanistan, Iraq, Crusades, western colonialism, economic globalisation and the like, which made ordinary citizens, educationalists, religious professionals and those in high political office across the world angry, but an anxiety about a religious worldview under threat.

For some reason the paranoia virus seems all too prevalent. The faithful are feeling encroached upon by 'others' who harbour unsavoury intentions. Jews fear anti-semitism, Muslims Islamophobia, Christians the tauntings of New Atheists and putative Aggressive Secularists. Mental territory, it seems, is in danger of being invaded and that is more serious than the invasion of any slice of earth territory. Such is the anxiety behind paranoia, whether reasonably founded or menacingly imagined. Paranoia sometimes masquerades as the fear of survival. As one Muslim dialogue partner once said to me: 'I say to my children that you can be as western as you like, but don't give up your Islam.' But could that Islam stand a better chance of being retained if it transmuted into a different shape for a different context? How changeable, adaptable, malleable can any religion afford to be? And is the experience of dialogue a new context which masks its own expectations of change? If so, it is small wonder that many remain cautious about it.

The rabbi and his congregation were incorrect, but not for the reasons they supposed. We're not alright. Only now, the 'we' means all of us.

A PARADOX

I have long observed the following paradox for relations between religions: a world in desperate need unites the basic compassionate impulse of the varied religions as never before but the inherited worldviews of the religions themselves drive them apart (as they have always done, though perhaps with a few historical exceptions). If there is any truth in the rumour of a 'clash of civilisations', then it has this paradox at its heart. But we don't need rumours; those of us involved in interfaith relations know it in our own experience: we are 'thrown together' and have to make sense of it. Those involved in the problems theologically, academically, pastorally and politically, know it as perhaps the most puzzling and challenging issue on their agenda.

So why be involved in interfaith relations? Many reasons can be proffered. Perhaps I want to know more about my religious neighbours' ritualistic and social habits, or the reasons for their moral advocacy on certain matters, or why they see the world as they do. If so, then getting to know neighbours more than superficially might help me figure out some answers. Or perhaps, in a more spirited civic mood, I might sign up for the social cohesion agenda, and I inevitably find myself having to unravel whether or not religious commitment is supportive of or inimical to social cohesion in a diverse society. Or, perhaps in a more politically resistant-minded mood, I join with others in protest, say, against aspects of foreign policy or home office immigration narrow-mindedness. In this instance I observe that the dynamics of globalisation are so intimately bound up with the history of civilisations, cultures and religions that statecraft can no longer afford to bracket the issue of 'ultimate commitment' out of the political reckoning. It seems that at every level of human interaction the business of what we think of and how we respond to people of different religious or ideological conviction matters.

Another way of entering into my fundamental paradox is to observe that we are creatures of both empathy and distancing in

Beyond the Dysfunctional Family

relation to those whose ways are not my ways. Empathy entails a sharing among human beings at existential levels where we experience, for example, joy, fear, anxiety, wonder, love etc. It leads to a mutual interest in discerning what constitutes a good and fulfilling life, and to a desire to be known, loved and valued as we know, love and value. These associations of empathy draw us into a common humanity and an ability to see the world as others see it. But then the opposite tendency follows close on empathy's heels. We are creatures who make distinctions: we distinguish between what is wholesome and what is demeaning, between good dreams and bad nightmares about the future, between what enhances our potential and what diminishes it. In empathetic mood my religious instinct might reach out to join with other traditions immersed in a common human quest. But in distinguishing mood I may be tempted to place the others in a negative light and see them as responsible for all things threatening.

In a post-psychoanalytic world we are familiar with the psychology of 'splitting', the phenomenon whereby we project on to others, who are different in some cultural or religious sense, the unattractive or hated aspects of our own nature. These 'others' become repositories of danger: they pollute our minds and morals, and they entangle us in their deceits. Is this what has been happening through our histories of religious intolerance, teachings of contempt and demonising of others – the distancing overwhelming the empathising?

The task for interfaith relations now, it seems to me, is to forge more creative ways of living existentially with the paradox of simultaneously being drawn together and yet thrust apart, and to do this with some self-conscious theological grounding. It won't do any more to perpetuate the 'splitting' – the splitting, so far as the church is concerned (others will have their own versions), for example, between other religions and Christianity conceived as a division between, say, 'impersonal law' and 'personal grace', or between 'preparation' and 'fulfilment', or between 'types and shadows' and the 'newer reality'. In the present globalising

Religious Absolutism, Violence and the Public Square

context this looks simply like a strategic bid for superiority when the historical record affords no such evidence. Not that I am suggesting that we should adopt the attitude that 'anything goes' in interfaith relations; clearly there remains a need to distinguish between good and bad, adequate and inadequate, and true and false religion. I am simply questioning why the line between these divisions should run between Christianity (or Islam, or Judaism) and the other religions and not right through all of them. Discerning the criteria for what counts as good and bad in religion is becoming a shared challenge in a globalising world.

DIALOGUE AS THEOLOGICAL

The promotion of dialogue between faith-commitments has many motivations, as I noted above. We can correct stereotypical impressions of one another by the hard work of empathetic listening and we can create a sense of shared endeavour for the common good by committing ourselves to working together. But at its deepest religious level the motivation for dialogue is theological, that is, we expect that something of 'God' is encountered in dialogue. Without this we are simply behaving as all good neighbours should do to one another.

In dialogue we learn about the religious lives of others and we learn of their search for that truth which we intuit in experience as ultimate mystery. But how can we know when we have encountered something of that 'mystery' in dialogue? As Christians, once we set aside the temptation to think that sheer difference between traditions automatically entails the rejection of the other, we are likely in dialogue then to 'measure' others by their closeness to our own Christian outlook. In other words, we seek inevitably and naturally to interpret the other in terms of the framework of our own faith. A moment's reflection, however, will tell you that that strategy is impossible. Traditions are different – because of root experiences, history and geography and politics as well as philosophical speculations. To 'measure'

Beyond the Dysfunctional Family

the other is already to place oneself at the apex prior to what might be learned from the other in dialogue itself. But then, the dialogue as such is presumably never-ending. This is one reason, at least, why dialogical theology represents something of a paradigm shift in religious belonging and believing.

Yet we continually shy away from the full implications of this new dialogical threshold. How do we do justice to the transforming power of universally-minded religions in the context of dialogue and plurality? This is the unavoidable task of the theology of religions. Yet it is my contention that this is precisely what is being side-stepped in the current social and political climate. The urgent need to address issues of 'religiously-motivated violence' and 'religion in public life' for the sake of a society shaped by some sense of sustainable future hope, is entirely reasonable, even urgent. But the theological question presses: is 'working for the common good' sufficient as a sole motive for interfaith dialogue? The religions, to be sure, will have their part to play in working for the common good. Dialogue, however, as I have already indicated, expects greater things than that.

But there is more. Already, the dialogue is producing positive fruits: the Abrahamic sibling rivalry is being addressed. We have begun to move forward from the position which was content simply to agree that our religious differences were a stubborn fact of history and tradition and that nevertheless this should not dissuade us from declaring a willingness to work together on common projects for the greater social good. This book itself is a witness to the endeavour to venture further. So the dialogical section of Part II demonstrates some fascinating interactions which are echoed in many projects, experiences and theological explorations world-wide. First, for Christians in relation to Jews, the fruits have involved a root and branch reversal of the Christian doctrine of supersessionism. God does not renege on promises, the mainstream churches have declared (as scripture has taught), and therefore the covenant with the Jews has not been overturned by the Christian dispensation. Then second,

Religious Absolutism, Violence and the Public Square

in relation to Islam, there are intense debates on 'the meaning of prophethood' or 'the Qur'an as the word of God', 'religion as a whole way of life', and so on. The view of Christian faith as the final repository of revealed truth is becoming less plausible.

So a gap has opened up between the permission for dialogue, given and embraced more than four decades ago in the churches, and the fruits of dialogue. There are some who say: let us at least keep our distinguishing finalities, our sense that divine reality has spoken definitively among us, for this is what motivates us at the deepest levels. Dialogue, the nervousness continues, should not be allowed to erode this sense of final connectedness with ultimacy, which represents the foundation of religious commitment as such. Yet the reality is that this is an assumption which the practice of dialogue in effect does seem to call into question. If dialogue leads us to expect to learn something of the reality of 'God' from the other, then we should not be surprised if this is actually what transpires: surprisingly we do learn! Yet the more this happens, the less our clinging to our different finalities makes sense. A form of cognitive dissonance between theory and practice opens up.

SEDUCED BY THE CONTEXT

Earlier I mentioned the twin features of our present day western context as being dominated by concerns over 'religiously-motivated violence' and 'religion in public life'. Both have come to the fore in relation mainly to the resurgent presence of Islam around the world. Islam has been burdened both with the image of violence as a result of the attacks in the USA on 11th September 2001, in London on 7th July 2005 and in other places around the world, and with the accusation of being the faith community least able to adapt to western democratic cultural habits and expectations. Rightly or wrongly, it is Islam which has thrust debate about the twin features of violence and religious relations with secularised culture into the public arena.

Yet there is every reason for seeing these twin features as functions of all three religions represented in this book, in their

Beyond the Dysfunctional Family

negotiations with society as a whole. Christianity and Judaism too continue to have their tangles with violence and both exist, in varying degrees, in tension with perceived increasing secularity. Islam on its own deserves no demonising. In fact, given our Abrahamic relationship, might it not be incumbent for Christians and Jews, precisely at this cultural moment, to join forces in solidarity – albeit critically – with a sibling under threat? Our shared dialogue could surely demand and embrace it.

Nevertheless, I contend that the allure of the maelstrom of both 'religiously-motivated violence' and 'religion in public life' is a convenient, if also understandable, distraction from the theological tasks. Yet theological tasks are also contextual. Therefore, if our dialogue is easily seduced by my twin features then let us be seduced and discover the theological challenges at the heart of the issues. If the horrors of religiously motivated violence and the debates about religion in public life are faced head-on then it seems to me that the same theoretical issue will be raised within both arenas: what to say about absolutism in religious conviction in an age of dialogue? This remains, I believe, the bottom-line question for interreligious understanding. Therefore let me take both issues in turn. It is my belief that the challenge to surrender our hold on doctrines of finality – the dialogical challenge – is brought into sharp relief in these two areas.

RELIGIOUSLY-MOTIVATED VIOLENCE

We know that religiously motivated violence exists. Not only 9/11 and 7/7, but around the world it seems to erupt constantly. And we know it is not the preserve of one religion only, but has examples in every tradition. (There is non-religious ideologically-motivated violence too).

The explanations for this violence are harder to unravel. Social scientists analyse it in terms of injustice, poverty, globalisation, political grievances, land, and so on. There is much credibility in these explanations. The problem, however, with these explanations is that the circumstances of religiously motivated violence might be so different that valid explanations in one context might not be valid in another. Young suicide bombers, for instance, are often well educated and not necessarily stuck in poverty.

Other explanations involve us in cultural analysis. The work of Mark Juergensmeyer has been seminal here. His book, *Terror in the Mind of God*, gave us not so much an explanation but an observation: much of present terrorism, he claims, is a form of 'performative violence'. That is to say, there is no rational strategy behind the acts, no master-plan with envisaged outcomes, but simply the desire to make a statement. They are, he says, '*dramatic events* intended to impress for their symbolic significance'[2] – a kind of ritual intended to alter how we view the world. And they have achieved that for many of us. Even so, there must be more to terrorism than theatre.

Closer to what I consider to be motivations behind religiously motivated violence are explanations to do with cultural displacement and loss of identity. This is the likely the explanation behind the UK's 7/7 bombers' actions, for example. Young Muslim men alienated from their elders because they have adopted elements of western lifestyles (especially the desire to choose their own marriage partners), and yet not fully accepted by indigenous British society either, find themselves occupying a cultural no-man's land, a land into which ideologues come and peddle their views.[3] It would not be too far wrong to call it a case of identity crisis.[4]

Therefore it is not a sufficient explanation of religiously-motivated violence to say that religion is being used by criminal minds for non-spiritual purposes. If religion can be appealed to in support of violence then there must be something in the religions to allow it to be so (mis)used. And there is: we call it 'texts of terror'. Our traditions are available for terror, because they contain stories of terror or recommendations about the rightness of terror.

What is the theological question arising from all this? Rowan Williams, as part of his response to the 38 Muslim scholars'

Beyond the Dysfunctional Family

Open Letter of 2007, 'A Common Word Between Us and You',[5] suggests that it relates to what we count as absolute, and that assuming responsibility for defending the absoluteness of God is not what faith intends. God's love or compassion is constant irrespective of human activities that measure up to it or fail it: 'God does not fail,' he says, 'because we fail to persuade others or because our communities fail to win some kind of power.' Terror and religious wars stem, he believes, from precisely the opposite motivation. If we perceive that we are in competition with another faith and we go into the business of defending God, then violence will result. Dialogue, Williams goes on to suggest, could well be the mechanism for breaking cycles of violence and retaliation because it is not built on protecting God's interests.[6]

All of which is wonderful grist to the dialogue mill. And yet, the defence of God is exactly what is embodied in our traditions. I take an example from a colleague, Perry Schmidt-Leukel, who has pointed out that even a major theological heavyweight such as Thomas Aquinas has a version of defending God. Aquinas makes the (to us) startling claim that heretics could be killed not because we might hate them but because of the command to love our neighbour. Loving the neighbour entails obliterating the heretic whose sole object is to lure the true believer away from true religion. God's offer of salvation needs protecting from the evil intentions of heretics. For the purposes of my argument here, instead of heretics read 'other religions'. (It is no accident that other religions have often been cast as Christian heresies). For example, this is why Dante placed the Prophet Muhammad (Peace be upon him) in the deepest regions of hell; and it is why the great twentieth century theologian, Karl Barth, once thought of Mahayana Buddhism as a kind of Lutheran heresy – they had a structure of grace-filled religion of sorts but it was not the grace of Christ. Thus it is the exclusive or finally superior hold on absolute truth which has given permission for religiously motivated violence. As Schmidt-Leukel has written: '... the religious root of the potential for interreligious conflict... lies in the explicit or implicit intention to supersede all other

Religious Absolutism, Violence and the Public Square

religions and in the readiness to defend one's own religion against analogous ambitions on the part of the others.'[7]

How does this account compare with that of Rowan Williams? Williams is clear that religions are not to be viewed as rival communities where 'my' hold on God is pitted against 'your' hold on God. Given this basis, Williams is then free to encourage dialogical interaction in order to find the best forms of living in a plural environment. The difference between Williams and Schmidt-Leukel is that Schmidt-Leukel wants to surrender supersessionist views and superiority claims as part and parcel of the theological appreciation of the religious other; Williams, on the other hand, is content simply not to concern himself with notions of superiority as this in turn seems dependent on notions of interreligious competition which he has insisted are to be put aside. His real objection is to notions of neutrality in the weighing up of divine truth and human dialogue: '... we cannot expect to find some neutral positions beyond the traditions of our faith that would allow us to broker some sort of union between our diverse convictions.' And further: '... our views are not just human constructions which we can abandon when they are inconvenient.' Yet this seems to me to be a potential weakness in this argument. Surely, whatever revelation we believe our tradition to be founded upon, our views are precisely our human constructions. The alternative would be that we hold the notion of revelation to be best envisaged as some propositional essence, and yet that runs counter to most Christian estimates of the meaning of revelation over at least the last hundred years. If we do not abandon notions of 'religious superiority' and 'religious absolutism' are we not landed with that competitive rivalry between faiths which Williams rightly deplores and which harbours the potential for violence which we are seeking to transform? It is the theological logic of 'religious absolutism' which Schmidt-Leukel has so clearly put before us.

To sum up: having to deal with religiously motivated violence could be thought to be, at one level, a distraction from the real business of interreligious dialogue. But once enquiry uncovers

Beyond the Dysfunctional Family

some of the religious factors at work within such violence it is far from a distraction. The real culprit, however, is that sense of religious superiority over the 'ownership' of salvation, and which is generally thought to be intrinsic to religious identity and absolutism. The agonising over the religious roots of violence leads the dialogue straight to the logic of absolutism which the churches had hoped to avoid by embracing the equally necessary pastoral practice of demonstrating solidarity in the face of societal atrocity.

RELIGION IN PUBLIC LIFE

My second example concerning the issue of religious absolutism in a dialogically mindful age centres on debates over what role the religions should or could play in the life of a pluralistic democracy. In a post-Christendom society the churches are freer than in previous ages to embrace the notion that a religiously plural society can be enriching for everyone, even if it is also rather messy. However, the spectre of different religions competing in the public square by responding to social change from out of very different sets of values and by being unwilling to restrain religious convictions to a private sphere, has unnerved some secularists. Therefore we have witnessed in recent years some fairly bad-tempered polarised debates. These debates are variously portrayed as ones of Religion versus Secularism, Multiculturalism versus Integration, and Political Liberalism versus Theocratic Traditionalism.

One reason why the polarisation of views has happened concerns the enormous success in western countries of political liberalism in theory combined with secular pragmatism in policy-making. But there is a feeling now that secular liberalism has not brought all of the benefits it perhaps once promised. For example, it has not had the strength to confront the corrosive effects of unrestrained economic globalisation, or its half-hearted commitments to an ecologically sustainable future have become all too clear. More than that, in separating off the material bases

Religious Absolutism, Violence and the Public Square

of living from spiritual needs many wonder whether it has any convincing answers to the basic question of what goals we should be pursuing as human societies other than the satisfaction of individual self-expression for its own sake.

However, I do not wish to be overly negative: political liberalism has brought many benefits, not least an end to the over-weaning power of religious institutions and the opening up of a new sense of dignity for individuals. Nevertheless, wholesale accommodation to the processes of secularisation which accompanied political liberalism was bound to remain problematic for the religious mind. The dispute is mainly with what is sometimes termed the Rawlsian contract theory of liberal democracy, from John Rawls the American political scientist.[8] Theoretically speaking, Rawls proposed that our reasoning over public policy should be based on that which no reasonable person could reasonably reject. It is a sort of highest common factor or pragmatic approach: put simply, decisions are made according to what works and what citizens will accept.

From a similar point of view, the philosopher Richard Rorty has said that when religion enters political/public debate it acts as a 'conversation-stopper'.[9] So when the religious person says that God commands this or that policy, it is difficult to know what sense can be made of it by citizens who do not subscribe to that particular framework. Therefore religious believers ought to keep God's commands for their private selves. This is a familiar secularist argument. How else can pluralist societies hold together other than by secular politics and pragmatic policy-making?

The difficulty for many believers is that this immediately rules out religious beliefs as a basis for moral decision-making in relation to public policy. (Something similar could be said for ideological secularists whose worldview extends beyond policy-making based on simple pragmatism). Religious voices want to ask questions of purpose and meaning in the making of public policy, but a government shaped by Rawlsian assumptions has no mechanism for answering those questions. In law, government

195

Beyond the Dysfunctional Family

might maximise human liberties and even assist civil society in developing intermediate mechanisms for influencing public policy, but it is simply at a loss when it comes to policy-making from a single comprehensive point of view. In the debate between 'human goods' and 'human rights', the religions are likely to be on the 'goods' side and the governing powers of a liberal democracy on the 'rights' side of the equation. Finding a decent balance between the two seems continually precarious, to say the least.

Furthermore, there may be a contradiction at the heart of the social contract theory. If the social contract is meant to allow freedom of expression and argument for all citizens and yet cuts out the reasons a great number of citizens give for arguing the way they do, then how can the social contract facilitate proper freedom?

There is a feeling, therefore, from many educated religious voices – Jews, Christians, Muslims and others – that public debate requires deepening. Where are the virtues that create human character and habits of relating based on respect and dignity? Political arrangements must surely have some connection with what human life is for. Liberty is good but there is liberty 'for' as well as liberty 'from'. Liberal democratic governments have no answer to what our liberty is 'for'. This might be a standard religious riposte.

So what is to be done? We do not want to return to the theocratic state, yet a polarised stand-off between 'Religion' and 'Secularism' seems equally unattractive, not least because it oversimplifies everything. Ideological secularists want to confine comprehensive convictions to the private sphere and consider public debate about moral direction in society to be purely instrumental. Sometimes this is backed up with claims that secularism represents moral neutrality in the face of comprehensive convictions. [10] For the convinced Christian (and other) believer this seems insufficient: the claim to neutrality is intellectually mischievous. On the other hand, why can we not imagine a public square crowded with argument, which will

196

be necessarily untidy and risky in terms of orderly debate, but where religious voices take their place alongside others in open exchange? As the Yale Law Professor, Stephen Carter, has it: liberalism needs to develop a politics based on 'a willingness to *listen,* not because the speaker has *the right voice,* but because the speaker has *the right to speak.'*[11]

What emerges from such an open exchange will not necessarily be the outcome of a kind of free-for-all ethical slanging match but, in the best possible world, the fruit of listening and rational persuasion – rational, that is, in the desired sense of seeing the persuasive reasons for something, even if one disagreed with the comprehensive view of life lying behind them.[12]

So much is commendable. However, there still remains the increasingly unsettling issue of religious plurality. This brings me to a positive proposal in trying to move beyond the stand-off between ideological secularists and convinced religionists.

What seems to be necessary is a model of participation in public democratic debate which allows for the particularities of religious and secularist voices and which relies on seeking common ground while respecting differences, and balancing compromise where necessary with critical solidarity, for the sake of a greater good. As we cannot know what that greater good might look like in advance such a model must surely be dialogical at heart if the religions are to develop their democratic political relevance. Most of all, the model must involve the religions self-critically if they are both to overcome their historic mistrust of one another and to learn the values of provisionality and humility that are necessary in the context of interpreting and negotiating plurality. A report prepared by the Millennium Institute for the third Parliament of the World's Religions in 1999 expressed the view that 'the greatest single scandal in which Earth's faith traditions are now involved is their failure to practise their highest ethical ideals in their relations with one another'. Thankfully, this may be slowly changing, partly as a result of the permission for dialogue that has been hard-won over four decades of scholarship.

Beyond the Dysfunctional Family

So for religion in public life to be healthy what seems needed is not so much an empty public square but what we might call a dialogically filled public square. We accept critical reasoning which means that we explain to one another the reasons we have for believing the things we do and why we want to act on them, whether we are confessionally secularist or religious. Why can we not come to mutually agreed decisions based on that mutual listening and mutuality of respect?

This is why I believe our interreligious dialogue is so necessary. It is not only good for our own learning from one another; it could well pose itself as a kind of model for helping us to move beyond the stand-off between 'Religion' and 'Secularism'. Yet the religions should only be allowed their voices if they transcend their historic antagonisms and mistrust, and in the process becoming aware of the limitations of different worldview perspectives even as we might cherish them.

The public square should not be filled with theocratic religious voices or be left hostage to a liberal secularist absence of religious reasoning, but be occupied by a dialogical conversation where each values the other even as it might disagree with them. This seems to me to be the next step in the religious support for liberty and democracy in a plural society. There is, however, one major problem in taking such a step. It will likely require us to suspend, if not surrender, our religious senses of absolutism. And the trouble is, the religions don't generally recommend that.

To sum up this section: religion has not disappeared in the way that many predicted would happen in the modern period. During this same period we have also realised that pragmatism, which has served us well and is preferable to ideological or theocratic politics, too has limitations. Add to this the plurality which stems from globalisation and increased immigration and the stage looks set for a change of direction. A politics which upholds pluralism requires a dialogue built not simply on respect or hospitality but on an acceptance which affirms separate identities even as it might not approve of everything those belonging to any particular tradition want to promote.

FINAL REMARKS

Interreligious dialogue, I suggest, is both what the world needs from the religions and what the religions at their best potentially offer the world. The dialogue between Jews, Christians and Muslims has made enormous strides in recent years and can be a spur to extending dialogical encounters in a myriad directions. As siblings in rivalry they are learning to appreciate their shared ethos and their divergent differences. Their contribution to interreligious dialogue more broadly carries an enormous potential.

This essay has asked the awkward question whether the dialogue about the two preoccupations of religiously-motivated violence and the place of religion in public life can avoid the fundamental issue of whether or not Christian faith (or any faith) can for ever postpone the theology of religions question about the place of other faiths in God's purposes. I have argued that this question cannot be forever side-lined. More than that, I have suggested that the issues at the heart of 'religiously motivated violence' and 'religion in public life' actually reveal what is at stake. Do we accept one another as theologically and religiously valid? And are we able to respond Yes to that question, even as we might be puzzled by some of the substantive matters that we each affirm?

NOTES

1. Akbar Ahmed (2007) *Journey Into Islam: the Crisis of Globalisation*. U.S.: Brookings Institution.
2. Mark Juergensmeyer (2003) *Terror in the Mind of God: the Global Rise of Religious Violence*. 3rd edition, revised and updated. Berkeley: University of California Press. p. 125.
3. Shiv Malik (2007) 'My Brother the Bomber' in *Prospect*. June. pp. 30-41.
4. Jim Kenney (2008) 'The Dark Side of Religion' in *Interreligious Insight* Vol 6, No 2.
5. http://www.acommonword.com/. The official web site, accessed: 1st August 2009.

Beyond the Dysfunctional Family

6. http://www.archbishopofcanterbury.org/1892. Rowan Williams's response to the Muslim scholars' Open Letter. Accessed: 1st August 2009. Follow through to Related Downloads.

7. Perry Schmidt-Leukel (2007) *Interreligious Insight*. Vol 55, No 2. p. 58.

8. John Rawls (1993) *Political Liberalism*. New York: Columbia University Press. Rawls claimed to have modified his view later, in: (1999) 'The Idea of Public Reason Revisited' in *Collected Papers*. Columbia University Press. But many have not been persuaded that his basic argument is altered.

9. Richard Rorty (1999) 'Religion as a Conversation-stopper' in *Philosophy and Social Hope*. London: Penguin Books. pp. 168-74.

10. See the defence of secularism as a benign force by Julian Baggini, 'A Heavy Cross to Bear', *The Guardian g2*, 15 February 2012.

11. Stephen Carter (1993) *The Culture of Disbelief*. Basic Books. p. 230. See also, Jeffrey Stout (2005) *Democracy and Tradition*. Princeton University Press.

12. I have discovered a similar optimistic argument from the public theology think tank Theos: Jonathan Chaplin (2008) *Talking God: the Legitimacy of Religious Public Reasoning*. London: Theos.

9

Faith and Engagement: A Reflective Journey

Ataullah Siddiqui

Growing up in a multi-cultural, multi-lingual, multi-religious, and multi-ethnic environment was at once confusing and a blessing. My parents arrived at a mountain region in the Himalayas as teachers and scholars of Islam. I grew up amongst a largely Hindu community. There were varieties of aboriginal tribes in the region; some retained their tribal roots, others considered themselves as Hindus, but one particular tribe was closely drawn towards Christianity, and their conversion was rapid and total. The region has a long history of Buddhism and trade links with Tibet. A small number of Muslims were traders from central India and they were largely seasonal migrants. My parents' priority was to revive a faltering primary school and provide a stable education for the migrant Muslim community, but also for those who were the third or fourth generation of Muslim children of mixed marriages. Pupil numbers were relatively low, with three teachers including one who was not a Muslim. My father was employed by the local Muslim community to teach and look after their social and religious needs.

My parents left their cultural, ethnic and linguistic roots behind and entered into a new state of 'strangeness'. The only thing left to them was to cultivate generous relationships amongst all faiths and across cultural divides. These relationships were tested when my mother fell seriously ill and took almost five years to recover. It was difficult to remember everything, but when I become aware of my surroundings my early memories were the hospital where my mother was admitted, which was a Christian charity where some of the doctors and nurses were

Beyond the Dysfunctional Family

from Scotland. Our neighbours, apart from a very close Muslim family to which our family owes much, were practicing Hindus and Christian converts. In my mind, they were part of my family and they too treated me as one of them.

Into this complex socio-ethnic mix entered yet another dimension: the incursion into Tibet by China created a huge refugee crisis. The Tibetan refugees arrived in thousands into the small town were we lived. For many this was to be a sojourn of one to three years until they found another place where they could move to, but for others this small town became their home. Among the refugees there were many who were Muslims. Their children were admitted to the primary school where my father taught, but in my mother's opinion girls needed special care and attention. As a result she opened a school for them, and with support from the local and Tibetan Muslim community, accommodation and food were provided for them. Slowly and gradually they moved to other parts of India and some decided to migrate outside the country.

VEILED PREJUDICES

This interfaith and intercultural living provided me with a rich experience of trust and an understanding of caring for each other. But what was so baffling about it was that while the overall community trusted enough *of* each other in the social sphere, they did not trust enough *about* each others' beliefs and practices. It was obvious that we knew very little about each other's faith and the role that it crucially played in the respective communities. This was also true of the tribal religions. Such perceptions were far more evident in the school playgrounds. Two illustrations will make things clearer:

It is now common knowledge that Muslims face, in their ritual prayers, towards the Ka'ba, a cubic building in the heart of Makkah, though of course Muslims do not worship the building as such. This is my first example. From Britain Muslims face towards a south-east direction, while from South Asia they

Faith and Engagement: A Reflective Journey

face towards the west. This sits very oddly with the Hindus. A devout Hindu will begin his/her prayers by offering water and facing the rising sun in the east. The general perception in our neighbourhood, as well as in the playground, was that this act of Muslims facing west in their prayers was considered a deliberate act in defiance of the Hindu observance of prayers. While such observations continued to be believed by many Hindus, it was especially notorious where minority Muslim children in dominant Hindu schools were taunted. Such perceptions, if not addressed, create their own problems. This difference of faith took on a more sinister tone when in the mid-1960s India and Pakistan were locked in a fierce battle over the issue of Kashmir. Muslim students were tormented, and even the Christian-run schools where I was a student accused Muslim families of being Pakistani spies.

My second example stems from my experience of daily Bible class, which was compulsory for all students. I had attended every year, for seven years, but this particular year the Bible class became a burden. My Bible teacher was in a hurry to convert us. He regularly demonised not only my faith, which he thought was very close to the Christian concept of salvation, but he treated the Hindus, Buddhists and especially one Roman Catholic student even more harshly. In no uncertain terms I was reminded again and again that there is no salvation in my faith and there is no other way to heaven except through Jesus. His understanding of Jesus obviously excluded mine, but also the Roman Catholics'. The students and the teacher were locked for the next few months in polemics which I had never experienced before. Eventually we moved on to the next grade, but this experience posed a serious question: do I know my own faith enough to face such challenges? This motivated me to take my faith more seriously and has led me to read and understand various dimensions of Islam ever since. It will not be out of place to mention that my parents wanted to send me to the Christian school because they had this great trust that the school would provide their son with some moral and ethical values which

203

Beyond the Dysfunctional Family

they did not feel could be gained from a secular non-faith based school. In 1967 when the Arab-Israeli war took place, my Bible teacher was exhilarated; he was full of joy and confident that the second coming of Jesus was no longer a distant prospect. He proudly showed to everyone the photograph of Moshe Dayan published in an Indian magazine. He was his unmistakable hero. A crisis in the Middle East brought home my own vulnerability, my own crisis of identity and my own search for belonging.

THE QUR'AN AND THE COMMUNITY

The Qur'an remains central to a Muslim's life. It is also the central point of the community's activities – Ramadan being one such example. The first revelation of the Qur'an took place in the month of Ramadan, the ninth month of the Islamic calendar and fasting and special evening prayers are focused on the events of the Qur'an and its place in Muslim society. The festival of Eid is also attached to the Qur'an. I was deeply connected to such events. But more importantly I was also raised in a household where the Qur'an was not only a book of guidance but also a book of personal and spiritual piety.

The relation between the Qur'an and the Muslim community in general was largely ambiguous. While all considered the Qur'an as a book of guidance, the community where I lived reflected the majority Muslim attitude that the Qur'an was to be recited at the death-bed or after a person's death, and used occasionally for opening ceremonies of, for example, shops, or at social functions. The Qur'an fulfilled the role of a celebrity for all seasons. Respect for the Qur'an was such that it was kept at the highest place in many Muslim homes. What was conveyed was that the Qur'an is something which is unreachable, yet the community subscribed to the view that the Qur'an is the solution to every nuance of society, and above all that it contains all the answers. To explore its meaning and message, and its relevance to contemporary society was not considered. What was even more unthinkable was to say that

Faith and Engagement: A Reflective Journey

its understanding is also changeable and contextual. This was for some blasphemous.

The paradox of the community was obvious – the Qur'an is a Book of Guidance that holds all answers, yet the community was deliberately oblivious of its essence and message. The 'illiterate' audience requires a literate interpreter and as a result the Qur'an and the audience become perhaps the prisoners of its interpreter.

The literati of the Qur'an were the religious scholars, in common parlance known as *maulvi sahibs*. The role of a *moulvi* was at once teacher, jurist and mediator, interpreter of the faith and leader of prayers in a mosque. The interpreter of faith and jurist part was largely and possessively denominational, with a hint of dislike for other denominations. Such an illustrious job description needed a qualification which the *moulvis* acquired in religious seminaries known as *dar al-uloom*. Such seminaries in South Asia were set up, especially during the late nineteenth century, with the prime objective of saving the religious legacies of the past generations in the hostile environment of the British Raj and increasing secularisation of education. The new breed of religious scholars had the inbuilt capacity to resist anything new, particularly if it is European. Generation after generation groups of *moulvis* graduated, until recently, without any job prospects in the public sector. The only option left to the new graduates was either to establish a new seminary replicating the syllabus that they had gone through, or to join an already existing one. The free food and lodging attracted many pupils from rural areas where the poverty was acute.

The Qur'an in Islam is eternal but its interpretation is not. Throughout the generations it has been interpreted and explained in the context in which people lived. Interpreters are human beings, and their thoughts and ideas are conditioned by the environment in which they live. Therefore there is no ultimate and final interpretation. The Qur'an and its understanding have to continue to provide new meanings and new answers for new questions. Yet I believe that the Qur'an should not simply be seen through the eyes of exegetes; it is also important

Beyond the Dysfunctional Family

to be aware of the fact that for Muslims like me it is a book of recitation and healing. The recitation of the Qur'an demands a continuous reading so that one must think, practice and heal again (*Fussilat* 17:82).

The reckless and authoritarian nature of Qur'anic discourse that permeates largely in South Asian religious culture, and which I believe is not unique compared to other parts of the Muslim world, has successfully inhibited Muslim consciousness from recognising the role of interpretation in understanding and receiving the Qur'an's message. The faithful believer approaches the Qur'an in many ways. One may read, recite or seek inspiration, but to read the Qur'an in only one way and to interpret it only literally would be an abuse of its status as holy scripture. One cannot limit the sources of the Divine and make it subservient to one interpretation.

I need to point out one important factor in relation to revelation in the Qur'an and the Prophet Muhammad. I have come across the issue of the finality of the Prophet in various encounters with Muslims and with others outside of Islam. Islam understands that the Revelation of the Qur'an and the recipient of the Revelation are interconnected. If one believes that God spoke to humanity through the Qur'an and that the Prophet demonstrates how one should live on this earth, then this combination in turn demands from Islam's followers a certain belief in the sufficiency of the faith, and it is in this sense the finality of the Prophethood needs to be understood. However, those who do not believe in the Revelation and the recipient of the Revelation as Muslims believe in them, then these others are certainly not bound to believe in the finality of the Prophethood of Muhammad. For Muslims, the Qur'an and the example of the Prophet will remain the guiding principles of spiritual living. Other faith communities will subscribe to different worldviews or faiths where they may believe and practice the religious life in ways entirely different from Islam. In the process of interfaith dialogue Muslims have accepted *de facto* that there could be

Faith and Engagement: A Reflective Journey

another religion after the Prophet, by engaging with Sikhs and Baha'is for example.

SEARCHING FOR MEANING AND IDENTITY

In the mid-eighties I used to share a house with a few Muslim students. At that time, in British universities, their presence was becoming increasingly more noticeable. Though the Islamic Societies had increased in numbers and local Muslim students were beginning to play a role in such societies, they were not active leaders. For a large number of them the idea of an Islamic Society was an exhilarating prospect, where they could discuss their faith and beliefs without the mediation of an Imam or their parents' ever-present gaze. They were free to discuss matters concerning their faith in ways which they were not able to do in their 'mosque years'. While they could be free to explore and assess, they were largely at the mercy of the foreign students who led such societies and were articulate and 'well versed' in Islam. The young Muslim students were impressed by their knowledge and performance and the way they conducted themselves. They were mature and well aware of the socio-political realities and various trends and movements of their part of the world. The local young Muslims were not exposed to those realities; rather, compared to their foreign student friends, they were mostly aware only of their mosque's local denominational, tribal and clan intra-fights which they could neither understand nor relate to. The discourse in mosques and communities was largely conducted in a language which they could understand on the surface but could not engage with existentially; nor could they relate to the cultural norms that shaped the socio-religious discourse.

Two young students with whom I shared the house were targeted by some young British Muslim students who had already been baptised in the ideology of Hizb ut-Tahrir by the foreign students. One Saturday five of them arrived on their head-hunting project of the local students in our house. The targets were two young Brits. I have seen their methods of

207

Beyond the Dysfunctional Family

approach and workings. They spent more than four hours there and intermittently I listened to the conversation. The evils of the modern world, the role of America and Israel, dictatorship in the Muslim world and the drawbacks of living in an un-Islamic society all came up for discussion. They also brought up the problem of the inability of the elders in the mosques to grasp the situation. The solution was the establishment of a Caliphate under a Caliph. At that particular point they turned to me and explained the significance of having a Caliph and that the solution to all our ills lay in one Caliph to whom we must give our allegiance (*bay'a*). I said I had a problem with this concept of a universal leader which presupposes a universal submission to this one man, which I believe, I said, possibly is not going to happen. In my reading of my faith it does not demand that kind of 'submission'. After all there was more than one prophet, not only in the same region simultaneously but even in the same family – Moses and Aaron are one such example. The day passed in a cordial manner but one issue they wanted to hammer in, other than *khilafa*, was the need and necessity of an 'Islamic State'. The people who came for the head-hunting later became some well-known Hizb leaders – some were public faces, others were heavyweights behind the scenes. The discourse of the Islamic state took centre stage during the 1990s and so the issues of democracy and nationalism on the one hand, and of 'puritan-Islam' on the other, became the battle ground for winning the souls of young people in Britain.

Let me also highlight a different but related issue of Muslims living as a minority. More than forty percent of the total Muslim population in the world lives as minorities. Generations of Muslims in Thailand and in South Africa or in India lived side-by-side with others. They have evolved a culture which instinctively finds its ways to social adjustment but remains anchored deeply in Islamic values. Though the issue of the Caliphate was a major topic of debate in early 1920s, in India for example, they looked at this institution as a symbolic institution of representation for Muslim aspirations at the international

Faith and Engagement: A Reflective Journey

forums. While the fall of the institution had a major impact especially on Muslims living in the Middle East, it had relatively little effect on Muslims living as a minority. But do Muslims desire to live in a Muslim majority country? It is difficult to answer 'yes' or 'no'. The current Muslim majority countries do not provide any attractive reasons for moving in that direction. Overwhelmingly the Muslims were drawn towards Muslim countries, particularly in the Middle East, because of economic reasons and not religious reasons. Anecdotal evidence suggests their experience of living and working in these countries would not encourage anyone to live there. It is interesting to note that Muslims who lived and participated, uninterruptedly and freely, in a democracy since 1945 are in India.

There were three broad factors that I believe were responsible for the proliferation of organisations of Muslim youth. First, the *Satanic Verses* controversy gave the impression to both younger and older generation of Muslims that if their faith and beliefs came face to face with the mighty machine of modernity and secularity their faith had to surrender, though not all other faiths had to do so. The special status of the Church of England and the Jewish community were compared and contrasted with their own situation. The second shock which young people faced was the Bosnian crisis and the cleansing of people from their land and property simply because they were Muslims. They looked at the crisis from the 'demand' point of view, where British/European society constantly demanded that their Muslim population needed to be integrated, and here was a population that was not only integrated with the Serbo-Croatian culture, but almost assimilated into that society. The Bosnian Muslims paid the price of their assimilation and that has sent a signal to the young Muslims in Britain and other parts of Europe that they will never be accepted within the wider society, no matter what welcoming rhetoric they may hear. Human rights and democratic values are there to be applied selectively. Third, the Gulf War which brought together a coalition of various countries led by the United States with the full approval of the United

Beyond the Dysfunctional Family

Nations, gave the impression that rights and justice are selective and at the service of economic interests. In the same region the state of Israel breaks the UN Resolutions repeatedly. The values such as Rights and Justice, Democracy and Accountability which the modern world was so proud of, seemed vague and elusive words.

As far as the West is concerned, it is the largest provider of goods and military hardware to the Muslim world, with several conditions attached. Western consumerism permeates the world but it is especially rampant in the Arab Middle East. Increasing tourism – in North Africa and other parts of the Muslims world – dents everyday life. However the overall perception of the west is not shaped, as such, by these encounters. What shapes their imagination of the west is its political domination. The encounters of the past such as the Crusades, direct colonisation of Muslim world, the Gulf War, the invasion of Iraq and Afghanistan and sustained political and military support to Israel reinforces those images of control and subjugation of people. On the other hand the western images of Islam are shaped by their encounters of Muslims in the past particularly through the Ottoman empire. The fall of Constantinople and the conquest of substantial parts of Europe have created an image of terror and alarm in the face of Islam and Muslims. In all these encounters what is lost is an ability to look beyond the single focus on political engagement to a West which is multi-dimensional, with its traditions of arts, music, humanism and intellectual engagements, all of which have something to offer Muslims. Similarly, the West also needs to recognise that in the shaping of its identity Islam and Muslims have played crucial roles. The west not only inherited from Jerusalem, Athens and Rome, but also from Madinah and Baghdad.

SHARIA

The modernity mediated by colonial South Asian experience was to limit my horizon of faith and its relevance to my life and practice. Following the recommendations of *Sharia* in the daily practices of life was informed largely by the 'Muslim Personal Law *(Sharia)* Application Act of 1937', an Act which, even today, is largely concerned with issues of marriage, divorce and inheritance of Muslims in India. After the partition of India in 1947 it also became part of the legal system of Pakistan and Bangladesh. The arrival and settlement of Muslims in Britain raised the issue of *Sharia* and its recognition, particularly the aspects concerning personal law. On the whole, what it meant was the adoption of a similar law to that adopted in India – marriage, divorce (including child custody) and inheritance was to be 'domesticated' within the British legal system. The demand for the incorporation of such a law was begun in 1975 by the Union of Muslim Organisations and its Secretary General Dr Aziz Pasha. Perhaps the model they had in mind was the *Batei Din*, the Jewish rabbinical courts set up by statute more than 100 years ago and which is a recognised practice within the legal system of the UK. However, support for such a law from Muslim communities within the country has been lukewarm.

There is an interesting comparison to make between the approaches of the two Muslim communities, one in India and the other in Britain. With Muslims living as a minority in the Indian context, the 'Muslim Personal Law' came into existence as a result of British initiative. When the Law became part of the Indian Constitution in 1950 the fate of Muslims to whom the Law was intrinsically linked became inseparable from it. Muslims were assured that their identity and self-expression as a community in an independent India was protected by the Law. Any attempt to visit and address the Law afresh was seen as interference from the political lobbyists and government. In the early 1970s a government initiative to bring in a 'common civil code' was perceived by Muslims as an abolition of the Law. This brought dispirited Muslim groups to a common platform of protest in order to work together on an agenda of 'no change'. Pressure groups were formed to oppose the code. But the problem was that even if the Muslim community saw the

Beyond the Dysfunctional Family

irrelevance of some parts of the Law, they were fearful of opening a can of worms and an opportunity for the government and far right national political parties to meddle in the community's internal affairs. The unexpected result was the development of the *Fiqh* Academy, established in 1988, that gradually brought together scholars of various denominations to discuss the current challenges posed by modern knowledge and scientific developments. This, on the one hand, allowed the issue of *Sharia* within the Indian legal system to remain untouched, and, on the other, it engaged with modern challenges faced by the community at social and communal levels. Discussions were published and agreed positions were pronounced, and this fed into the legal system, thus helping the community, to some extent, to re-think and recognise the challenges.

In contrast, the place of *Sharia* in the British context is emerging differently. In the absence of any statuary recognition of Muslim Personal Law or the equivalent of having a *Batei Din*, the community has largely created its own *Sharia* 'courts' to address their religious needs, particularly in areas such as marriage, divorce and inheritance. The proliferation of community radio, TV stations, newspapers and particularly developments in the area of Islamic Finance with '*halal* products' is making its own mark and creating a *fatwa* industry. *Sharia* is not only about marriage, divorce and inheritance but much more. What shape and which route this course will take is too early as yet to judge.

After the 7th July bombing in London, the government initiated a series of meetings with Muslim communities in Britain in order to prevent such a thing happening again. In one such meeting, Dr Aziz Pasha (UMO) reminded the Minister responsible for communities that one way of combating extremism is allowing them to have Islamic law (*Sharia*) within British legal framework which will help to convince young people that they have been treated equally. But I believe *Sharia* is more than that

The *Sharia* for Muslims is also about their prayers and spirituality. A close connection with God and living a life in accordance to the teaching of the Prophet, for many Muslims,

Faith and Engagement: A Reflective Journey

sums up the meaning of the *Sharia*. For others it is a means of seeking justice in public and personal life. It is popular in modern times because it has become a means of redressing perceived injustices and exploitations. *Sharia* under competent Muslim jurists was the balancing factor against the excesses of the government, providing a forum for the accountability of rulers and protection for the poor and needy – the *ulama* (Islamic religious scholars) became the unofficial guardian of the law. After the decline of Muslim rule and the beginnings of colonisation the power of the jurists and the *ulama*'s authority were curtailed considerably. In many Muslim countries they are practically – if there are provisions in place – judges of family courts. The rampant corruption of rulers and the control of natural and national resources in a few hands and families have not benefited the citizens. Rulers are not accountable to their people, nor do the citizens have any say in the running of the country and use of resources. Decades of public misfortune resulted in broken trust between the ruler and the ruled. Against this background a tussle is going on between the two. The hope is, in some respects unrealistically, that the jurists and *ulama* will play the same role they once did, but the reality now is completely different. Military generals and dictators in the past used this expectation of the people. Every time a ruler was threatened or felt his power slipping away, he unashamedly declared the implementation of *Sharia*, largely meaning flogging and amputation, and people feel once again cheated, having no means of expression or a way out of this maze.

CONNECTING WITH THE MODERN WORLD

The *ulama* have been largely out of touch with modern science and technology and other areas of epistemology. Their acquired knowledge hardly prepares them to be more innovative or engaged with their surroundings. The combination of the knowledge of the Qur'an, the Prophet's traditions recorded in the *ahadith*, the acceptance of analogical reasoning and emphasis

213

Beyond the Dysfunctional Family

on consensus all require to be connected with the modern world. As a result, those who demand the establishment of an 'Islamic State' have little faith in the role of *ulama*. The change they perceive is to capture the existing state and then change all the apparatus of modern government and eventually change the constitution and process of legislation.

One thing that I have noticed which is common between those who are in favour of an 'Islamic state' and those who hope for a return of the Caliphate, is that they have to function essentially within the paradigm of a nation state. Even a universal aspiration to a *Khilafa* is practically bound within that paradigm. The search for an Islamic state immediately raises a few questions. The nation state and its essential components as political scientists suggest are four-fold: territory, population, sovereignty and government. Territory is defined within a geographical context. An aspiration to a universal Muslim *ummah* will remain an aspiration and spiritual connection and nothing more. The population within a nation state is largely defined by the nature of citizenship and no longer by faith identity or by a faith community living in a Muslim territory.

The classical definition of belonging was clear where each faith group had their rights, collectively and individually recognised and set in the legal system. But the modern state demands/requires the relinquishing of that collective faith identity. The sovereignty in an 'Islamic state' only belongs to God and is not derived from the people. The Government is largely a guardian of Islamic values, but accountable to the people and responsible for their welfare. The equalising factor is the citizenship. The definition of citizenship involves four components: rights, responsibility, participation and identity. A citizen has not only a legal identity but is also linked with a national identity. Today this link is breaking down along with all of the four components of citizenship. They do not constitute a model of citizenship, e.g. the participation of a citizen is no longer bound within the limits of a state. Modern communication has made it possible to bring together interest groups to put pressure on governments

Faith and Engagement: A Reflective Journey

for the rights of others, which the participant individual may not have directly experienced, but they feel passionate enough to join a protest.

Against this background, the search for an 'Islamic state' with *Sharia* will continue with some vigour for the foreseeable future. The aspirations of people for a rule of law and social justice will be the main motivating factors, especially in Muslim countries. Anyone who comes to power with an Islamic agenda, including an elected leadership, will have their legitimacy tested on the criteria of rule of law and social justice. If they prove they are equally as corrupt as the secular dictators, people will not only blame them but also the belief system with which they came to power. In countries like Britain, where they find that the rule of law and remedies for injustice exist, the aspirations of *Sharia* will be more of a spiritual fulfillment; but at times this could be used by one section of the community against the prevailing cultural practices such as forced marriage. In both cases the protagonists will have to go through the process of renewal and rebuilding. Renewal – so that they will not betray the core values of Islam; and rebuilding – where they will have to adopt and adapt the modern 'vocabularies' to make sense of their existence.

Finally, I believe that the intrinsic values of religion are not the same as the management of a political society. Religion, and particularly Islam, is for the self-fulfillment of spiritual and social need on a large scale. While Islam provides the basic inner strength in fulfillment of key Qur'anic values such as Mercy, Forgiveness, Justice and *Ihsan* (excellence in our behaviour), its expression of such values requires taking note of its interconnectedness with other human beings. Islamic norms and values cannot be constructed in isolation: they always need to pay attention to the context of their surrounding environment.

10

In the Footsteps of Dinah:
A Feminist Perspective on
Jewish/Christian/Muslim Dialogue

Elizabeth Tikvah Sarah

PREAMBLE

Before I focus on some key issues in Jewish/Christian/Muslim dialogue, I would like to illustrate the problematic context in which a Jewish woman relates to Jewish tradition, and speaks as a 'Jew' with 'Christians' and Muslims', by exploring a narrative included in the *Torah*.

In the Book of Genesis chapter 34, we find a little-remembered story which is rarely included in the litany of the famous tales of the Jewish ancestors. It is curious for this reason (and for many reasons): because it represents a sub-plot to the main story about Jacob, the last of the three forefathers, who was re-named Israel, and whose descendants later became the people Israel; because it is about Dinah, the only daughter of Leah and Jacob (Genesis 30:21); because it seems to centre on Dinah and what happened to her when she ventured out on her own into the city of Shechem, near to where her father had camped on his return to Canaan after his twenty year exile, but actually is about how Dinah's *brothers* responded to what happened to their sister; because it opens with what is, arguably, one of the most remarkable and the most mysterious verses in the whole of the *Torah* (34:1):

> Now, Dinah the daughter of Leah, whom she had borne to Jacob, went out to see the daughters of the land.

Beyond the Dysfunctional Family

In a clear echo of her father's journeys, Dinah 'went out' (*va-teitzei*) – she headed out on her own, purposefully – perhaps even eagerly. With the exception of Judah', who 'went down' (*va-yeired*) from his brothers, the *Torah*'s way of signalling that he went astray (Genesis 38:1), and Joseph, who was 'brought down' (*hurad*) to Egypt as a captive, after his brothers sold him to travelling merchants (Genesis 39:1), among the children of the family, Dinah alone 'went out' on her own journey. But she didn't just step out of her own volition, 'she went out to see the daughters of the land'. Why? Who were 'the daughters of the land'? Why are 'the daughters of the land' mentioned? We don't find answers to these questions by reading what follows or by investigating any other texts in the *Torah*. The *Torah* usually tells us about individual 'daughters', when relating something about particular male characters. For example, when Judah 'went down from his brothers, and turned towards a certain Adullamite whose name was Hirah, he saw there a daughter of a certain Canaanite, whose name was Shu'a; and he took her, and came in to her' (Genesis 38:1-2). Otherwise, 'daughters' don't get a mention – let alone a *collectivity* of daughters.

How ordinary it seems to a modern reader that Dinah 'went out to see the daughters of the land', but how extraordinary in the context of this ancient text and the patriarchal society it reflects. And then, how disappointing that Dinah experienced the fate of so many daughters, who dare to go out on their own, in every age: she was raped (34:2):

> Then Shechem, the son of Hamor the Hivite, the prince of the land, saw her, and he took her, and he lay with her, and humbled her (*va-yy'anneha*).

Is the story of a solitary 'daughter' going out 'to see the daughters of the land' a cautionary tale, perhaps? *Va-yy'anneha* – the three-letter 'root' of this word in the intensive (*pi'el*) form as we find it in this verse means to 'humble' or 'afflict'; in relation to a man 'afflicting' a woman, 'humbling' is a euphemism for rape. But do we need to be told that 'he humbled her'? Don't the words,

218

In the Footsteps of Dinah

'... saw her, and he took her, and he lay with her' already tell us everything? If we turn again to the story involving Dinah's brother, Judah, we learn that after 'Judah saw a daughter of a certain Canaanite... and he took her and came in to her' (38:2), the unnamed woman simply bore Judah's sons (38:3-5). There is nothing unusual about a 'daughter' being seen and 'taken' by a man – indeed that is how 'marriage' was practised in ancient times before it was ritualised as a social institution. The difference in the case of Dinah is that, in addition to having a significant father, she also had *brothers*. And so it was that after Shechem fell in love with 'the young woman' and wanted to marry her (38:3-4), her brothers entered into negotiations with Shechem's father, Hamor, concerning an 'alliance', which was conditional upon all the men of Shechem being circumcised (34:14-17). But that wasn't the end of the matter: three days following their circumcisions, when the men of Shechem were 'in pain', 'two of the sons of Jacob, Shimon and Levi, Dinah's brothers, took each one his sword, and came upon the city unawares, and slew all the males' (34:25).

Years later, at the end of his life, in Jacob's final address to each of his sons, he condemned Shimon and Levi for their violence (49:5-6). He had come 'in peace' to the city of Shechem (33:18), and they had destroyed any hope of this (34:30). So, the text is clear that Shimon and Levi did wrong – and the narrative may even be read as a polemic against brothers engaging in 'honour killing'. But as soon as the reader accepts this resolution – she or he is in danger of colluding in a double betrayal: Dinah 'went out to see the daughters of the land'. Instead of finding them, Shechem 'saw her, then took her and lay with her and humbled her' (34:2) – and from there on the text centres not on *her* experience – having stepped out, Dinah is then completely passive and silent throughout – but on how the male members of her family set about dealing with the offence against *them*: 'The sons of Jacob came in from the field, when they heard it; and the men were hurt (*va-yita'tz'vu*), and they were very angry because he had committed a vile deed in Israel by lying with Jacob's daughter; which should not be done' (34:7).

Beyond the Dysfunctional Family

INTRODUCTION

Why have I begun my reflections on Jewish/Christian/Muslim dialogue with this story from the *Torah*? According to the central narrative of the *Torah* about Jacob and his sons, 'the sons of Israel' – *b'ney Yisrael* – joined Joseph in Egypt (Genesis 46:8-27), and generations later, their descendants were liberated by the Eternal One, with whom they entered into a covenant in the wilderness at Mount Sinai (Exodus 19-20; 24). Then, after forty years of wandering in the desert, and the deaths of Miriam, Aaron and Moses in the desert, the descendants of the 'sons of Israel' crossed over the Jordan into Canaan (Joshua 1:10-15). How does Jacob's only daughter, Dinah, fit into the great story of 'the Israelites'? How does her mother, Leah, the mother of Reuben, Shimon, Levi and Judah, Issachar and Zebulun, fit into it? How does Jacob's favourite wife, Rachel, the mother of Joseph and Benjamin, fit into it? How do the concubines, Bilhah, the mother of Dan and Naphtali, and Zilpah, the mother of Gad and Asher fit into it? The sister of the brothers; the mothers of 'the sons of Israel': the wives and daughters came along too (Genesis 46:5-7), but what is their inheritance?

Of course, according to the *Torah*, two women did play significant roles in the narrative of the emergence of 'the Israelites': Sarah, the wife of Abraham, took action to ensure that her son, Isaac, inherited the covenant (Genesis 21: 8-13); and Rebecca, the wife of Isaac, took action to ensure that the younger twin, Jacob, received his father's blessing as the 'first-born' son (Genesis 27: 5-17); strong, resourceful women both. And later, Moses and Aaron's sister, Miriam, played a part in the liberation of the slaves and in leading the people in the wilderness. But with just thirty-three verses in all devoted to Miriam in the *Torah* – ten of which don't mention her by name[1] – although the eldest sibling, she, too, like the midwives, Shifra and Puah, who saved the baby boys threatened by Pharaoh's genocidal decree (Exodus 1:55-22), basically serves the unfolding story, which centres on the key male characters.

220

In the Footsteps of Dinah

A JEWISH WOMAN IN INTERFAITH DIALOGUE

So, how do I as a Jewish woman living in Britain in the 21st century, heir to an inheritance, which has centred on 'the sons of Israel' and their male descendants for millennia, engage in Jewish/Christian/Muslim dialogue? Is it possible for me, a Jewish woman, to speak *as a Jew*? And what difference does it make to my participation that I am a Jewish *woman*, rather than, simply, *a Jew*? What difference does it make to my participation that after two thousand years of an exclusively male rabbinate, I am one of the new breed of female rabbis that began to emerge in the 1970s, as the Women's Liberation Movement found its way into parts of the Jewish world in the United States, Britain and Europe?

The trope of interfaith encounter, conducted as if gender were an added 'extra' brought into the otherwise gender-free interaction when women are involved, has been well rehearsed over the decades since Jewish-Christian, then 'multi-faith', and then Jewish/Christian/Muslim dialogue was established in this country.

Before I explore my own responses to these questions, let me turn to another Jewish woman, also a feminist (but not a rabbi) – Susannah Heschel – whose own questions about the interfaith enterprise get to the heart of the matter:

> How am I to engage in theological discussion if I believe my partner in dialogue is engaging in oppressive and immoral subjugation of women? Moreover, being a woman in the context of theological discussion automatically puts one in a position of alterity; how am I to represent a tradition that has failed to represent me? Who is the 'we' of the questions formulated for this session? Am I expected to speak in the name of a tradition that has excluded and oppressed me?[2]

The session in which Susannah Heschel participated, was held as part of a ground-breaking conference of Jewish and Catholic theologians at the Sternberg Centre in London in the late 1990s – and the questions she was asked to address were as follows:

Beyond the Dysfunctional Family

a) How do we respond to the values of egalitarianism, autonomy, pluralism and democracy?
b) How do we respond to the values of secularism and contemporary humanism?

As long as Judaism and Christianity – and indeed, Islam – whether of the pre-modern, modern or post-modern varieties – maintain theological systems and institutional frameworks predicated on male-experience as the norm, women who engage in interfaith encounter can only participate in the 'we', either as the gendered other – women – prepared to add our gendered-perspective to the discourse, or as honorary men, excluding our gender from the equation.

So, to the questions with which I began: I can't answer them. I don't know how I as a Jewish woman can do anything else except disrupt the encounter by bringing in the anomaly of my femaleness – and insisting that it is acknowledged. This is what I do – all the time. The fact that I am a rabbi makes it both easier and more difficult: wearing the mantle of ordination helps me to imagine that I am, indeed, like my male rabbinic colleagues – one of them – and that my femaleness is irrelevant. At the same time, my rabbinic status is misleading: just because I, the rabbi, who is also a woman, participate on equal terms with my male colleagues – and meet other religious representatives, both Christian and Jewish, on equal terms – doesn't make the ground on which we stand together any the less patriarchal.

I struggle with an irony: as a Jewish woman and a feminist, I wanted to move from the margins to the centre, lay claim to my Jewish inheritance and make it my own. Indeed, as a radical feminist, who was also a lesbian separatist at the time, I made a conscious decision to come into the Jewish community, to include myself, and do what I could to play a part in transforming Jewish life from within, rather than remain 'excluded' on the outside. In practice, this great adventure, which began when I first started learning the *Aleph-Beit* in the autumn of 1983, and became institutionalised when I started

In the Footsteps of Dinah

studying at the Leo Baeck College as a rabbinic student in the autumn of 1984, has meant that I have been forced to deal with my marginality and 'otherness' as a woman and as a lesbian each and every day of my professional life. The fact that the choice of participation and engagement I made – and other Jewish women have made – has had a 'reforming' impact on Jewish life, making enclaves within it more egalitarian and inclusive, does not mean that Judaism has re-formed into an arena, defined and controlled by women and men alike. More to the point, these changes – mostly within Progressive Judaism – have made very little difference to the patriarchal dynamics of interfaith encounter.

THE 'ABRAHAMIC FAITHS' – THE SONS OF THE FATHER

Let me return to Susannah Heschel. In the same paper she writes (p. 148):

> Under the influence of postmodernist thought, feminism is rooted in the assumption that knowledge and truth are embedded in political interests that impose their will through coercion and power. Religious thought is understood less as a matter of ontology, but a matter of politics. At stake is not discovering 'truth', but unmasking regimes of power that have succeeded in imposing themselves as if they were true and natural. Feminists have unmasked Western philosophy not as the mirror of nature, but of men's experience, ideas and power, and Jewish feminists have similarly unmasked the Bible, Talmud and even modern Jewish thought, as regimes preserving patriarchal power. There is no ontology of gender, but gender identities produced as the effect of cultural regimes.[3]

And so if we turn to Jewish/Christian/Muslim dialogue, we can see that it continues to be a site of the encounter of three patriarchal traditions: the 'Abrahamic Faiths'. The construct for Jewish/Christian/Muslim dialogue over the past few years asserts the common roots of these three complex religious civilisations and demonstrates, clearly, their family connection:

Beyond the Dysfunctional Family

theologically, linked by the faith in One God, Jews Christians and Muslims also share one father in Abraham.

But there is a problem with this construct, which only serves to reinforce the patriarchal frame of Judaism, Christianity and Islam that almost half a century of dialogue has not transformed: all three sibling-religious civilizations remain, essentially, the sons of the Father.

There is no doubt that the feminist movement, which began to develop in the west in the 1960s has born fruit in the significant changes that have taken place in the more amenable manifestations of Jewish, Christian and Muslim life – so that there are now, for example: progressive women rabbis, church denominational women priests and ministers (with female Church of England bishops on the way) and female Imams in some quarters. Additionally, within all three worlds there has been a huge amount of feminist scholarship, which has begun to fill what Rabbi Marcia Plumb, in 1992, called 'the half empty bookcase'.[4] Nevertheless, despite these developments, the frame of all three sibling religious civilizations, individually, and collectively, remains Patriarchy.

So, dialogue has not made a difference; feminism has not made a difference. In one sense it is obvious why: we can't turn back the clock. The fact is, the roots of Judaism, Christianity and Islam lie in a patriarchal past – and all we can do is modify the patriarchal legacy.

But this, like the half-empty book-case, which has been steadily filling for a quarter of a century now, is only half-true. Let me explain what I mean by reference to the foundational narrative of the Jewish people. I have already mentioned Sarah. According to the *Torah*, when Abraham (Abram at this point in the story), left his land, his kindred and his father's house to go to the land, which God promised to show him, he 'took' his wife, Sarah (Sarai at this point in the story) with him (Genesis 12:1-4). Abraham was the prime-mover. God speaks to Abraham; Abraham acts. The continuing narrative demonstrates that Sarah is a powerful character – but nevertheless, Jewish tradition, reflected in the blessing included

In the Footsteps of Dinah

in thrice-daily prayer known as *Avot*, 'fathers', crafted by the early rabbis, talks of 'the God of Abraham, and the God of Isaac and the God of Jacob'. However, despite a patriarchal God, a male-authored text, and the primacy of the patriarchs in Jewish tradition, the act of Jewish women today, engaging with the *Torah as women* and re-reading the *Torah* from the perspective of Sarah and Rebecca and Leah and Rachel, and also from the perspective of the unofficial wives of the patriarchs, Hagar, Bilhah and Zilpah – as well as stepping into the shoes of Dinah – has involved a re-framing of the foundational narrative from a female perspective.

However, this re-framed narrative remains, like the unofficial wives and the forgotten daughters, the unofficial narrative: it is the 'other' view; the 'other' voice – other than the authoritative male standpoint. The insight of the French intellectual, Simone de Beauvoir, concerning man as 'self' and woman as 'other', in her monumental work, *The Second Sex* (*Le Deuxieme Sexe*), which pre-dated the 'second wave' feminist movement by more than a decade, remains as true today as it was in 1949, when it was first published. Even today, as long as the women in all three 'Abrahamic Faiths' belong to a sub-set – the Jewish woman; the Christian woman; the Muslim woman – *the* Jew will continue to signify the *male* Jew, *the* Christian, the *male* Christian, *the* Muslim, the *male* Muslim.

So, here I am offering an*other* view, a *fourth* perspective, an adjunct to the voices of the three official Jewish/Christian/Muslim dialogue partners, because as yet Jewish/Christian/Muslim dialogue is a meeting of the three 'Abrahamic Faiths' and defined by that construct. How can it be otherwise? That is where we are right now: the reality is the perspective of women remains marginal; it has not yet been integrated into the official narrative. But this is not because we can't turn back the clock and change the past. Of course, we cannot. But we can do something – at least three things – that could make a significant difference to the nature of Jewish/Christian/Muslim dialogue, so that it ceases to be purely a brotherly affair, a meeting of the sons of the Father. We could:

Beyond the Dysfunctional Family

- Acknowledge, not only the patriarchal past of Judaism, Christianity and Islam, but also the continuing impact of the patriarchal legacy, expressed, in particular, both in the marginalisation – and in some contexts, the oppression – of women, and in the linked phenomena of fundamentalism and extremist violence.
- Create more opportunities for Jewish, Christian and Muslim women to dialogue with each other.
- Cease to focus exclusively on the unifying construct, the 'Abrahamic Faiths', which, by definition, marginalises the perspectives and experiences of Jewish, Christian and Muslim women, and journey together, as women and men, towards a new terrain of Jewish, Christian and Muslim encounter.

The last step is the most crucial, but it is also the most uncertain: how do we leave the old way behind and embark on a new one – and how might we begin? Let me share an experience. For several years, the Hedwig Dransfeld Haus in Bendorf, in Germany – a dialogue centre that, sadly, no longer exists – played host each year to two annual Jewish/Christian/Muslim week-long conferences – one of which was run by and for women. I remember participating in a drama activity at the women's JCM that focussed on the conflict between Sarah and her servant, Hagar, as related in the *Torah* – in the Book of Genesis, chapter 16. All the participants were presented with a simple challenge: to take it in turns to role-play Hagar and Sarah. For the Christian women present it was a more complex experience, but as each Muslim Sarah and Jewish Hagar played out the conflict between them, the possibility and the inevitability of each one of us identifying with both protagonists became more and more evident. And, somehow, we managed, both, to stand in the shoes of the other and to re-craft the narrative so it became a story about women struggling to define themselves in a patriarchal culture – then and now.

I can imagine that if groups of Jewish, Christian and Muslim women and men participated in a similar exercise – the women

226

In the Footsteps of Dinah

of all three traditions stepping into Abraham's shoes, the men, into Hagar and Sarah's – the impact could be very powerful, indeed, perhaps, even transformative. The challenge is daunting – but it is also possible; the way ahead is uncertain, but as soon as we begin to take steps, it becomes clearer. We may not know yet how to make a start, but if Jewish, Christian Muslim encounter is to evolve so that dialogue, reconciliation and action between Jews, Christians and Muslims may become a reality, Jewish, Christian and Muslim women cannot remain a sub-set, with our perspectives and experiences relegated into a sub-category, focussed on 'women's concerns', we need to be equal partners with men and part of the main event that is defined by all of us.

PRE-MODERNITY, MODERNITY AND POST-MODERNITY: THE IMPLICATIONS OF MULTI-DIMENSIONED SOCIETIES FOR JCM DIALOGUE

So far, while exploring the issue of gender, and the historical antecedence of patriarchy in Jewish tradition – it is for Christian and Muslim women to reflect on the patriarchal antecedence of Christianity and Islam – I have treated the socio/political/ religious context as if it were somehow constant, and as if it was possible for Jewish, Christian and Muslim women and men to encounter one another imagining that Judaism, Christianity and Islam were fixed entities, unaffected by time. Of course, we live now, but even 'now' is not, simply, present time. We live in confusing times; in *different times* – depending on where we live around the world. The capitalist economic system may be global, but cultural and religious variations between societies mean that some remain pre-modern, and that contemporary societies in many parts of the world today, combine in varying ways, pre-modern, modern and post-modern elements.

In no arena is this more evident than in religion. In the aftermath of the French Revolution, which led to the destruction of feudal society in central Europe, Jewish life changed dramatically over the next one hundred years as the ghetto

Beyond the Dysfunctional Family

walls came down and Jews became citizens of the host-societies in which they lived. It was in this context that traditional forms of Jewish existence that varied from place to place gave way to, sharply contrasting, Orthodox and Progressive responses to Modernity. Since that time, even if we simplify the picture somewhat, it is evident that active Jewish life in modern Britain today, for example, encompasses at least three major strands: Orthodox expressions of Judaism, which strive to preserve pre-modern modes of Jewish thought and practice that entail maintaining communal control over the lives of their members; Progressive expressions of Judaism that, having embraced modernity's rationalist imperative, continue to adapt the Jewish heritage to reflect modernist democratic and egalitarian values, rooted in the rights of the individual; and various innovative responses to the emergence of postmodernity in the second half of the twentieth century. Plural and eclectic the latter include: cyber-space face-book encounters; counter-cultural satirical happenings; creative reconstructions of rituals; and new engagements with the source texts of Judaism that conflate the binary distinction between traditional and critical readings, and emerge out of the reader's experience.

And, of course, it's not just that pre-modern, modern and post-modern forms of existence co-exist in the world today – individual lives may also encompass all these dimensions. I am the child of two Jewish parents whose backgrounds spanned both the pre-modern and the modern worlds: a mother from an orthodox family, whose parents fled pogroms in eastern Europe for London in the early 1900s, and a father, who grew up an upper middle-class liberal Jewish home in Vienna and was educated in French, and whose own father was incarcerated by the Nazis in Dachau in November 1938. My paternal grandfather was one of the lucky ones: he escaped the 'Final Solution' because my father, who had left Europe for South Africa in 1936, managed to arrange domestic permits for his parents and siblings that enabled them to travel to England. My parents came from different Jewish worlds, but they did have much in common:

In the Footsteps of Dinah

although my mother enjoyed the ritual of *Shabbat* candle-lighting, neither considered themselves to be 'religious', and apart from when my brother was studying for his *Bar Mitzvah*, we didn't belong to a synagogue. They also both voted Labour and were fervently anti-Apartheid and anti-racist.

Nevertheless, there were major differences between them. My mother spoke *Yiddish* and sang *Yiddish* and Hebrew songs, both ancient and modern, and was an ardent Socialist Zionist. My father was a liberal with a lower case 'l', who hated all forms of nationalism, and who would walk out of the room in protest when my mother began to sing or speak *Yiddish* – objecting both to what he saw as the 'insular' culture of the Jewish ghetto and to Zionism. I imbibed all these influences, and my life reflects my encounter with my parents' complex legacy as I have journeyed and continue to journey in my being in their worlds – and also in my own worlds: as a feminist lesbian Jew, who spans and reconstructs both traditional and liberal Jewish elements in a spirit that is less about faith, and more a process of 'struggle', like Jacob/Israel, 'with God and with humanity' (Genesis 32:29), and *in* and *with* the wilderness of Life.

In different ways, unless we live in totally segregated communities, each one of us inhabits different cultures and even different times. To make matters even more complicated, the distinctions between pre-modern, modern and post-modern dimensions in many contemporary societies are not absolute. Although pre-modern Jewish communities, like the ultra-orthodox in Britain, remain hostile to modern ways, while rejecting modernity's ideas, they often use modern conveniences, albeit in a controlled way – for example, telephones, cars, and the internet. Meanwhile, during the course of the 20th century, and in particular, after the *Shoah*, modernist, Progressive forms of Judaism, true to their dynamic, progressive impulse, cannot help but be in the process of grappling with postmodernity.

The challenge that modernity presents to pre-modern forms of religious life is clear: since the French Revolution of 1789, there have been myriad examples of traditional societies confronting

Beyond the Dysfunctional Family

modernity and either resisting change or submitting to progress. The challenge that postmodernity presents to modernity is, on the other hand, by definition, multi-dimensional, because it is in the nature of postmodernity that modernity is incorporated rather than overcome or banished. But what does this mean in practice? If the impulse of modernity, rooted in reason and the quest for objective truth, is *singularity* and coherence, how is it possible for modernity to co-exist with postmodernity – with plural approaches to existence that encompass subjectivity, and multiple perspectives and truths? And, most important, what are the implications of all this postmodern complexity for Jewish/Christian/Muslim Dialogue?

It is more important to ask the questions, and to engage in a questioning way, than it is to try and find the answers. But there are three obvious implications:

First, since JCM dialogue exists in a nexus of plural religious expressions, it may become necessary for it to diversify to include opportunities for encounters with the other players – both JCM encounters with other religions and individual Jewish, Christian and Muslim encounters with others – for example, with Hindus, with Buddhists, and so on.

Second, even in the context of JCM dialogue work, awareness of and respect for a plurality of other religions, and experiences of encounter with them, will, in time, involve modifying our assumptions, as JCM dialogue partners, about our particular – and superior? – monotheistic credentials.

Third, since plurality is an intra-religious issue as well as an inter-religious one, JCM dialogue will need to proliferate to enable multiple and varied dialogue initiatives reflecting the diverse range of perspectives and experiences within Judaism, within Christianity and within Islam, including the perspectives of women and other, as yet, marginalised elements and constituencies.

I have stated these implications very starkly and in somewhat formulaic terms. But there is another way of thinking about them that might help us to grasp what is really at stake when JCM dialogue comes to terms with the complexity of contemporary reality. Whoever you are – whatever your bundle of identities, whatever your gender – imagine that you are Dinah, taking the risk of venturing outside the confines of your family and your community in order to see and meet the daughters – and the sons – of the land: all the different people and peoples, who constitute our plural societies today. Imagine that you have stepped out because you are eager to meet others and learn about their lives. Imagine that, no longer content to 'belong' in a particular place, being who you are in all the complexity of your past and your present, you want to inhabit the world. Imagine what 'dialogue' might become if we all 'went out' to meet one another.

THE CHALLENGE OF ENCOUNTER: FROM INTERFAITH DIALOGUE TO INTERFAITH SOCIETY

But I am running ahead of myself. JCM and interfaith dialogue in general faces many challenges, not least the challenge of finding ways of having an impact on the respective individual religious traditions of the participants, and on society at large. But how to do this? During the twenty-five years that I have participated in Jewish-Christian-Muslim encounter, it has become increasingly obvious to me that the very process of engaging together has generated both a new form of dialogue-partner identity – I am a Jew in relation to Christians and Muslims – and created a gap between the Jews, Christians and Muslims who have experienced encounter with one another and the Jews, Christians and Muslims who have not – with important implications for the possible impact of JCM dialogue on Judaism, Christianity and Islam.

Let me just take the JCM group that has created this book as an example. It began and became a viable entity because the individual Jews, Christians and Muslims involved wanted, both, to speak to 'the other' and to listen to 'the other'. Rabbi Dr Jonathan Magonet, a long-time member of our particular group, and co-founder with Rabbi Lionel Blue of the Standing

Beyond the Dysfunctional Family

Conference of Jews, Christians and Muslims in Europe over forty years ago, which organises the annual Leo Baeck College eight-day JCM conference in Germany, has spoken of the terrain of interfaith dialogue as a 'border-land': the very act of meeting together involves participants in moving from the centre to the edge of their respective traditions; it is here, in this 'border-land' country, on the margins that participants are able, not only to meet the other, but also, from that vantage point, look over into other lands, and note both the similarities and the differences between these other lands and their own. The JCM group meets in such a border-land – indeed, has been meeting for so long now on the same border-land, that it has become a very particular JCM country – indeed a veritable nation, with its own language, culture, rites and practices, which distinguish it from other nations – not least the long-established nations of Judaism, Christianity and Islam.

Of course, it's not quite a simple as that. JCM nation remains a border-land of temporary settlers, which means, not only that the surrounding nations are always in evidence across the way, but also that without border-controls in any direction, people come and go freely, and newcomers are always welcome. Nevertheless, the gap between JCM nation and the nations of Judaism, Christianity and Islam is real – and those, who venture out into the border-land and dwell there awhile can't help being changed by the experience and adopting strange ways that feel alien to 'the folks back home' when they return.

So, what to do? For most of its life our JCM dialogue group has concentrated on talking together, albeit a lot of our talking has taken the form of writing papers, which we then discussed. But following 9/11 and the subsequent military offences launched by the United States, Britain, and their allies against the Iraqi regime of Saddam Hussein and the Taliban in Afghanistan, we began to feel that perhaps the time had come for us to communicate what we had learnt from our dialogue experience to the outside world. And so it was that during 2003, we began to work on crafting a Platform Statement, which subsequently

232

In the Footsteps of Dinah

was published in 2005, simultaneously, in Jewish, Christian and Muslim journals, under the heading, 'Welcome and Unwelcome Truths for Jews, Christians and Muslims'.[5]

Producing the statement was very hard work. Getting everyone involved to agree a single text that we could all sign up to was a great challenge – and, indeed, a couple of people felt unable to sign it. Every word was scrutinised, analysed and interrogated and there were several re-writes. One of the main reasons for this was that we were determined, not only to state our common bonds, but also to challenge, in particular, fundamentalism, past and present, and the history of exclusive truth claims in all three traditions. Further, in making it clear that 'We must welcome religious diversity and concede that no single religion can claim a monopoly of truth', the statement is also a call to action to promote reconciliation through initiatives in the arenas of education and politics, as well as religion. The Platform statement was an attempt to say something radically new about Judaism, Christianity and Islam and the challenge of encounter; it was also a deeply felt plea summed up in the closing paragraph:

> We can only achieve our vision of a repaired and transformed world by pooling the best of our respective teachings and talents in partnership and shared endeavour. Only full and effective partnership can end conflict and bring peace, with opportunities to ponder together the wonders of creation and the mystery of God.

Was anyone listening? What changes need to take place to enable those who are not engaged in interfaith encounter to listen to the voices of those who can only say what they say because they have been listening to one another?

Clearly, the religious leaders of the respective traditions need to engage in interfaith encounter themselves – and then take responsibility both for speaking and teaching from the perspective of their interfaith experiences and for creating opportunities for encounter in their localities. Religious leaders,

Beyond the Dysfunctional Family

Jewish, Christian and Muslim, need to preach and practice respect for and acknowledgement of other religions than their own.

But for this to happen, something much more fundamental needs to take place, which brings us back to the multi-dimensioned pre-modern/modern/post-modern social nexus. By definition interfaith encounter involves transgressing the boundaries of a separatist milieu; by definition interfaith encounter entails engagement with modernity and its ethos of rational critical enquiry, individual autonomy and progressive development; by definition interfaith encounter is a post-modern phenomenon; an expression of multiple truths and perspectives and experiences of life.

So, the question arises, is it possible for those who are engaging with modernity and postmodernity to enable those who are not, to open the doors to their self-enclosed worlds and step outside? I'm not sure it is. But that doesn't mean we can't do something. On the contrary, by continuing to do what we do and broadcasting our activity – not least, on the internet – and keeping the pathways to the border-land open, we can create new possibilities for those who might feel inclined to venture outside, if they only knew where they might go.

It is impossible to change the views and ways of those who do not wish to change, unless one resorts to force – the option adopted by totalitarian regimes the world-over, which is, of course, self-defeating. However, it is possible to foster a dynamic social environment in which multiple understandings of life and ways of living are available. In response to ethnic and religious tensions and, in particular, the outbreaks of violence during the summer of 2001 in the northern towns of Oldham, Bradford and Burnley, as well as the bombings of July 7th 2005, the last British government (May 1997 – May 2010) began to promote a 'community cohesion' agenda, centred on maximising social interaction between different groups in society and fostering social integration.[6] On a practical level, creating 'community cohesion' means funding initiatives that bring together people from different social, religious, ethnic and racial groups for joint

In the Footsteps of Dinah

ventures. If it isn't scraped and is funded at the level required, 'community cohesion' could make a significant difference up and down the country. We might speculate, for example, that without in any way challenging Judaism, Christianity and Islam directly, if the young people of all three traditions – and more – came together each week, in both same-sex and mixed-sex groups, to play football or jam in a band or rehearse a musical, there is a very good chance that their views of one another – including of their different religious traditions – could be radically transformed, and that they would also feel valued and included.

Perhaps the most crucial arena for taking action to foster 'community cohesion' is education, where initiatives have already taken place.[7] But as soon as we turn to the area of educational provision, it is all too apparent how much needs to be done to overcome social, cultural, ethnic and racial divisions within and between schools. Perhaps, if government determined to fund education in such a way that every school had the resources needed to become a real locus of learning for all, encompassing provision for both same-faith as well as multi-faith and multi-cultural activity in both same-gender and mixed-gender settings, perhaps they might begin to provide an environment capable of generating social interaction between students from across the social, ethnic, racial and religious spectrum. Perhaps, if this happened, it might become normative for all schools to be in a position to develop their existing religious education curricular, with input from the different faith communities, in such a way that the teaching of the different faiths might also foster an appreciation of our shared values and a real understanding of the reality and meaning of religious pluralism. Of course, none of this will have any chance of success unless the government, simultaneously, makes more resources available to deal with hate crime directed at minority groups and to ensure equal opportunities, so that all the different constituencies within society, both large and small, feel valued and included.

The education of young people, both formal and informal, holds the key to the development of openness towards the other

Beyond the Dysfunctional Family

and respect for difference in society at large. Schools, youth clubs and sports centres all have a crucial role to play in creating attractive and engaging environments that enable young people from different religious and ethnic communities to encounter one another, and which would also involve appropriate staff training, as well as workshops for young people. I know of one particular example – the Young People's Centre in Brighton – where providing a meeting place for different youth programmes, including Allsorts, a project for LGBT (lesbian, gay, bisexual and transgender young people, aged 15-24) and RASP, a project for young refugees and asylum seekers, also encompasses celebrating the major festivals, and creating contexts in which young people with very different backgrounds and life issues experience something of each other's cultures and traditions.[8]

There are a growing number of examples of initiatives across Britain that enable those involved to encounter others and engage in shared activities. If 'community cohesion' projects proliferate, perhaps in time, in addition to opening their doors for school visits, synagogues, churches, mosques and temples might also play their part by creating opportunities for their members of all ages to get together with others, from different communities, for both age-related and cross-generational activities. The great majority of people in Britain today still live largely in segregated communities, particularly those who have a strong religious affiliation. If we make progress in the wider society but leave religious congregations to themselves, the 'community cohesion' agenda will be in danger of isolating the different religious communities and widening the gap between those who engage with others in a plural social milieu and those who do not. Again, the example of Dinah comes to mind: if we are going to make the leap from interfaith dialogue taking place in specialised border-land enclaves to a genuinely interfaith society – that also makes space for those who see themselves as atheist or agnostic – each one of us needs to put our best foot forward and go out to see and meet all the other daughters and sons of the land.

CONCLUSION

I have identified several issues raised by interfaith dialogue: the reality of patriarchy that continues to shape and determine how the faiths encounter one another at the expense of women; the implications of a multi-dimensional pre-modern/modern/post-modern society for the nature and range of interfaith encounter; and the challenge of extending interfaith encounter, so that it becomes a feature of the wider social landscape, in the interests of fostering religious pluralism and mutual respect between all the different faith communities. We have achieved much so far in the arena of Jewish/Christian/Muslim engagement, but it is only a beginning.

NOTES

1. Exodus 2:1-10 does not mention Miriam by name. The other texts in the Torah about her are: Exodus 15:20-21; Numbers 12:1-16; Numbers 20:1; Numbers 26: 58-59; Deuteronomy 24:8-9.

2. Susannah Heschel (2001) 'The Challenge of Modernity and Postmodernity' in Eds. Tony Bayfield, Sidney Brichto, and Eugene J Fisher. *He Kissed Him and They Wept: Towards a Theology of Jewish-Catholic Partnership*. London: SCM Press. p. 149.

3. *Ibid*. p. 148.

4. Rabbi Marcia Plumb took the lead with her women rabbi colleagues in establishing *The Half-Empty Bookcase* in 1992, which became a framework for organising conferences, study materials, a quarterly newsletter and Jewish women's groups during the 1990s.

5. See pp. 263-268 in this book.

6. See the following web-sites: www.idea.gov.uk/idk/core/page. do?pageId=8799365; www.communities.gov.uk/communities/racecohesionfaith/communitycohesion; www.cohesioninstitute. org.uk/PolicyResearch/PolicyFramework.

7. See: www.teachernet.gov.uk/wholeschool/Communitycohesion/.../info/doweneed.

8. The Local Government Agency Children and Young People Bulletin, March 2009, includes a report of the Youth Action and Engagement case study set from the National Youth Agency (available from www.

Beyond the Dysfunctional Family

nya.org.uk), which looks at young people and community cohesion. The five very different youth projects featured – from around the country – include Allsorts Youth Project in Brighton. Based at the Young Peoples' Centre in Brighton, Allsorts provides a 'drop in' and support services for young lesbian, gay, bisexual, transgender and unsure young people aged under 26 in *Brighton and Hove. See: www.allsortsyouth.org.uk. Also based at the YPC,* RASP – Refugees and Asylum Seekers Project – is a mentoring and befriending project for young refugee and asylum seekers living in *Brighton and Hove.* See: www.bhvolunteers.org.uk/rasp.

PART FOUR

Analysing Our Encounters

11

Differences and Common Ground

Tony Bayfield, Alan Race, Ataullah Siddiqui

This book reflects a rich process of dialogue, embracing elements of honest engagement, personal risk, building trust and coming to care about one another. It has also involved us in what the American Catholic theologian of interreligious dialogue, Leonard Swidler, has called 'a whole new way of thinking',[1] a pursuit in mutual accountability for what we are prepared to affirm as people of faith and committed human beings. The journey has been both unnerving and exhilarating. The analysis that follows draws together the different parts of this book.

PART ONE: THE BASIC THEMES

The process of our dialogue is reflected in the choice and style of the three opening chapters. Michael Hilton, Elizabeth Harris and Dilwar Hussain agreed to bring a strong personal perspective to a consideration of how the British Jewish, Christian and Muslim communities come to be where they are today. 'What does it look like and how does it feel to you?' we asked.

So the starting point wasn't 'a brief history of Christianity/Judaism/Islam in Britain' or 'a guide to the main tenets of Christianity/Judaism/Islam today' but three people, professionally committed to their respective faiths, narrating a personal perspective.

There is, of course, a potential pitfall with this approach. Interesting and engaging as our three contributors are, they speak only for themselves. What we also wanted to do was to convey something about Judaism, Christianity and Islam in

Beyond the Dysfunctional Family

Britain today. Jews frequently tell the story of two Jews who were shipwrecked on a desert island and built three synagogues – one each and one that neither of them would be seen dead in. It is reflective of Britain's tiny Jewish population, still with diverse backgrounds, who rejoice in what they assert as a history of debate, disagreement and driving their own personal taxi. It's an interesting perspective on Jewish history but it's not unique: Muslims in Britain today manifest a far greater cultural diversity than is often appreciated and denominational differences and internal disagreements are not unknown within Christianity. Therefore we asked our three opening authors to include a dimension 'which is not wholly autobiography and broadly reflects the other members of the same faith in the group'. Of course even the collectivism of group members is atypical. Relatively few Jews, Christians or Muslims have either the time or the inclination to commit to exploring the three Abrahamic faiths and what they might contribute to 21st century British society.

So it is our job, as co-editors of this book, to draw out from the individual contributions that which sheds light on the larger narrative.

We start with Michael Hilton, who was born into a well-established Jewish family, and in whom there is no sense of being foreign or not British. Yet he has a strong sense of minority status and being different. He says, 'My Judaism was important to me, because it was about rigorous honesty, a secure and loving family and *being different* from Christian boys at school.'

Michael is not typical in having been brought up within Liberal Judaism, at that time the most anglicised denomination within Britain's Jewish mainstream, but his experience is in no sense unusual. What he brings out is that, as a child in the 1950s and 1960s, he met a degree of non-comprehension from committed Christians as to how he could both persist in error and miss out on the greatest Truth of all and also enlist sympathy for the horrors of the Holocaust. He identifies a turning point which he relates to the history of the State of Israel and the rise since the 1970s of renewed Jewish insecurity. The contemporary

Differences and Common Ground

Jewish agenda is dominated by the sense that an already tiny community – only 267,000 in a population of more than 60 million – is further diminishing (as a result of assimilation, marrying out, secularisation, and failure to maintain a significant enough birth-rate); by a resurgence of anti-Semitism and by being implicated in an increasingly hostile view of the state of Israel. Not even a marked upturn in the quality of Jewish life in Britain over the last thirty years stops Michael from contemplating the disappearance of British Jews and asking 'would we be missed?'

Nevertheless, Michael ends with a passionate message: dialogue is not peripheral but central (as it was to his choice of the rabbinate as a career). Society continually needs reminding of the spiritual and the personal and these are central to the processes of dialogue itself. 'We have to trust each other more, and we have to be aware as individuals of the spiritual longing that exists in all of us. We have to be more aware of our shared experiences as human beings, experiences of alienation, of migration, of loneliness, of love, of searching.' After all, we are all minorities today.

If Michael is correct – and we believe he is – then the plea for dialogue is not a call for involvement in something peripheral to our humanity. It is an intrinsic part of what it is to be a human being at all! The dialogue between religious outlooks, therefore, exists in order to deepen our sense of humanity by directing us to the spiritual nature of who we are.

That leads us on to Elizabeth Harris. In many ways Elizabeth's story – particularly the context – is radically different. She recounts a story both national and international which reflects the sheer size of the Christian world (2 billion Christians) as refracted through Empire and then Commonwealth. In some ways the discovery of the 'other' is a feature of the post-Second World War period.

Her personal narrative touches on Jewry. Harris' grandfather, disillusioned by the First World War, embraces the radical, co-operative, socialist tradition – and pacifism. The pacifism is inherited by Elizabeth's father, a Methodist Minister, who

Beyond the Dysfunctional Family

is then forced by post-war revelations to recant in the face of something more evil than war itself – Nazism and the Holocaust. Awareness of the Jewish 'other', notes Harris, predates the Shoah but was confined to a tiny minority of British Christians. It did not stem the horror 'made possible because of centuries of Christian anti-Semitism.'

But for Elizabeth personally, and perhaps for Britain in general, the 'other' is not confined to Jews but consists of Buddhists and Muslims and even Black Christians.

The horrors of the Second World War and perceived Christian failings led, for some, to radical opposition, for instance, to The Bomb. Awareness of growing secularism also goes back to the 1950s. As the 50s and 60s pass, liberal Christians begin to question traditional images of God as well as grow indignant at the global inequalities between rich and poor. This liberality extended to the Roman Catholic Church and the Second Vatican Council. The World Council of Churches speaks of a need for 'new openness to the world in its aspirations, its achievements, its restlessness and its despair.'

However, by the mid 1970s a gap was emerging between those Christians, who emphasised their concern for the poor and dispossessed together with a conviction of the imperative of a new openness to the other on the one hand, and those Christians whose concern was primarily with 'personal salvation and evangelism' on the other. Elizabeth identifies the 1970s as a pivotal decade for Christians in Britain (and elsewhere).

The liberals continued to press forward, as exemplified by the shift from comparative religion – 'where other religions are studied through mainly Christian eyes and each analysed according to a Christian pro-forma' – to religious education in which faiths are encouraged to learn about each other through the eyes of a practitioner of that faith.

But the Christian world in Britain is changing – with a growing anxiety about the loss of Britain as a Christian country. So a significant part of the Christian world in Britain finds itself unable to move beyond an exclusivist theology. As

244

Differences and Common Ground

a result, a worrying bifurcation, a disturbing retrenchment emerges which, says Elizabeth, is not the way forward for Christians in religiously plural Britain. 'More than ever before, people from different faiths need not only work together but to share their wisdoms. They also need to engage positively with secular society and the new forms of spiritual and religious belonging present in the West. If Christians fail to do this, they risk irrelevance.'

Though very different personal narratives, Michael and Elizabeth share much in common – not least a sense of minority status, anxieties about the future, a conviction that the way forward lies in the abandonment of exclusivism and the recognition that God is to be discerned in the 'other'. For Elizabeth, the renewal of the international struggle between the West and the Muslim world, highlighted by 9/11 and ever rising tension, has become the disturbing focus for those who take the path of 'retrenchment'.

This makes it appropriate to turn now to Dilwar Hussain. He begins by making the point that the Muslim experience in Britain should not be seen as something radically different and unique to Islam. It follows very much in the pattern of immigration to Britain going back to the major Jewish immigration of the late 19th century and, before that, to the Irish and the Huguenots. It does not help to exceptionalise Muslims as they too go through the process of 'migration, settlement, establishment of communities, negotiating new identities, dealing with poverty, racism and changes in family dynamics' which are common traits. He distinguishes between the first generation who are migrants, the second generation who see Britain as their home and the third generation, many of whom regard questions around identity and loyalty as either silly or in need of reframing. The echoes of Michaels' narrative are loud and clear.

Just as Elizabeth saw 9/11 as compounding negative British attitudes to Muslims, so Dilwar underlines how international events have politicised Muslim identity and increased the extent to which it is 'forged in oppositional terms [and] becomes more defiant'.

Beyond the Dysfunctional Family

Dilwar emphasises that the push-pull effect of the British need for labour and the unsatisfactory economic and educational conditions in former colonies brought to Britain an ethnically diverse and culturally vibrant community of communities – youthful, with a heightened sense of religious identity in an otherwise increasingly secularised society. Dilwar wants above all for this community of communities to become normal and normalised – not assimilated but in no more need of a member being defined as a Muslim as the British Prime Minister needs to be defined as a Christian.

He deplores the radicalisation caused by foreign events but asks Muslims to own some responsibility: 'Muslims were not able to challenge strongly enough the preachers of hate and the peddlers of simplistic solutions who were able to tap into that frustration. Nor did they create adequate religious institutions that could connect with young people and educate them in an idiom they would understand, something that could have protected them when challenged by extremists.' There are strong echoes of this in Elizabeth's anxiety about the extremes of Christian entrenchment (and progressive Jewish fears about *charedi* – ultra-Orthodox Jews).

Dilwar has little sympathy for those who long for a return to a romantic monochrome 'Christian Britain'. He looks to a future in which Muslims are integrated, fully participating members of society. He sees Britain moving forward and changing, with Muslims making their own contributions (as Jews long have). As he says: 'This is not about a clash of civilisations or even a clash of values; after all, much of what we all aspire to are human needs, desires and values. Think of freedom, equality, justice, accountable governance, rule of law, prosperity, education, charity, protection of rights, etc – such values and ideas have no single creed, no specific culture, and no particular civilisation. They are now truly universal and human aspirations.' It is interesting to us that Dilwar does not frame these universal values as hallmarks of modern, western culture *to which Islam has contributed.*

Differences and Common Ground

Dilwar laments the growing sense of victimhood amongst Muslims in Britain. He acknowledges the challenges to Islam – loss of temporal authority in the face of the nation state; secular values pushing religious traditions to the periphery; the spread through globalisation of people as consumers rather than citizens; the increase in the pace of life and the impact of hi-tech. But he positively welcomes a response from Muslim intellectuals: 'It is a long term struggle, nothing short of creating a revitalised, reformed Muslim intellectual paradigm.'

Dilwar's is a challenging, exciting vision. In many ways he offers the most enthusiastic and optimistic vision of the three. Any uncertainty, moreover, about its realistic possibility should not deter us from whole-heartedly endorsing it as the next phase in Islamic development in this country. We might also add that it would be a strengthened paradigm if it was forged in a spirit of interreligious dialogue.

We have, then, three different individual stories and journeys, each with their own distinct voice and concerns. Yet they sit together remarkably well – they share concerns over the minority status of the religions, religious reactionary forces which display an unwanted and unwarranted arrogance and a positive desire for a future which is born from sharing insights between the faiths.

PART TWO: THE COMPLEXITIES OF THE ABRAHAMIC CONCEPT

This book assumes that there is something special about the relationship between what have become known as the three Abrahamic faiths. By special we do not mean that this relationship is of greater importance than that between, say, Islam, Hinduism and Sikhism, but simply that there is a 'sibling relationship' which is historically distinctive and worthy of exploration.

From time to time, the term 'Abrahamic faiths' was vigorously challenged. This first challenge came from Elizabeth Tikvah

Beyond the Dysfunctional Family

Sarah (Elli), who pointed out the intrinsic patriarchal nature of the terminology. The second came from Muslims with a background in the Indian subcontinent, for whom the particular configuration seemed remote. After all, what is the significance of a relationship with a tiny faith group, the Jews – seen very much as a subset of the Christian-European-Western cultural entity – when compared to the relationship with Hinduism? Some voiced the awkward observation that the construct 'Abrahamic' is interpreted differently in the three faiths and is therefore not easily applicable to all three on comparable terms.

Tony Bayfield was the most insistent on the validity of pressing the metaphor of siblings. He argued – radically for a Jew – that Judaism and Christianity are siblings, defining Judaism as Rabbinic Judaism which emerged at the same time as Christianity and out of the same milieu. On this thesis the Hebrew Bible, very largely synonymous with what Christians term (uncomfortably for Jews) the Old Testament, is a shared inheritance containing a shared story which begins with Abraham and Sarah. To view Jews and Christians as siblings – though not identical twins – then makes sense.

But what of Islam? There is clearly a deep connection between Torah and the Qur'an, with many shared figures and stories. Just as the emergence of Rabbinic Judaism and Christianity was characterised by mutual misunderstanding and rejection in the fraught Roman empire setting of the first century of the common era, so the emergence of Islam is accompanied by a similar sense of mutual incomprehension and rejection between Jews and Muslims, on the one hand, and Christians and Muslims, on the other. Yet there are many shared commitments and characteristics between the three faiths, at least embracing basic monotheism, prayerful dependency on God and fundamental ethical values. Tony argues passionately that even if Muslims share only one parent, Abraham, whilst Christians and Jews share two (Abraham and Sarah rather than Hagar), the term sibling is appropriate. We are clearly part of the same family – albeit an extremely dysfunctional family!

Differences and Common Ground

It is above all else that very dysfunctionality – we are inextricably involved in so many of the geo-political conflicts of today's world – that makes engagement and dialogue essential. What the group did not bargain for was the full extent of the individuality of the bilateral relations within the dysfunctional trinity! The second section of the book brings this out and we turn now to explore these.

The first dialogical exchange between a Christian and a Muslim displays a significant level of misconnection. For Shanthikumar Hettiarachchi (Shanthi), a Sri Lankan-born Christian (with significant empathy towards Buddhism), Islam was something initially in his life quite remote and puzzling. Moreover, the 'reification' of the Qur'an is as puzzling and disturbing to him as the 'deification' of Jesus is to Sughra Ahmed, his dialogue partner. (Shanthi observes that the deification of Jesus is also puzzling to some Christians!) He writes: 'All peoples, cultures and religions are fallible by definition. Even the theological notion of revelation operates under historical contingency. How can it be that the meaning of the whole is wholly represented, contained or reflected solely in one moment of historical vulnerability?' That observation, *concerning the Qu'ran*, underscores a hugely important theme that we will return to, a theme running through many of the Jewish and Christian contributions to the book and 'unpacked' by Alan Race. It is there, perhaps in more subtle form, in some of the other Muslim contributions, notably in Ataullah Siddiqui's, and in the probing of Elizabeth Sarah. In fact, how believers in dialogue regard the linked issues of revelation, the role and authority of our respective scriptures and the absolutism of beliefs in our three traditions proves to be the most troubling and yet exciting common task between us.

Shanthi is much impressed by the 'meticulous discipline of prayer' within the Islamic tradition – as is Sughra with the centrality of love in the Christian tradition. However, he is troubled by the lack of 'owned' symbolism in Islam and tries to find it in facing the Ka'ba in prayer. Eavesdropper Miriam Berger points out that Islam shares with Judaism a clear and

249

Beyond the Dysfunctional Family

distinct determination not to portray or symbolise God. That points to a very important discussion: is it possible to avoid the operation of a symbol system within religious conviction, even as we protest against any human or worldy 'depiction' of the divine? Still more crucially, Miriam points out the importance of acknowledging the pre-judgements we bring to dialogue and the imperative of trying to stand in the shoes of the other. That way leads to positive change for all of us.

Finally Shanthi addresses two fears in the western world which have arisen through world political circumstances: the Islamic revolution in Iran and the 'terror-induced chaos' caused by Al Qaeda. He acknowledges the effect of the 'War on Terror' and the media's negative approach to Islam as having placed many Muslims in a terrible situation and laments the insufficiency of dialogue, of what he calls 'decent conversations'.

Sughra agrees: 'Religions often find themselves betrayed by the very people who claim most vociferously that they follow the faith in truth and are the closest to the teachings of the Prophets who bring messages of love, mercy, honour and justice.' But she sees the greatest challenge as coming not from those who pervert their faith tradition but from secular ideology.

The rise of so-called secularism, fears about religiously-motiovated terrorism and the role of religion in public life are a troubling bundle of issues fiercely argued over in present day discussions with the so-called New Atheists and others. They are analysed further by Alan and come close to the central concerns of this book. Suffice it to say that it is the Christian-Muslim dialogue which brings these issues out into the open.

Norman Solomon and Abdul Jalil Sajid become embroiled, as Marcus Braybrooke points out with characteristic gentleness but clarity, in historical disputes. Much of their respective contributions are devoted to the long and complex historical relationship between Judaism and Islam. We have already noted that Muhammad was not supported by the 'Jewish tribes' amongst whom he lived and worked. Jews play, for Norman, an ambiguous role in the Qur'an which Abdul Jalil, always

Differences and Common Ground

committed to positive and fruitful relations between Jews and Muslims, is determined to see as much more straightforwardly positive than ambiguous.

Norman describes the experience of Jews over more than a thousand years as a minority in Muslim lands as 'good times and bad': 'Jewish attitudes to Islam and to Muslims have ebbed and flowed with the changing conditions.' Abdul Jalil, on the other hand, stresses the historic commonality between the two communities and regards the deterioration in relationships as a function of 'the dominance and control of the Western powers'. The 'dark-shadows' of the present-day Middle East crisis are seen against that background too.

Reverting back to the dialogue between Shanthi and Sughra, it is Sughra who refers briefly to the crusades and the history of Muslim-Christian relations. The dimension of history which is so present in the Jewish-Christian and Jewish-Muslim relationship is also present as a potent force in the Christian-Muslim bilateral dialogue – but far less openly acknowledged, at least in this book. Meanwhile, we can ask: why is it that the Muslim-Jewish dialogue seems scarcely able to rise above the tragic relationships of the past and present? The dialogue reflected in the short exchange here is indicative of much Muslim-Jewish conversation more generally.

Finally, we turn to the bilateral dialogue between Rachel Benjamin and Jane Clements, with Humera Khan reflecting as the eavesdropper. Rachel details the characteristics of the moderate, liberal Jewish attitude towards Christianity in Britain today. She acknowledges the role of a desperately difficult 2,000 year old history (though, as Michael pointed out, not without its light as well as its terrible shade) and the lack of realism in expecting it to be easily, if ever, completely put behind us. She acknowledges the problems on the Jewish side of diminishing numbers, lack of self-confidence and suspicion. She identifies the theological challenges emanating from Christianity – supersessionism, for example – and makes the important point, taken up by Tony later, that Christians

251

Beyond the Dysfunctional Family

need to recognise Jews and Judaism as distinctive and not as forerunners of a later Christianity.

Jane responds with deep empathy and understanding, acknowledging the role of history. She also acknowledges Elizabeth anxiety about the bifurcation in the Christian approach to Judaism and the lack of penetration of new attitudes into the grass roots. 'One reason for this sense of retreat may be that, having for centuries been the default position of most people in Britain, Christianity now finds itself with an identity crisis. Not only must it compete with a rapid secularisation of society, but it must also stand its corner alongside other faith communities. This crisis of confidence has led to a sense of the "re-affirmation" of Christian identity in recent years. One of the casualties of this process has been the removal of any sense of collective guilt for centuries of anti-Judaic teachings.'

But empathy would not be true empathy without some questioning of the 'other' as well. 'Yes', says Jane, 'everything that you say Rachel is correct. But are Jews also prepared to be open, engaged and receptive to dialogue?'

This is a reminder of the Jewish tendency to present a shopping list of demands to Christians, to be enthusiastic about explaining and teaching about Judaism, but to be less interested in finding out about Christianity. It is a reference to a slowness, even refusal, to engage in *theological* dialogue, which is a feature of some currents of Judaism in Britain today. The relationship, says Jane, cannot go forward on the basis of guilt alone. It also demands an engagement with and a sharing of those things which are most important to both parties.

Humera's reaction to this conversation is wonderfully clarifying. She points out the special nature of the relationship between Judaism and Christianity, its intimacy, its sibling nature. She says with the utmost honesty: 'I have not always found it easy being on the outside of Jewish-Christian dialogue primarily because it is not directly part of my personal history nor is it central to my sense of self. I have said in many dialogue groups, as a second generation British Muslim of Pakistani

252

Differences and Common Ground

heritage, I struggle with my own history and so do not always have the space to immerse myself in someone else's.'

In listening to the Rachel-Jane conversation she veers from empathy to frustration, as the apparent ignoring of the Muslim here and now gradually dawns. She struggles with the word 'alien' and asks: 'how can we say we are from the Abrahamic family and then say that our faiths are 'alien' to each other?' She feels marginalised, unequal. Her Muslim identity (spiritual, historic and political) seems not fully acknowledged.

Humera's experience of as being somehow a Muslim 'add-on' to a long-running Jewish-Christian bilateral conversation in one sense raises the question of the credibility of our 'Abrahamic' dialogue project. Yet it is also symptomatic of the complexities of relationships which are many-sided. All three traditions bring their 'baggage' to the dialogue table as well as their aspirations for a different future and a desire to grasp new opportunities beyond past antagonisms. There are relationships within relationships, and our dialogue perhaps needs to become more sophisticated if it is to do justice to the realities of history. For all our parts, there is also the need to transcend victimhood, if we are to escape the captivities of the past. As Humera says: 'Dialogue, as Jane and Rachel's essay reflect, can only be meaningful when we come to the table as equals.'

PART THREE: DEVELOPING AND CLARIFYING THE THEMES

For us, as editors, what emerges from the discussions of Part II is confirmation of the rejection of the view that 'all religions are essentially the same and should be viewed and categorised through a common lens, a single pro-forma'. But what we also reject is the notion of exclusive difference which should simply be respected and accepted. If the epithet 'Abrahamic' is not intended to mix up the three traditions, neither does it condemn us to life in confined spaces. Moreover, although our dialogue has concentrated on the impact of our different historical

Beyond the Dysfunctional Family

developments, we are also mindful that dialogue which does not include core beliefs – engagement with the authority of Torah, the Qur'an and the divinity of Christ – simply isn't dialogue.

Furthermore, the metaphor of dysfunctional family, whatever its limitations, is proving helpful. We are neither identical triplets nor polite strangers who pass in the night. The life blood of birth, shared history and constant interaction demands an honest and creative response, which is always painful and risky.

In reflecting on Part III let us start with difference or, better, distinctiveness – that which insists we are not identical twins but siblings with, in the cases of Judaism and Christianity, two shared parents and, in the case of Islam, one shared parent. Tony Bayfield, Alan Race and Ataullah Siddiqui each have their individual particularities which, though personal and idiosyncratic, can stand as metaphors to remind us that each faith (and even the term 'faith' may be a compromise) is unique in itself.

Alan articulates an impatience with the past, a feature which many Christians may share but feel too insecure in dialogue to express. He doesn't put it quite as baldly but it goes something like this. 'For the last sixty years our most significant other, our Jewish sibling, has been hitting us over the head with responsibility for anti-Judaism, anti-Semitism and anti-Semitism in the guise of anti-Israel sentiments. We have been so shamed that it is hard to retain self-respect. Now, along come the Muslims and one can't have any kind of conversation without being hit over the head by them and just as hard. Ten minutes into any dialogue and up come the Crusades, 300 years of humiliation experienced during the gradual decline of the Ottoman Empire and the imperialism and colonial arrogance of the allegedly Christian West. Can Christianity – never mind my generation of Christians – be held responsible for all the woes of Judaism, Islam and the world?'

We think that the question should be allowed to hang in the air because it is a valid question even if it springs from frustration and impatience.

254

Differences and Common Ground

Tony Bayfield's comparable frustration is very different. He insists that Zionism – the right of Jews to a land of their own somewhere within the historic borders of the biblical land – has a theological as well as pragmatic dimension. Judaism, he claims, has a geography as well as a history. The re-establishment of the state represented the opening of a new paradigm in Jewish history and presents a *religious* challenge to both Christianity and Islam. Told that this is a far less palatable or even comprehensible piece of particularism than his more attractive liberal universalism, he stamps his foot somewhat petulantly and says that if you don't accept him as a package then you don't really love him.

Ataullah's particularism, his 'otherness', is differently expressed but equally dramatic. For him what is most tragic about the situation of contemporary Islam is the intercession of seekers after power between the individual and the text; the seizure of a wonderfully humane, sensitive and endlessly open interpretative tradition by those who tell their fellow Muslims what it is that they must believe. It is this politicisation, this abuse of power, which has leached from Islam the personal spiritual dimension which is what Islam means to him and many others.

What is perhaps idiosyncratic is that Ataullah does not address directly the challenge of Islamic fundamentalism, the vision of world domination expressed by a small but attention-claiming minority through the doctrine of the Caliphate. Nor does he write at length about the seeming inability of the Arab world to find a form of government which is neither a theocratic nor secular dictatorship. Instead, he focuses on the role of the Muslim as a minority citizen of secular, democratic Europe. In a subtle and restrained way Ataullah is wonderfully eloquent about his vision for Islam and the way forward.

In no sense are we the same. Christianity, so anxious not to be captive to the past; Judaism, with its highly inconvenient sense of geography as well as history; Islam, so alienated from a West to which it has contributed so much, are different in both form and substance. Yet we are related in every aspect of our being and bound together by the challenge of present and future.

Beyond the Dysfunctional Family

CITIZENS OF THE SECULAR, DEMOCRATIC STATE AND HAPPY TO BE SO

There is one particular tune which plays a number of times in Parts I and II of the book which Alan, Tony and Ataullah turn into a major theme. We are – Jews, Christians and Muslims – citizens of Britain and very happy to be so. Anti-Semitism and Islamophobia persist but we all, it seems, want to be here. Opinion formers within British society have moved on a long way since Norman Tebitt's obtuse cricket test and the concept of multiple identities suits us just fine. We want desperately to contribute as Jews, as Christians, as Muslims. We want to work together as mainstream exponents of essentially liberal religious traditions. We wish to play a significant part in the building of a just, equitable, open and tolerant Europe, a Europe composed of nation states which preserve their particular traditions but collaborate. We make that last point about secular, democratic states preserving their particular traditions because it is clear that most, if not all, of the Jewish and Muslim voices acknowledge, either explicitly or implicitly, the Christian history and ethos of Britain and have no wish to eliminate Christmas or silence church bells. The Jews and Muslims ask only for respect for their independent traditions, the right to practice them according to their own rhythm as freely as the larger Christian community and the opportunity to contribute to society.

Here Alan and Tony become specific in embracing the concept of the public square. They refute the accusation that religion has no place in the public square because the discussion would allegedly be halted by a veto before it begins. Rather they affirm that democracy is synonymous with discussion. They ask how that process of discussion might be institutionalised – through establishing a contract or compact or covenant? Through some form of consultative body? Through an effective public space which can accommodate both intra- and inter-religious differences and also give effect to the many shared values and aspirations expressed in this book?

Differences and Common Ground

Tony approaches this last point in a particular way. He argues that the rise and rise of religious fundamentalism – not just in the three Abrahamic faiths – over the last half of the twentieth century has not only disfigured the world with its perversion of the faiths that it purports to represent but has also caused untold damage to the faiths and to religion itself – for which we, mainstream liberals must take our full measure of blame. Dilwar makes the identical point. We have all done, for quite different social and historic reasons, far too little to combat extremism. That said, we move now to the heart of 'our message'.

NO-ONE HAS A HOTLINE TO GOD

It is Alan who cuts to the chase and articulates clearly the core of this book. He moves us from the past and says that all the anguish over history is displaced angst for a religious world view under threat.

He is certainly right that the fundamentalist perversions of religion (Tony), the perpetration of violence in the name of religion (Alan), the disastrous politicisation (Dilwar) and seizure of power (Ataullah) by radicals, the retrenchment (Elizabeth) by conservative forces, have their roots in the shaking of old beliefs and their reassertion in a banal and obtusely literalist form. This has fed a sinister lust to proclaim absolute Truths as the word of God which can therefore be imposed upon others by whatever means, however unethical. Alan argues with penetrating insight and conviction that at the core of the dilemma of religion today *is the need to renounce absolutism.*

He writes: 'Having to deal with religiously motivated violence could be thought to be, at one level, a distraction from the real business of interreligious dialogue. But once enquiry uncovers some of the religious factors at work within such violence it is far from a distraction. The real culprit, however, is that sense of religious superiority over the "ownership" of salvation, and which is generally thought to be intrinsic to religious identity and absolutism.'

Beyond the Dysfunctional Family

He poses the question that raises the *sine qua non* of real, progressive dialogue: 'Do we accept one another as valid theologically and religiously? And are we able to say that, even though we are simultaneously puzzled by some of the substantive matters that we each affirm?'

Bayfield expressly and clearly agrees, arguing for a much greater degree of philosophical humility within each faith, for an acceptance that none of us has Truth with a capital T, but only fragments of truth – fragments of truth which have particular affinities within the Abrahamic family by virtue of the family ties. Ataullah affirms more obliquely: 'Allow the individual Muslim to engage directly with the Qur'an as a spiritual rather than political text.' Absolutism – we have a monopoly on truth, ours is the only way – has to go. At one level, this is of course simply a function of the provisionality of the human condition.

MODERNITY, POSTMODERNITY, SECULARITY: FRIEND OR FOE?

Tony is the most explicitly positive about modernity (and postmodernity). He recognises the inroads made by secularism but embraces what he explicitly terms the *revelations* of modernity. These include the understanding that many of the old Truths were only partial truths, that the faiths can only authentically exist today in relationship to each other and that the power of faith wedded to the power of the State is too much to be held by the same hands. For Tony, Alan and Ataullah, engagement with the 'fourth dialogue partner', acknowledging the rich but acutely challenging culture called secularity or modernity or postmodernity or 'the west' – to which we have all contributed and to which we all wish to contribute – is not just threatening but also exhilarating. In fact, the extent of agreement amongst the contributors to this book is quite remarkable. It manifests both in the desire to contribute ethical values to our society and in the yearning for a spirituality and experience of a God who is not exclusive or totalitarian.

258

Differences and Common Ground

We should, however, add that for British Jews and Christians the challenge is considerable but one we have worked at over many decades. For British Muslims the challenge is far greater. Ataullah shows enormous courage in focusing on a vision and task of immense proportions. It is no less than the reframing of the Muslim identity as collaborative citizens of modern, western, secular democracy and recasting Islam as a faith of depth and wisdom for the individual rather than the tool of those in search of power or bemused by the indignity heaped on Islam by history.

FAITHS AND POWER

It is fascinating how we have come to these points from radically different positions with regard to power. The Christians have come from the shock of having lost power but not wanting to retreat into theocracy. The Muslims come – with almost a sense of liberation – to the challenge of affirming the values of Islam whilst experiencing something new, living as a minority within Europe. The Jews come from 2,000 years of powerlessness, in which they had to manipulate the system in order to survive, to the challenge of surviving as a free, if tiny, minority and also as a people inextricably bound up with those facing the extraordinary challenge of exercising power presented by the state of Israel.

Ridding our faiths of absolutism, coming to terms with the new realities of power, re-engaging with society and its challenges, reaffirming the spiritual dimension of life and doing things together, the tunes become major themes. But stop.

DON'T GET TOO TRIUMPHANT

Elli is a champion of the outsider but who nevertheless operates from the inside. She has survived several decades of confronting colleagues with perspectives that most of us miss most of the time. She has fulfilled that role tenaciously within our group for many years. Her place at this point is crucial.

Beyond the Dysfunctional Family

First she quotes the American Jewish feminist intellectual, Susannah Heschel: 'How am I to engage in theological discussion if I believe my partner in dialogue is engaging in oppressive and immoral subjugation of women? Moreover, being a woman in the context of theological discussion automatically puts one in a position of alterity; how am I to represent a tradition that has failed to represent me? Am I expected to speak in the name of a tradition that has excluded and oppressed me?' In the face of furrowed brows and objections that much progress has been made or 'we are much more egalitarian than you think', Elli challenges us most succinctly in her own words: 'Just because I, the rabbi, who is also a woman, participate on equal terms with my male colleagues – and meet other religious representatives, Muslim, Christian and Jewish, on equal terms – *this doesn't make the ground on which we stand together any the less patriarchal.'*

Secondly, she returns to her critique of the formulation of 'Abrahamic faiths', 'which, by definition, marginalises the perspectives and experiences of Jewish, Christian and Muslim women', and calls on us 'to journey together, as women and men, towards a new terrain of Jewish, Christian and Muslim encounter.'

New terrain? She challenges us with the implications of the shift from modernity to postmodernity, with its plural approaches to existence that encompass subjectivity, multiple-perspectives and truths. Here Elli is at one with Alan and his call for the abandonment of absolutism and with Tony in his plea for much greater humility.

Elli goes on to observe that, by definition, dialogue takes place in 'border-land country with participants moving from the centre to the edge of their respective traditions'. What we say is important but does anyone listen? She asks: 'What changes need to take place to enable those who are not engaged in interfaith encounter to listen to the voices of those *who can only say what they say because they have been listening to one another?'*

Elli is far from sure that the contributors to this book and those like us can readily influence the mainstream, still less move interreligious dialogue to the mainstream. But she is

Differences and Common Ground

certain that whatever can be achieved can only be achieved through education. Indeed, every contributor to this book would agree that education – and new forms of dialogically-focused, post-modern education – is key. Yet the word education has not featured large up to now. It will certainly need to appear significantly in the recommendations with which the process and this book conclude.

Elli rightly mutes any triumphalist conclusions, underlines the provisionality of the place we have reached so far, and highlights the immense challenges that lie ahead. The future of interreligious dialogue will not be able to ignore her probing and prophetic call.

CONCLUSIONS

There are some major themes which, though played on different instruments by the three faiths, are common and encouragingly so. But each includes a significant degree of uncertainty, pain and messiness which it is important to acknowledge. Let us offer the following brief concluding summary. Somewhat arbitrarily, we have identified seven points:

(1) We are now all minorities in Britain and that draws us closer together. We all experience ourselves as minorities under pressure. Particularly in terms of numbers, the Jews will raise their eyebrows and mutter 'if you think you've got problems' (in Britain, there are roughly only 267,000 Jews), but minorities we are in a secular environment. We see secularity/modernity both as a major threat, when it presents itself also as a new exclusivist absolutism, as well as a potentially exhilarating and even revelatory presence.

The Muslims and Jews see themselves as victims and struggle to recognise that a competition for victimhood is not the best recipe for being contributing citizens of Britain and Europe.

Christians and Jews find it hard to recognise just how challenging life is for Muslims. They need to read and re-read

Beyond the Dysfunctional Family

Dilwar and Ataullah, acknowledge the courage of these authors and the enormity of the task they set the multiple Muslim communities of Britain today.

We are all fearful – of anti-Semitism, of Islamophobia and of secular fundamentalism – of the way religion is often misconstrued at the beginning of the 21st century. Whilst recognising the traps of assumed victimhood, Christians and Muslims should not lose sight of the fact that it is only Jewish institutions – synagogues and schools – that have to be guarded by their own members and parents.

We all have a sense of loss, some of power, some of old certainties, some of threatened heritages. Loss is endemic in the exponential rise in the pace of change. Yet we recognise that loss is inevitable because we cannot afford 'to pay the ever increasing price of remaining the same'.[2]

We struggle with identity – what does it mean to be a Jew or a Christian or a Muslim today? – and with the complexities of multiple-identities.

(2) We are each experiencing bifurcation. We are under pressure because we are each minorities, even within our respective Jewish, Christian and Muslim communities, and the border-lands are a frustrating and pressurising place to live. Nevertheless, we acknowledge the strength and richness that lies in our situation of post-modernist pluralism. The fact that no one has a monopoly on truth and there is no one way of walking the Jewish/Christian/Muslim walk is liberating.

But we are deeply disturbed by those who will not continue the journey that is faith but seek stasis; and by those who have retrenched, turned back, retreated into an illusory world of fake certainty with the arrogance, the hubris of their hotline to God. We could wish that our institutions be prepared to exercise more courage in this matter.

(3) We are people of faith, determined that our faiths and traditions shall continue. The nature of faith has undergone

Differences and Common Ground

radical change but that is not necessarily a bad thing. Faith needs to connect imaginatively with the spiritual searchings alive in society at large, and it has much to offer in terms of connectedness, meaning and being willing to approach some of the mysteries of existence itself.

Given that faith is not, for any of us, a matter divorced from society and its values, we are committed therefore to our religious purpose which is variously described as 'repairing the world' (Jewish), 'building the kingdom of God' (Christian) and 'creating a just world' (Muslim). We are committed to negotiating with government and society ways in which both individually and collectively we can be constructively part of civil society, a lively voice in democratic discussion, and contribute to the national debate.

(4) We are deeply pained by the patriarchal nature of our respective traditions. It is reflected in the language of those traditions and the way in which God is conceptualised and spoken of. It is present in the way power is exercised within many of our institutions. Above all, there is the undeniable fact that we stand, even as individuals determinedly committed to equality, on traditions fashioned largely by men, which subordinated and often excluded the potential contribution of women. We are still the three children of *Abraham* and the process of transformation has much further to go.

(5) We recognise that it is both our task to affirm and also to be critical of our respective religious traditions. The challenge of dialogue brings us to the threshold of some fundamental theological questions. In particular it demands a renunciation of absolutism – whatever form that absolutism takes in our particular tradition – and the recognition that what each of us witnesses to is but a fragment of truth, each fragments of incalculable value but fragments nevertheless. Our theologies must express a greater humility and much more respect for the other.

Beyond the Dysfunctional Family

In particular, we have done far too little to stand up to the extremists and fundamentalists whose perversion of faith threatens both the peace of the world and the good name of religion.

(6) We see interfaith dialogue as neither peripheral nor a luxury but as an imperative of our times. It is in engaging with others and building trust at the deepest level that we are all transformed. Dialogical commitment is both a place in which we can deepen our understanding of God and a place in which we can learn how to behave better towards each other and thereby work together not just for the benefit of society but also for our own personal, spiritual development. One of the keys to interreligious dialogue is education and in evolving new materials and new approaches for interfaith dialogue we can develop materials that can contribute to new and better forms of relating within society at large.

(7) Dialogue has taught us that there is no substitute for the quality of relationships. Even after many years of engaged dialogue there is much the group has never discussed – the nature of our personal faith itself, for instance. But learning to stand in the shoes of the other, striving to understand what causes the other pain, trusting, caring, listening out for the echoes of divine life in one another – there is no substitute for that.

Of course we acknowledge just how hard it is to stand in each other's shoes and see the world through the eyes of the other:

- for Christians and Muslims to understand the obsession of Jews with numbers and the psychological implications of so much victimhood;
- for Jews and Christians to understand Humera's cry of pain and the enormity of the task set by Ataullah and Dilwar;
- for Muslims and Jews to grasp Christian fears for the future of a society in which the heart remains stirred by Blake's Jerusalem ('and was the holy lamb of God …'), the landscape

Differences and Common Ground

defined by ancient churches and the Cup Final evoked by the singing of a Christian hymn.

How else but through dialogue – a dialogue of respect for equals about those things that matter to us most – can we embrace the other and see ourselves more honestly? Is that not a task in which every Jew, Christian and Muslim can participate?

It all sounds very serious. But we have learned to tease each other and to laugh at ourselves in the presence of the other. 'Love, trust and laughter' may not be the key to unlock all the secrets of the universe but they are essential to interfaith relations.

NOTES

1. Leonard Swidler (1990) *After the Absolute: the Dialogical Future of Religious Reflection.* Minneapolis: Fortress Press. p. xi.
2. Norman Mailer.

PART FIVE

Looking to the Future

12

The Platform Statement (2005) – a Staging Post

A Group Agreement (1)

Our dialogue as Jews, Christians and Muslims has embraced issues of historical and political legacy, interrogation over beliefs and practices, anxieties about survival and present-day dialogical mutual learning, the place of interreligious cooperation in public life, puzzles about 'otherness' and religious absolutism, the rise of religiously-motivated violence in our day, and many other matters. This is can be hardly surprising, given that dialogue involves the whole of what it means to be religious. The period following 9/11, however, has involved all religious communities in profound searching, having to face disturbing questions about why religion can become so entangled with violence. 9/11 was connected with Islam, but the fact is that none of us can claim immunity from having been or having become embroiled in violence. This Platform Statement represents the first attempt at summarising the fruits of dialogical endeavour after a prolonged discussion about the relationship between religious commitment, truth, violence and interreligious dialogue.

It represents a staging post on the way to deeper dialogical encounter. In this sense it was 'truth for the moment' and involved the members of our group who are named at the end of the Statement. Since then some members of the group have either died or ceased their membership. But the issues with which it wrestles are still with us and have found their way into the substance of our dialogue reflected in the pages of this book. Therefore the present members of the group are happy to endorse the Platform Statement as a record of those people at that time and are grateful for the work which was done to that

Beyond the Dysfunctional Family

point, recognising that not every word would be repeated by everyone who has participated in the group which has produced the present book.

We reproduce the Statement here also as a means of honouring dialogue partners who have contributed to the momentum of the group over many years.

Unwelcome and Welcome Truths
a Platform Statement from a Dialogue Group of Jews, Christians and Muslims

UNWELCOME TRUTHS

While rejecting the widespread notion that religion is always and necessarily divisive, we believe that Jews, Christians and Muslims should acknowledge some unwelcome truths:

1. At various times in history relations between the three communities have been marred by discrimination and violence, and within each community religion has also been a source of sectarian strife.

2. In Jewish, Christian and Muslim scriptures and traditions one can find passages that have often been interpreted to support exclusive truth claims and a sense of superiority.

3. In practice, each faith has been notably self-centred and lacking in self-criticism, claiming for itself a superior position and a unique authority. Humility has often been notably lacking, and in its place arrogance and triumphalism have been all too evident.

THE DANGER

There is a real danger now that these unwelcome truths, combined with political injustice, human rights abuses, poverty,

The Platform Statement

hatred, fear, ignorance, globalisation, war as an instrument of imperial policy, and the failure to respect international legal or ethical principles, will aggravate conflicts, intolerance, and even anarchy around the world.

THE REMEDY

Jews, Christians and Muslims must not allow their religion to be abused in this way by exclusivist ideologues. We must make a stand together for peace, understanding, compassion and justice. We must welcome religious diversity and concede that no single religion can claim a monopoly of Truth. We must each put our own house in order, recognising what we have in common, accepting that our scriptures and histories are interconnected, and acknowledging our interdependence. Each faith has its contribution to make both separately and together: indeed, at this era in history we need each other far more than in the past, and the future of our world demands that we teach to our communities the value and benefits of dialogue, co-operation and interdependence.

WELCOME TRUTHS

Jews, Christians and Muslims can be inspired to change their mind-sets for the better by considering the following welcome truths:

1. We worship and serve the God who created and sustains the universe, the One God of Abraham, Moses, Jesus and Muhammad. Behind our differences lies the unity of the One.

2. We share the same general code of ethics, which condemns murder, theft and adultery, and demands that we secure the rights of those who have been denied their rights, to care for those in need, the sick, the suffering, the widow and the orphan, to welcome the stranger, the outcast and the persecuted, and to offer shelter and refuge to the homeless and the dispossessed.

Beyond the Dysfunctional Family

3. Each of us inherits a broad and rich religious tradition within which many different views can coexist.

WHAT WE BELIEVE

We believe that:

1. Religious and cultural diversity should be valued and celebrated, in the full knowledge that each faith tradition is unique and invaluable.

2. As human beings with human limitations, we will never be able to grasp the full meaning of the Truth or comprehend God's nature.

3. Our respective religious traditions are capable of exploring the implications of new insights and dilemmas presented by modern science and technology and that we have a duty to reinterpret our religion with this aim in mind.

4. Our religious scriptures must not be used in a simplistic way; they need careful interpretation, bearing in mind both their historical context and their relevance to present needs.

5. Our religious traditions can best flourish in just, pluralistic and democratic societies, where there is freedom of worship and where the rights of all individuals are respected.

6. Missionary work which provokes antagonism and resentment should be strongly discouraged.

7. God is the true Owner of everything, that we are finite, and that all that we have is a loan or gift from God; we therefore have a duty to look after this planet and protect its natural resources and its variety of interdependent life forms, for the sake of future generations.

8. The sanctity of all life is defiled by war, terrorism, genocide, torture, rape, extra-judicial killings, and detention without trial.

9. Scripture should not be used to justify violence, oppression, exploitation, military aggression, or claims of superiority.

The Platform Statement

10. That which binds us to God also binds us to one another as a single human family.

WHAT NEEDS TO BE DONE?

1. There is a desperate need for education in Judaism, Christianity and Islam. Too many are ignorant of the teachings of their own faith, and know even less about the other faiths. Our day schools and religious institutions have a duty to teach not only adherence to our own traditions but also knowledge of other traditions, placing special emphasis on the ethical aspects and what they have in common.

2. Through school programmes and the mass media, social harmony should be promoted by making us more aware of the contribution to civilisation made by other religions, cultures and civilisations.

3. Jews, Christians and Muslims should work together as equal partners. Equal respect and theological space should be accorded to each faith. A just and peaceful world can only be achieved in partnership.

4. Jewish, Christian and Muslim scholars should be made more aware of their duty to demonstrate how their sacred texts and religious traditions are relevant to current needs.

5. Since it is God's will that we should strive to become, as best we can, the servants of his love and compassion, we should seek to resolve disputes by means of forgiveness, empathy and reconciliation, and encourage others to do the same. We should all be able to answer affirmatively the question posed by the other: "Do you know what causes me pain?"

6. We should refute exclusivist perversions of Judaism, Christianity and Islam that glorify war and aggressive behaviour, and we should condemn those who spread false stereotypes of the Other.

7. We, as Jews, Christians and Muslims, have a duty to challenge the misuse of power and to demand that governments tackle

Beyond the Dysfunctional Family

the roots of terrorism, using diplomacy as a first resort, with respect for human dignity, human rights and the due process of law. We have a duty to defend the right to asylum where this is wrongfully withheld, and to seek to abide by ethical and humanitarian principles both at home and abroad.

8. We have a duty to truth and reconciliation which demands of us that we recognise we are all the victims of different and irreconcilable accounts of current and past public events, and that only together can we build shared narratives based on accurate testimony and records.

We can only achieve our vision of a repaired and transformed world by pooling the best of our respective teachings and talents in partnership and shared endeavour. Only full and effective partnership can end conflict and bring peace, with opportunities to ponder together the wonder of creation and the mystery of God.

SIGNATORIES:

Jewish:
Rabbis Tony Bayfield, Michael Hilton, Jonathan Magonet, Elizabeth Tikvah Sarah, Norman Solomon

Christian:
Revds Eric Allen, John Bowden, Marcus Braybrooke, Alan Race, Dr Jenny Sankey

Muslim:
Mr Rumman Ahmed, Dr Roger Abdul Wahhab Boase, Imam Abdul Jalil Sajid, Dr Ataullah Siddiqui

13

Recommending a Way Forward

A Group Agreement (2)

1. PREAMBLE

1.1 Attitude to modernity and contemporary culture

We live in a modern, western, liberal democracy with a strong secular ethos. All of these five terms are less well defined than many of us might like but we are agreed that they characterise the culture in which we live. It is a culture which both offers many opportunities and throws down some significant challenges to aspects of our respective faith traditions. We are a group that welcomes the opportunities and the challenges, and recognizes their impact on the development of our respective faiths. In fact, all three of our faiths have contributed extensively to modern, western culture and we very much want them to continue to do so.

Sadly, the world in which we live often looks bleak and depressing. The decline of the religious perspective on life may not have helped but neither have fundamentalist distortions of religion, in our three faiths in particular.

1.2 Attitude to disillusionment with religion and global despair

The world needs a renewed sense of hope. Offering hope should come naturally to the followers of our three religions. Our raison d'être is to provide hope. Those of us who have been involved in this dialogical engagement over many years believe that our religions share a prophetic understanding of God as the One who calls, leads and sustains people in their efforts to build the good society, a society based on justice, peace and compassion for one another and for the world. However, we also recognize

Beyond the Dysfunctional Family

that it is possible to be caught in a spiral of despair about the future such that all life force is drained from us. As a group, we have found renewal of hope through dialogue.

1.3 Attitude to dialogue

In this book we have been responding to one another out of our respective traditions as individuals and not as representatives of our faiths. Our dialogue over the years has taught us that while it is essential to be empathetic and receptive to the feelings of our dialogue partners, it is also to the good that we are frank and critical when necessary. We have come to the conclusion that such engagement is essential for religious commitment and understanding in the future. The integrity of Judaism, Christianity and Islam is increased by virtue of active engagement with one another.

We have also learned that while we are engaged in dialogue with members of other faiths, we are at once engaged in intra-faith dialogue with those from our own tradition and in an internal search for new meanings and understandings in our respective faiths in the light of new encounters. Thus we develop both through the self-examination that dialogue prompts and through the new dimensions to faith that we learn from our partners.

1.4 The need for concrete proposals

The following outline recommending a way forward builds on our 'Platform Statement' of 2005 (see p. 270) and extends it as a result of our continuing experience of dialogue itself. We believe that a programme of action is needed and the following recommendations represent achievable aims.

2. FOR OUR RESPECTIVE FAITHS AND THEIR LEADERSHIPS

2.1 Positive engagement with contemporary culture

Our faiths must work together to ensure that all three continue to play a significant role in the development of contemporary

Recommending a Way Forward

culture. We must do everything to enable our full and positive participation in Britain's public square [see below 3.2]. We must also redouble our efforts to engage with the development of global ethics and human rights. In particular, Jews and Christians need to assist Muslims in recognizing their contribution so far.

2.2 Leading change in attitudes with regard to other faiths and belief systems

Religious leadership plays an obvious, crucial role in both our respective traditions and society generally. While it is important to have a deep and thorough knowledge of faith, it is equally important that leaders should recognise that they cannot ignore the contextual reality in which we are all placed. The plural nature of society demands that religious leadership must acquire new skills, strategies and theological openness for the exercise of leadership in new situations. This entails that religious leaders must reflect on their respective religious texts with a keen generosity in respect of other faiths and engage with others as they wish themselves to be engaged with.

2.3 Rejecting absolutism

Perhaps the most radical and far reaching conclusion of more than fifteen years of dialogue and the writing of this book is the conclusion that progress – in dialogue, in mutual understanding, in collaboration and in healing the rifts between the three Abrahamic faiths – lies in renouncing that form of religious absolutism which blocks any meaningful process of shared learning between us. However difficult it is to move beyond long-cherished articles of faith, the claim that we have a monopoly on truth or that our faith is somehow truer or better than the faith of our siblings – or that 'my faith' has the final word for everyone – is not compatible with the genuine respect which siblings demand. We must show far greater humility in our truth affirmations.

Beyond the Dysfunctional Family

2.4 Responding to the challenge inherent in the Hebrew Bible, the New Testament and the Qur'an

Our sacred scriptures all contain narratives and verses which are open to political exploitation and interpretation which justify violence, unethical behavior and disrespect. It is a matter of urgency and great importance that we find ways to prevent political manipulation, unethical interpretation and the presentation of a false picture of the values that our respective traditions embrace.

2.5 Developing genuine respect

Religious leaders, scholars and others must recognise that they need to compare and contrast Judaism, Christianity and Islam *in their entirety,* fully encompassing the history, culture and civilisational aspects of faith. Any inflated generalizations which do not take note of intra-religious pluralism will create enormous misunderstandings. We must learn to see the other as a richly-complex, global tradition and not as a simplified, distorted stereotype which is four-square with our particular model of faith – only inferior. We must also be constantly aware that culture, history and practice frequently fail to match the religious ideals of our own faith – as well as others.

2.6 Tackling gender issues

Each of our three faiths has strongly patriarchal traditions. Modern culture has revealed the unacceptability of gender inequality based on religious patriarchy. In order to advance core values of justice and fairness it is essential that gender relationships in each of the faith traditions are fully appreciated and that due attention is given to changing patterns of relationships. This is significant for both internal and public life. There are inherited cultural and religious prejudices, particularly against women, which must be challenged. Even those who recognize the shortcomings of the past and have made radical change do not always give sufficient attention to the inescapable truth that we each stand on the shoulders of a patriarchal tradition.

Recommending a Way Forward

2.7 Developing greater insight into the way we tell our own narratives

We need to pay much more attention to our histories. Our three histories are inextricably interwoven and are deeply embedded in the world view of our respective faiths. We recount history very differently.

We have both to understand the way in which we employ history and rehearse our respective narratives through very specific lenses and also to learn from how others view the history of our relationships. This will enable us to appreciate the past without being confined to one view of it. Given that many conflicts in the present are fuelled by a partial view of history, adjusting to multiple perspectives will potentially bring a new awareness.

We have also to wrestle with the asymmetrical nature of our historical relationships, our differing contributions to conflict and violence within the Abrahamic family. In particular, we should exercise a degree of critical suspicion when it comes to theologies of triumphalism.

2.8 The impact of issues of power and numbers on our psychology

History in general and changes in relationship to power in particular have had a profound impact on our three faiths. The Christian community needs to work on the psychological implications of its loss of power in Britain. The Muslim community needs to work on what it means to live as minority citizens in a modern, western, liberal democracy. Britain's Jewish community has a complex but equally challenging and important task in considering its relationship to the exercise of power in the re-established state of Israel. Jews, Christians and Muslims need to reflect on the impact of that exercise of power on the image of the Jew and the reality of Jewish life in Britain.

We should not underestimate the psychological impact of the dialogue over the history of Christianity in relation to Judaism and Islam. Full and explicit acceptance of the past is, of course, necessary but there is a limit to how much guilt Christians of today's generation can deal with.

Beyond the Dysfunctional Family

At the present time it is accepted that there are roughly 2 billion Christians in the world, 1.4 billion Muslims and 14 million Jews. In Britain, according to the official 2001 Census figures, there are roughly 42 million Christians, 1.5 million Muslims and 267,000 Jews. While Census figures are by nature only rough estimates, and incorporate nominal as well as more active adherents, nevertheless Christians and Muslims need to reflect on this disparity and how it is reflected in Jewish concerns and psychological responses. On their part, Jews need to understand how justified anxieties about survival colour their approaches to dialogue and collaboration.

Muslims are the most recent of the three of us to life in modern, significantly secular Britain. Whilst their situation is in many ways familiar and not unique, it demands patience and understanding from Jews and Christians. We must stand shoulder to shoulder in rejecting and denouncing the Islamophobia that threatens so much of Muslim life in Britain today. It too has profound psychological consequences for Muslims.

Each group needs to be more aware of the implications of history, numbers and power for its own psychology. Each faith needs to be much more sensitive to the impact of history, numbers and power on the psychology of the other.

It is not helpful for each group to compete for the status of victim.

2.9 Interfaith collaboration and recent history

For apparently different reasons, each of our faiths has experienced a bifurcation, a dividing of the road we have been walking since 1945 towards interfaith and interethnic collaboration and harmony. Each faith includes significant numbers who have lost their nerve, retreated from the implications of a multi-faith and multi-cultural society and reasserted older, absolutist beliefs and views.

We have not been nearly as strong as we should have been in indicating just how damaging and dangerous this path, which ultimately leads backwards, has been and is. We are committed

Recommending a Way Forward

to continuing the forward march of interfaith conversation and collaboration with all their far reaching implications. We are deeply critical of fundamentalism and absolutism. We are clear that we represent not just the mainstream of religion but its only credible form and hope.

2.10 The centrality of education

Religious education plays a crucial role in our respective religious traditions. It is absolutely essential:

a) that we develop programmes of religious education for our respective faiths which produce people with strong cognitive and affective resources in the full range and richness of their own tradition. Such education must also emphasize religious pluralism and respect for diversity and difference. We must resist those whose approach is shallow, partial and doctrinaire.

b) that we develop educational programmes and tools to enable all within our communities to engage in dialogue. Learning how to stand in the shoes of the other and see how the world looks through their eyes must be given the highest possible priority.

c) that collaboration between Synagogue, Church and Mosque at a local level must also be actively and effectively encouraged. Education should be central and the development of educational tools to make the collaboration effective is vital.

2.11 The interfaith dimension of 'clergy' education

In order to generate trust and mutual respect, our experience tells us that creating partnerships for mutual learning between the theological schools and training institutions is essential. It is increasingly necessary to invite representatives from the different faith communities to give an account of their own religion. We recommend that Judaism and Islam be taught in Christian seminaries by Jews and Muslims respectively – with the same principle applying to Muslim and Jewish colleges. Furthermore, the theology of interfaith relations, interfaith dialogue and the engagement of faiths with contemporary

Beyond the Dysfunctional Family

culture and the institutions of the modern, western, democratic state should be obligatory aspects of clergy training.

2.12 Collaborating in areas of service to the community

One of the most useful ways of learning and engaging with one another is working together in situations of need and service. Chaplaincy – in public sector locations such as universities, prisons, hospitals, and work environments – is a good example where pastoral care displays the compassionate side of our faiths. Shared training in chaplaincy is necessary in order to match shared practice in public institutions. All three communities need to be given particular support by Government and the communities themselves, so that they can participate fully and not leave places with a vacuum to be filled by fundamentalists and extremists.

2.13 Our role in the public square

It would be difficult to overestimate the importance we place on our commitment to democracy and our participation and collaboration in what is often termed the 'public square'. We need to make it clear to ourselves and to others that it is a dual role. It is significantly a collaborative role vis-à-vis Government, engaging in conversation and debate about the values which govern public institutions and public policy. However, we also need to remind ourselves of our prophetic role, challenging the abuse of power, the exploitation of the individual and advocating for the poor, the dispossessed and the marginalized.

3. FOR GOVERNMENT AND BRITISH SOCIETY

3.1 Supporting and extending democracy

We have learned that democracy is discussion and debate rather than crude majoritarianism. Further, not least because of the much greater diversity of contemporary British society, renewed attention needs to be paid to the public square. Parliament and the media are vitally important but not, in themselves, sufficient.

Recommending a Way Forward

We are strongly opposed to theocracy as a form of Government in the modern world. History has demonstrated, time and again, that the concentration of religious and political power in the same hands is dangerous and unworkable. We are therefore supportive of the modern, western, liberal democracy which characterizes much of Europe, and not least Britain, whilst also reserving the right to offer critical responses in the face of democracy's inadequacies or failings, particularly in respect of being truly inclusive.

Since the second world war Britain has been transformed into a much more diverse society. All religious groupings are now minorities (albeit that Christians are by far the largest minority and, more than any other faith, have made and still make Britain, what it is today). Furthermore, public debate is increasingly polarised in the tussle for power between secular fundamentalism and religious fundamentalism.

In order to avoid this, Britain urgently needs to review the role of the faiths in discussions of public policy and develop an effective relationship with institutional public life in the twenty first century.

3.2 Making the public square real and effective

Given that all public policy is infused with values, public institutions and policy discussions cannot perpetuate the myth that the public square is supposedly 'neutral' in terms of its principles and values. Constant, detailed consultation and debate will be essential once this myth is identified.

To enable this process Government must establish mechanisms – perhaps additional institutions – in which consultation, discussion and debate can happen and to which it listens and responds. The discussion and debate will not, of course, be a solely religious one. It must include a range of ethical voices which have equal right to contribute. Of course not all voices will sound in harmony, but all need to be heard.

Faith communities themselves will not speak with one voice. Multiple perspectives are characteristic of all faiths today. This

Beyond the Dysfunctional Family

only adds to the richness of the debate, particularly because all mainstream exponents of the Abrahamic faiths speak out of long traditions of ethical reflection. The faiths have much to offer society particularly in the areas of social and economic justice, the values of mutual caring and compassion, and the vision of the good life.

As people of faith, we must recognize that in the public square we are obliged – as we always do – to exercise reason and that we have no power of veto. We have also to recognise that there are boundaries, beyond which we cannot go, in arguing for our position and limits to the extent to which we can seek to impose a view on others who do not share our values. Equally, society needs to be open to the possibility of granting faiths their own space and not having to abide exclusively by current, deeply held but contentious, secular values.

3.3 Supporting and encouraging integration rather than separation

We believe that it is of the utmost importance that faith groups are not under pressure to assimilate (i.e. lose their distinctive tradition and character). It is equally important that the faiths should integrate fully into society (i.e. participating and serving the whole of society, not just their own group). It is essential to us that we retain our rich traditions and distinctive identities. But equally we do not wish to live separate or 'parallel lives'.

It is for society to decide how much support it gives to those who do opt for a significant degree of separation and non-participation. However, we believe that Government should be positively encouraging the mainstream of the faiths, those who wish to deepen and strengthen their member's understanding of their own faith, so that they can collaborate and contribute to the building of the good society.

This means that we acknowledge the need felt some in all three religions for schools dedicated to the needs of their particular tradition, providing that the school takes the principles of religious pluralism and education about other faiths seriously, and fosters active engagement with children of other faiths, and

Recommending a Way Forward

indeed with children of no faith belonging, in collaborating for the good of society at large.

3.4 Considering contracts between faith groups and society

Given the importance of the underlying values of British society – democracy and equality for example – and given the rich and stimulating quality of multiple identities, serious consideration should be given to the development of explicit res publica 'contracts' with religious groups. Government could make explicit commitments to the faiths and the faiths could make explicit commitments to society.

3.5 Positive Government support for interfaith dialogue and collaboration

We believe that Government initiatives of recent years in Britain have begun to appreciate the value of interfaith dialogue and shared action. These need to be developed further. At the same time, it is necessary to move beyond the real but narrow concerns of national security in order to avoid the danger of 'co-option' of religion by Government and setting religions against one another.

We therefore urge that Government finds resources to support the educational initiatives set out above in 2.10 (a) and (b). It needs to continue to support and encourage local dialogue and collaboration initiatives as indicated in 2.10 (c). It needs to support and facilitate chaplaincy and other similar initiatives indicated in 2.12.

3.6 The place of both Christianity and Britain's minority faiths

We fully accept that the minority faiths need to respect the majority Christian history and culture of Britain and they should not collude with any secularization process which seeks to diminish it. But the faiths must also have every right to participate fully in society and live according to their own particular cultural rhythms. Christian festivals must be respected but Jews and Muslims should not be penalized, in

285

Beyond the Dysfunctional Family

employment for example, for observing their own customs and festivals. These are part of the cultural space we ask Government to maintain and protect.

3.7 Regulating the free market by values

Judaism, Christianity and Islam are not intrinsically wedded to any particular economic system. However, both the Hebrew and Christian Bibles, and the Qur'an, are deeply concerned with economic behaviour and insist that it should embody values of honesty and fairness. We are all deeply committed to economic as well as social justice. Recent history has taught us that free markets, unregulated by values and concerned only with individual liberty in the field of wealth creation, are a disaster. Government needs to work with the faith communities so as to ensure that whatever the economic system under which we live, it is regulated and governed by values.

3.8 Showing sensitivity to the impact of international events on national faith communities

One of the features of recent decades, reflecting the increasing diversity of the cultural inheritance of British citizens, is the impact of international events on British communities. We do not suggest that British foreign policy should be governed by its likely impact on British minority communities. However, Government needs to redouble its efforts to be sensitive to the consequences of international events for its multi-identity citizens. Engagement and understanding is crucial to the building of a cohesive society, the elimination of feelings of marginalization and victimhood.

4. FOR OURSELVES AS AN INTERFAITH GROUP AND ALL THOSE ENGAGED IN INTERFAITH WORK

4.1 This is a small beginning – there is so much more to do

We do not see this book and its recommendations as a once and for all blueprint. Interfaith dialogue is still in its infancy and those who engage in the work inevitably inhabit a borderland. There are many areas that require much further exploration. Communicating our insights to those who have chosen not to engage in the process or who do not have the opportunity to engage is an enormous challenge. This recognition is a recommendation in itself for redoubling efforts.

4.2 Those engaged in dialogue should practice what they preach with regard to social participation

Contemporary Britain is largely a secular, liberal society which provides a space where different religious voices can be heard. In principle, and the establishment of the Church of England notwithstanding, it prevents a particular group or faith tradition either from exercising a 'superior' influence or from claiming religious legitimacy in ways which lead to undemocratic action. However, people of faith have a religious obligation to hold power to account and become a prophetic voice for and on behalf of the whole of society, particularly those who are weak and vulnerable. Democracy guarantees the opportunity and Non-Governmental Organisations provide a platform for action. We encourage all those engaged in interfaith dialogue also to be involved actively and effectively in such organisations.

4.3 Dialogue must be extended beyond the three Abrahamic faiths

We are very aware of the distinct relationship between Judaism, Christianity and Islam. We are equally aware of the historic dysfunctionality of the Abrahamic family and the urgent need – of which more than a decade of dialogue has been a tiny contribution – for 'family therapy'. Yet we are also acutely aware of the fact that we need to involve and engage with other fellow citizens whose faith has historical roots in another geographical location and have different historical backgrounds, e.g. Hindus, Buddhists, Jains, Sikhs, Baha'is and others. Jews, Christians and Muslims also need to engage in dialogue with other forms of contemporary spirituality, humanists and the ancient religious traditions of Britain.

Beyond the Dysfunctional Family

4.4 The importance of learning from women in dialogue

We believe that there is an urgent need to create more opportunities for women to participate in dialogue, both in 'women-only' initiatives and as part of mixed gender groups. Experience reports that women-only groups generate different methodologies and dynamics, which in turn yield different outcomes and insights for the dialogical process as a whole.

4.5 Increasing the extent to which we challenge our own prejudices

Although already referred to, we cannot emphasise too strongly the importance of self-criticism. Specifically, we believe that it is essential that we challenge prejudiced views and misperceptions of other religions in conversation and through the written word as need arises. In turn, we should be prepared to challenge our own traditions to become more open to the perspectives of different faiths. The journey into other peoples' gardens should not only increase our knowledge of gardening but help us to recognize much better the weeds as well as the flowers in our own garden.

4.6 Tackling the relationship between religious law and British law

All three of our traditions have an important legal dimension – rabbinic law, canon law and sharia law. The ancient Jewish tradition that *'dina d'malkhuta dina*, the law of the land is the law' has guided Judaism in finding an appropriate place within society for Jewish law. The role of Batei Din in Britain may or may not be a useful model for Muslims to explore in order to discern whether or not sharia has a place in the context of a liberal democracy. As it is, all of us, Muslim and non-Muslims alike, need to understand the meaning of sharia much more than we do.

4.7 Collaboration in deepening spirituality and the quest for the Divine

All of us have a yearning to deepen our spiritual lives. All of us recognize the challenge to faith thrown down by modern secular

Recommending a Way Forward

society and the inadequacies of past expressions of belief that have been revealed. As this has not been the immediate focus of our group's dialogues, little serious engagement has taken place in these areas within our group. Along with working together to build the good society, the intensification of spirituality and the response to God should be a prime area for collaboration.

4.8 Responding to the process of change and the crisis of the environment

We live in a world in which change is not only remorseless but the pace feels as though it is increasing exponentially. Of course religions need to hold on to their eternal verities but they can all too easily become refuges for those who are shocked, frightened or disempowered by change and seek to turn their back on the world as it now is. We know that we can neither retreat nor close our eyes to change. We are obliged to engage with the world and its needs as change takes place, and with our traditions so that they can offer their perspectives, help and support. Not only *can* we do this together but we lack the strength and the authority unless we do it *together*.

LIST OF CONTRIBUTORS

Sughra Ahmed
is a Research Fellow in the Policy Research Centre of the Islamic Foundation. She has worked with a number of organisations to consider the issues young people face whilst growing up in the UK and the impact of this upon wider British communities and has recently published *Seen and Not Heard: Voices of Young British Muslims*. Sughra is a Trustee of the Inter Faith Network UK, Director at the Leicester Council of Faiths and previously co-ordinated the 'Women in Faith' interfaith project training British Muslim women to get involved in interfaith activity at a regional and national level.

Tony Bayfield
was born in London in 1946, read Law at Cambridge and received rabbinic ordination (*semikhah*) from Leo Baeck College in London. He served as a congregational rabbi in Surrey before becoming Director of the Sternberg Centre for Judaism and then Head of the Movement for Reform Judaism. In 2011 he became the Movement's President. For much of his career Rabbi Bayfield has specialised in interfaith dialogue between the three Abrahamic faiths. He co-edited *Dialogue with a Difference*, SCM Press 1992, (with Marcus Braybrooke) and *He Kissed Him and They Wept*, SCM Press 2001 (with Sidney Brichto and Eugene Fisher). In 2006 he was awarded a Lambeth Doctorate for his work in the theology of interfaith dialogue. Rabbi Bayfield teaches Personal Theology at Leo Baeck College and is a President of The Council of Christians and Jews. He is a widower with three children, the youngest of whom, Rabbi Miriam Berger, is also a rabbi.

Rachel Benjamin
was ordained at Leo Baeck College in 1998. She is proud to be the rabbi of the South Bucks Jewish Community. Rachel

Beyond the Dysfunctional Family

worked in investments and finance for several years, in London and then in Los Angeles, before joining the Hebrew Union College Skirball Museum (in LA), where she worked as the Assistant Curator of Judaica, and also gained an MA in Judaic Studies. While a student at LBC, Rachel worked as copy editor of the journal, *European Judaism*, and was on the planning team for the annual Jewish-Christian Bible Week in Bendorf, Germany. Since ordination, she has acted as a supply teacher of Bible Studies at LBC, and copy editor of the *Tanakh* volumes of Rabbi Sidney Brichto's *The People's Bible*. Rachel was also a visiting tutor at Heythrop College (University of London) during the 2003-4 and 2004-5 academic years, where she taught a core module, entitled 'Jewish Interpretation of the *Tanakh* (Hebrew Bible)', in the MA Biblical Studies programme. As well as Bible study, Rachel's interests include music and singing. Rachel is a keen sportswoman, and is proud to have represented England in tennis and Great Britain in squash at the Maccabi Games.

Miriam Berger
received S'micha – Rabbinic ordination – in the summer of 2006 from the Leo Baeck College. Having spent her final year at college as a Student Rabbi for Finchley Reform Synagogue, she stayed on to take up the post of Rabbi. In 2008 Miriam's role at the synagogue changed from associate to principal rabbi. Having known from a very young age that she wanted to become a rabbi, Miriam took a very direct path. On leaving The Henrietta Barnett School she went to read Theology at the University of Bristol and then to Hebrew Union College in Jerusalem. Miriam is married to Jonni and they have a son Benjamin.

Marcus Braybrooke
is a retired priest in Dorchester-on-Thames Team Ministry near Oxford. He has taken an active part in interfaith dialogue for over forty years. He was Executive Director Council of Christians & Jews 1984 - 87, and Chairman of the World Congresses of Faiths

Contributors

1978 - 83 & 1992 - 99, and is its current President. He is a Co-Founder of the Three Faiths Forum. He is author of over forty books on world religions and prayer, including *What Can We Learn from Islam?*, O Books, John Hunt Publishing, Hampshire, 2002; *Meeting Jews*, Christians Aware, Leicester, 2011; and *Beacons of the Light*, O Books, John Hunt Publishing, Hampshire, 2009. His Lambeth Doctor of Divinity was presented by the Archbishop of Canterbury in recognition of "his world-wide work for inter-religious understanding and co-operation."

Jane Clements
is the Founder and Director of the Forum for Discussion of Israel and Palestine (FODIP), an interreligious dialogue organisation which facilitates conversations between faith communities in the UK on this issue. Prior to that, she was Director of Programmes at the Council of Christians and Jews. Jane is a Trustee of the Holocaust Memorial Day Trust, and advises the Anglican Communion on matters relating to Israel as a member of the Anglican Commission to the Chief Rabbinate of Israel.

Elizabeth J Harris
is a Senior Lecturer in the Comparative Study of Religion within the Department of Theology, Philosophy and Religious Studies of Liverpool Hope University. Prior to coming to Liverpool Hope, she was the Executive Secretary for Inter Faith Relations for the Methodist Church in Britain, whilst also teaching within the Graduate Institute of Theology and Religion of the University of Birmingham and, as a Visiting Lecturer, at the University of Lund. Previous to this, she was a Research Fellow at Westminster College, Oxford. She has been involved in interreligious dialogue and encounter for about thirty years. Her publications include: *Theravada Buddhism and the British Encounter: religious, missionary and colonial experience in nineteenth century Sri Lanka*, London & New York: Routledge, 2006; *Buddhism for a Violent World: A Christian Reflection*, Epworth, London, 2010.

Beyond the Dysfunctional Family

Shanthikumar Hettiarachchi

has a PhD in majority-minority ethnic and religious conflict, from Melbourne College of Divinity, University of Melbourne, and is a Lecturer and Consultant in Religion, Conflict and Social cohesion. He has worked extensively with community groups and social movements in Sri Lanka and studied them at depth, both at community and post graduate levels. His primary research interests are in the Diaspora communities – their settlement processes, religious affiliations, political mobilisation, identity politics in social and cultural adjustments in the UK, Europe and Australia. His writings dwell on the radicalization of religious faith; land, history and notions of chosenness as political tools for defining identity. His most recent involvement has been in the rehabilitation, de-radicalisation and the community reintegration processes of ex-combatants in Sri Lanka's post conflict period.

Michael Hilton

studied Classical and English Literature at Oxford, obtaining MA and DPhil degrees, before moving to London and training as an English teacher. He worked as a Homeless Persons' Officer before entering Leo Baeck College in Finchley to train as a rabbi. For eleven years he was rabbi of Menorah Synagogue Cheshire Reform Congregation, and since 2001 has been Rabbi of Kol Chai Hatch End Jewish Community. Michael has been leading Jewish-Christian-Muslim conferences at the Ammerdown Centre, Somerset, for 20 years. He is married to Claire Hilton and has three sons.

Dilwar Hussain

is Head of the Policy Research Centre, based at the Islamic Foundation, Leicestershire; a Senior Programme Advisor to the Institute for Strategic Dialogue; and a Visiting Fellow at the Centre for Islamic Studies, Cambridge University. He has taught courses on Islam in contemporary society and has a number of published works in the field. He was a specialist adviser to the House of Commons Inquiry into the Prevent strategy (2010); Commissioner at the CRE (2006-2007); member of the Archbishop's *Commission on Urban Life and Faith* (2006); and co-chair of Alif-Aleph UK (2005), a network of British Jews and Muslims. His research interests are social policy, Muslim identity and Islam in the modern world. Dilwar is on the steering group of the *Contextualising Islam in Britain Project*, Cambridge University. He is married, has four children and lives in Leicester.

Humera Khan

is a founding member of the pioneering An-Nisa Society, an organization working for the welfare of Muslim families. She has been an activist and educator for over 25 years, working in race and gender equality, the voluntary sector and social services. She has written a series of books on Islam and sexual health, Muslim fatherhood and recently completed a twelve month project working with Muslim boys and young men entitled 'British Muslim or Wot'. Over the last 20 years, as a freelance consultant, Humera has written numerous articles for various publications including *Q-News*, *The Guardian* and the *The Independent*. She has also had various media and public appearances speaking on a wide range of issues from multiculturalism, Islamophobia and racism to social issues such as sexual abuse, generation conflicts, domestic violence and gender.

Alan Race

has spent many years involved in interfaith dialogue work, both nationally and internationally. His publications include *Interfaith Encounter: The Twin Tracks of Theology and Dialogue*, London: SCM Press 2001; *Christian Approaches to Other Faiths*, (Ed. with Paul Hedges), SCM Core Text, London: SCM Press, 2008. He is Rector at St.Margaret's Church, Lee, in south London, and teaches courses with the St.Philip's Centre, Leicester, on the theology of religious pluralism. He has been a member of the World Congress of Faith for many years and is Editor-in-Chief of the journal *Interreligious Insight*. He holds an Honorary Research Fellowship at the University of Winchester.

Beyond the Dysfunctional Family

Elizabeth Tikvah Sarah
is a London School of Economics Sociology graduate (1977), who went on to contribute to the development of Women's Studies. She was ordained in 1989 after training at Leo Baeck College. A teacher and tutor of rabbinic students for many years, she continues to mentor recently ordained rabbis. Since December 2000, she has been rabbi of Brighton and Hove Progressive Synagogue, and also serves as a chaplain at both Sussex and Brighton Universities. A participant in this dialogue group since 1994, she has edited three books and written over three dozen articles and several poems, which have been published in various journals and anthologies. Her book, *Trouble-Making Judaism*, a summation of her rabbinate and teaching so far, was published in February 2012 by David Paul Press.

Abdul Jalil Sajid
is Chairman of the Muslim Council for Religious and Racial Harmony UK (MCRRH); President for the National Association of British Pakistanis (NABPAK); President of Religions for Peace UK and Deputy President of European WCRP (Religions for Peace); Link Officer for Brighton and Hove Interfaith Contact Group (IFCG) for National and International Interfaith matters; European Representative of the World Council of Muslims Interfaith Relations (WCMIR); Vice Chair for the Muslim Council of Britain Interfaith Relations Committee and Adviser to the Muslim Council of Britain Europe and International Affairs Committee; and a founding member of MCB since 1997.

Ataullah Siddiqui
obtained his PhD in Theology from the University of Birmingham (UK). He is the Reader in Religious Pluralism and Inter-Faith Relations at Markfield Institute of Higher Education, where he teaches 'Islam and Pluralism', and is the course director of 'Training of Muslim Chaplains'. He was also the Director of the Institute from 2001 to 2008 and Academic Director 2009 – 2011. He is a Visiting Professor at University

Contributors

of Gloucestershire and is a Visiting Fellow in the School of Historical Studies, University of Leicester, as well as at York St. John University. He was founder President and Vice Chair of 'Christian Muslim Forum', and founder member of the Leicester Council of Faiths. He has published extensively on Interfaith and Christian-Muslim relations.

Norman Solomon
is a member of Wolfson College, Oxford, and the Oxford University Teaching and Research Unit in Hebrew and Jewish Studies. Born in Cardiff, South Wales, and educated at St John's College, Cambridge, he has served as rabbi to Orthodox congregations in Britain. He was founder-Director of the Centre for the Study of Judaism and Jewish/Christian Relations at Selly Oak Colleges, Birmingham, and from 1995 Fellow in Modern Jewish Thought at the Oxford Centre for Hebrew and Jewish Studies. His publications include: *The Talmud: A Selection* (Penguin Classics) and *A Very Short Introduction to Judaism* (OUP). *Torah from Heaven*, published this year by Littman Library of Jewish Civilization, London and Oregon.

We would like to acknowledge others who contributed significantly to the life of the Manor House Group during its life over the period 1993-2010. These include: Rumman Ahmad, Roger Boase, John Bowden, Harriet Crabtree, Michael Henderson, Jonathan Magonet, Jenny Sankey, Margaret Shepherd.

INDEX

Absolutism 194, 198, 249, 257, 258-9, 260, 263, 269, 271, 277, 280, 281
Anti-Semitism 31, 36, 93, 96, 103, 159, 160, 184, 243, 254, 256, 262

Barlas, Asma 74

Census 2001 19-20
Citizenship Survey 59
Contextualising Islam in Britain 69, 74
Covenant of Madina 74, 131, 132,
Critical thinking, 5, 7
CRPOF (Committee for Relations with People of Other Faiths) 39, 41
Crusades 25, 67, 184, 209, 251, 254

Dinah 217, 219, 220, 236

Emet, Dabru 86-7, 94

Faith Schools 20, 27, 176, 235, 273
Fundamentalism 4, 23, 172-3, 223, 255, 257, 262, 275, 283

Heschel, Abraham Joshua 170
Heschel, Susannah 221, 223, 260
Holocaust/Shoah 14, 85, 93, 98, 101, 104, 159, 229, 242, 244
Human Rights 67, 72-3, 196, 209

Inter Faith Network 44, 45
Islamophobia 46, 63
Israel-Palestine/Middle East 18, 89-90, 97, 129, 142-3, 147, 173, 209

Juergensmeyer, Mark 191

Modernity/Postmodernity 56, 73, 87, 102, 155, 159, 163-4, 166-7, 170, 175, 177, 194, 213, 223, 227, 229, 234, 246, 260, 261, 262, 275, 279, 283

Nazism 22, 31, 93, 103, 228, 244
NIFCON (Network for Inter Faith Concerns, Anglican) 49
Nostra Aetate 36, 49, 86, 94

Patriarchy 224, 225, 226, 227, 237, 248, 263, 278
People of the Book 102
Pinto, Diana 160-1, 176
Presence and Engagement 47

Quilliam, Henry William (Abdullah) 33, 57

Ramadan, Tariq 71, 74
Rawls, John 195
Religious violence/9-11/terror 5, 7, 17, 48, 59, 63, 76, 111, 189, 190-1, 232, 245, 250, 257, 269
Revelation 108, 206, 249
Rorty, Richard 195
Rumi, Jalaluddin 108, 116

Sacks, Jonathan 89, 104, 155
Satanic Verses 45, 61, 209
Schmidt-Leukel, Perry 192
Seal (Finality) of the Prophet 109, 206
Soroush, Abdolkarim 73
State of Israel 16, 17, 22, 26, 85, 90, 129, 135, 156, 158, 161, 162, 164, 168, 169, 243
Supersessionism 86, 94, 125, 188, 251

Theology of Religions 188
Three Faiths Forum 45

Vatican II 36, 135
Victimhood 61, 135, 159, 247, 264, 280

Wadud, Amina 74
WCC 36, 41-2, 90

Beyond the Dysfunctional Family

Williams, Rowan 191-3
Women's Liberation Movement/
    Feminism 221, 224, 225

Zionism 14, 143, 162, 229, 255